BUILDING AND SUSTAINING THE CAPACITY FOR SOCIAL POLICY REFORMS

Building and Sustaining the Capacity for Social Policy Reforms

Edited by
BELKACEM LAABAS
Arab Planning Institute
Kuwait

Ashgate

Aldershot • Burlington USA • Singapore • Sydney

Published by
Ashgate Publishing Ltd
Gower House
Croft Road
Aldershot
Hants GU11 3HR
England

Ashgate Publishing Company
131 Main Street
Burlington
Vermont 05401
USA

Ashgate website: http://www.ashgate.com

British Library Cataloguing in Publication Data
Building and sustaining the capacity for social policy
    reforms
    1. Arab countries - Social policy 2. Africa - Social policy
    I. Laabas, Belkacem
    361.6'1'09174927

Library of Congress Catalog Card Number: 99-85917

ISBN 0 7546 1191 4

Printed and bound by Athenaeum Press, Ltd.,
Gateshead, Tyne & Wear.

Contents

List of Contributors   vii
Preface   ix

1   Introduction   1
    Belkacem Laabas

PART I: SOCIAL DEVELOPMENT   15

2   Social Development Trends in the Middle East, 1970-95   17
    Richard J. Estes
3   Poverty and Social Development in Africa   47
    Arimah Benedict Chukuwka

PART II: POVERTY MEASUREMENT   89

4   What is Known about Identifying the Poor in Africa and the   91
    Middle East?
    Arjan de Haan and Shahin Yaqub
5   Priorities of Social Policy Measures and the Interest of Low-   125
    Income People: The Egyptian Case
    Karima Aly Korayem
6   Evaluating Psychological and Biological Deprivation in Low-   155
    Income Countries: Focus on the Angolan Experience
    Mwangi S. Kimenyi

PART III: SOCIAL REFORMS AND SOCIAL SECURITY   177

7   A Welfare Analysis of the Price System Reforms' Effects on   179
    Poverty in Tunisia
    Sami Bibi
8   Design Principles for an Efficient and Sustainable Social   207
    Security System
    Peter Sturm

9   Institutional and Regulatory Issues in Pension System   233
     Reforms: Country Experiences and Policy Options
     Iyabode Fahm

PART IV: BASIC HEALTH SERVICES   259

10   A Framework for Primary Health Care Reforms   261
     George L. Dorros, Marianne Jensen and Gary D. Robinson
11   Evaluating Health Care Policy Reforms in Africa: A Lesson   279
     from the Use of Precision Service Delivery Techniques in
     Animal Health Care Management
     Isaac A. O. Odeyemi, N.B. Lilwall and R.L. Wilson

List of Contributors

Sami Bibi
Assistant Professor of Economics
Faculty des Sciences Economiques et de Gestion de Tunis (FSEGT) -
Tunis

Arimah Benedict Chukuwka
University Lecturer
Department of Geography
National University of Lesotho - Southern Africa

George L. Dorros
Senior Consultant
Health Policy and Planning
World Health Organization - Switzerland

Richard J. Estes
Professor of Social Work
University of Pennsylvania - USA

Iyabode Fahm
Economist
Policy Intelligence Unit, Research Dept.
Central Bank of Nigeria - Nigeria

Arjan de Haan
Social Development Adviser
Department of International Development (DFID) – England

Marianne Jensen
Health Policy and Planning
World Health Organization - Switzerland

Mwangi S. Kimenyi
Economist
Associate Professor of Economics

African Educational Foundation for Public Policy and Market Process Inc.
UT. - USA

Karima Aly Korayem
Professor and Chairperson of the Economics Department
Faculty of Commerce (Girls)
Al-Azhar University, Cairo - Egypt

Belkacem Laabas
Economist
Arab Planning Institute (API) – Kuwait

N.B. Lilwall
Institute of Ecology and Resource Management
School of Agriculture
The University of Edinburgh - Scotland

Isaac A. O. Odeyemi
Health Care Economist
Institute of Ecology and Resource Management
School of Agriculture
The University of Edinburgh - Scotland

Gary D. Robinson
Manager of Human Resources Indicatives
Health Policy and Planning - World Health Organization - Switzerland

Peter Sturm
Economist
International Monetary Fund (IMF) – Washington D.C. - USA

R.L. Wilson
Institute of Ecology and Resource Management
School of Agriculture
The University of Edinburgh - Scotland

Shahin Yaqub
Research Economist
Poverty Research Unit
University of Sussex – England

Preface

This book is the fruit of a workshop on *Building and Sustaining the Capacity for Social Policy Reform* organized by the Arab Planning Institute (API) in cooperation with the African Training and Research Center in Administration for Development (CAFRAD) in Tangier, Morocco on December, 1-3, 1998. This workshop undoubtedly constitutes a major scientific event not only in the history of the API but also in that of the Arab and African academic and research community, and policy makers at large. It further reflects the API's determination to fulfill the mission entrusted to it by its 15 member countries, namely to support economic and social development issues as well as contribute toward improving policy making, decision making and development planning in all Arab countries. It is in this respect that the API takes special interest in the issues related to poverty alleviation policies, basic health care, social policies, and social security issues that are related to poverty alleviation.

The fact that a number of Arab, African and other developing countries are in the process of implementing structural adjustment programs and moving toward market economies, calls for active social policies to reduce the burden of these adjustments heavily borne by the most vulnerable in these societies. The experiences of these countries reveal that without such social policies, growth will not reduce human misery and inequality. Despite the recognition of this fact in the design of structural adjustment programs, it is the lack of proper and sound institutions and policies that build the capacities for positive policy reforms which enable advances in the human welfare of the populations. The papers certainly bring out the major trends, nature and soundness of policies designed to alleviate poverty, as well as suggest policies useful to policy makers in the Arab and African continents in the face of adverse social conditions. The emphases of this workshop as highlighted by the papers shed light and new evidence on the major issues related to the critical issues and priorities in social policy reforms, and major institutional aspects in these reforms. These issues will emerge from sketching a clear picture of the poverty profile. This identifies who the poor are, their characteristics, and the contributory factors for becoming or staying poor.

These facts should pave the way to providing help to the vulnerable and the needy through social security policies and providing basic health care, education, decent shelter and food security.

The main objective of this workshop is to provide a forum for discussion of the means to build and sustain institutional capacity for social reforms, and analyzing the link between these reforms and poverty alleviation policies, by focusing on reforming social security, pension funds and primary health care drawing on relevant theories and regional as well as international best practices. This workshop constitutes an important event coming as a result of fruitful cooperation between the API and CAFRAD, who both share a common interest in the issues of development, and mutually emphasizing the social implications of structural adjustment programs.

Essa Al-Ghazali, Ph.D.
Director General, Arab Planning Institute
Kuwait

1 Introduction

Belkacem Laabas

This book is the compilation of ten papers presented at a workshop organized jointly by the Arab Planning Institute (API) in Kuwait, and the African Training and Research Center in Administration for Development (CAFRAD) in Tangier, Morocco on December 1-3, 1998. The workshop aimed at discussing the means to build and sustain institutional capacity for social reforms, and analyzing the link between these reforms and poverty alleviation policies.

Poverty is concerned with the relationship between minimum needs of people and their ability to satisfy these needs. Research on poverty is extensive due to the complexity of the problem, the proliferation and availability of data from household surveys, and the interest of international agencies, governments, and scholars in poverty analysis. Despite the spread of poverty research worldwide however, empirical evidence on poverty in the Arab countries is very sketchy and only few studies are available[1]. Most of the research conducted on poverty in the ESCWA region is reported in the ESCWA (1997) publication.

Poverty constitutes one of the major social and economic problems. It reflects the malfunctioning of the social and economic systems. It stems from different sources, i.e. social, economic, and political factors, massive unemployment, low incomes, economic backwardness, social and economic exclusion and unequal income distribution, drought, environment deterioration, floods, civil wars, political instability and corruption. It also reflects the neglect by the governments of the most unfavorable and vulnerable people in the society, such as the disabled, the elderly, and female-headed households. Poverty also spreads out due to lack of proper social institutions (social security, pension funds, retirement plans, charities, etc.) and the lack of basic human rights and the proper laws and policies to protect them.

Poverty is a worldwide phenomenon and has degraded human lives for centuries. Despite the huge progress in poverty reduction, it is estimated by the UNDP (1997) that about 1.3 billion people still live in poverty as compared to 2-3 billion three decades ago. The pattern and dynamics of poverty worldwide are very complex. It is concentrated in the south of the globe, mainly in Asia and the Pacific, accounting for 950 million of the 1.3 billion still living in poverty. Sub-Saharan Africa has the highest proportion of people living in poverty and is considered a poverty stricken region and expected to worsen by the turn of the century. Latin America and the Caribbean also suffer from poverty but less severely. However, Eastern European countries have the highest growth of poverty. Despite the achievements of the industrial countries, it is estimated that about 100 million still live in relative poverty. Be that it may, poverty line is defined differently.

People in Arab countries (ACs) constitute a total of 258 million. Little is known about the detailed poverty profile of each AC. On aggregate, the UNDP (1997) estimates that around 4 % of the population have daily spending less than US$1. However, the ESCWA (1995) has recently estimated the percentage of the poor in total Arab population for 1992 as ranging between 3 and 45% with an average of about 27 %. This figure may be underestimated as it excludes many countries, some of them suffering with widespread poverty, e.g. Sudan and Mauritania. Despite the good position of ACs as far as the severity of poverty is concerned, the figure conceals some realities of Arab poverty. Some Arab countries, i.e. Mauritania, Yemen[2] and Sudan, are very poor and their situation is similar to that of Sub Saharan Africa. Other ACs with large population densities and severe economic problems such as the Maghreb countries and Egypt, might witness a tendency in poverty to worsen and acute urban poverty fueled by rising unemployment and inflation. Rich ACs, despite their financial wealth, still register some difficulties in eradicating poverty[3] as measured by the Human Development Report (1997). However, some countries register a good record in welfare such as in the case of Oman (HDR, 1997).

Poverty is traditionally measured by different statistical methods based on income and expenditure distribution which helps to establish some poverty line. Poverty indices include, among others, national and international poverty lines based on Purchasing Power Parity, head count, poverty gap, Gini index, and the P-alpha index. The UNDP(1997) distinguishes between poverty from an income perspective, based on a predetermined poverty line called income poverty, and poverty from human development perspective called human poverty. The latter is built to reflect aspects of human development and welfare. It is measured by the lack of social welfare and the level of basic needs fulfillment. Given the multi-dimensionality of this concept, the UNDP developed a composite index of human poverty called Human Poverty Index (HPI)[4]. The novelty of this index is that it gives a contrasting picture on poverty to that given by measures of income poverty. This conclusion is true for the Arab region. Research on poverty is also expanding toward using large data sets from surveys and using a micro approach in order to understand deeply this phenomenon and to design specific targeting policies. Some advanced econometric techniques are used to model poverty incidence using the Logit and probit models, and spell duration models to estimate poverty survival.

Constructing a precise poverty profile requires a rich body of data in order to identify the poor, their characteristics and their place in the society. Poverty lines derived from expenditure and income surveys are only aggregate measures which reflect the extent and severity of poverty. More information is needed to understand poverty, to determine who the poor are, their characteristics, their location, causes for their poverty , and measures being undertaken to minimize, if not to eradicate their poverty.

The research on poverty in Arab world is very sketchy and little is found in the literature. From available sources, only few ACs have estimated poverty lines (seven countries in the HDR, 1997). Country studies on poverty are very rare, probably with the exception of Egypt. Part of this situation is due to the lack of data[5] and the absence of the analysis of available data. In this respect, it is worthwhile trying to build a poverty profile for the ACs using both income and human poverty approaches.

If economic backwardness and explosive population growth which strains available resources are regarded as the major sources of poverty, by the same token, growth and distribution may also regarded a strong means of poverty reduction. However, without the proper social strategy and adequate institutions, growth could not lead to poverty reduction. In the fight against poverty, most governments try to implement policy packages adequate with the poverty profile of their countries. Rural poverty is mainly characterized by landless peasants. One strategy is to redistribute small lands and facilitate access to resources and assets. In the case of urban poverty, it is the fight against unemployment, easing access to informal markets (micro projects), providing shelter for the homeless, encouraging community help and charities in the process of fighting poverty and exclusion. It is also part of the poverty alleviation to provide social services and to enhance social security, to help the elderly and the disabled and all poverty-vulnerable groups.

At the heart of the poverty alleviation program lies the role of the social security system. This institution provides social assistance in the fields of basic health care, unemployment benefits, old age pensions, employment injury, family size, maternity, invalidity and widowhood (ILO,1952). In developed countries, a formal social security system usually performs quite well, despite actuarial and fiscal imbalances, and most vulnerable groups depend on it. However, in most developing countries, social security suffers from many shortcomings which effectively reduces its role in poverty alleviation (Guhan, 1994). This is primarily due to: (a) Availability varies across contingencies; (b) Limited coverage and widespread exclusion; and (c) Formal social security systems are inefficient and run into fiscal imbalances.

Clearly, exclusive reliance on formal Western-type social security systems in the least developed countries (LDCs) would be inappropriate to alleviate poverty, since the incidence of poverty is very high, has been persistent overtime and is rooted in several structural features of their economies.   Social security is mainly restricted by the limited scope of the credit and insurance markets. Social insurance is also limited by the labor market structure. This is mainly dominated by informal employment and extensive rural labor market. For this reason, neither Beeveridge, nor Bismarck's social security type can provide a model for LDCs.

Social security in LDCs will have to be viewed as part of and fully integrated with anti-poverty programs. Given a persistent poverty trend, the concept of social security has to extend considerably beyond the conventional social insurance model and encompass a large measure of social assistance.   On the aggregate, these measures may be categorized into promotional, preventive, and protective.

- Promotional measures include the wide array of macroeconomic measures of major importance to poverty reduction, operating at the macro and meso level and addressed primarily to the prevention of actual types of deprivation, such as primary education, primary health care, housing and shelter provision.
- Preventive measures include direct measures for poverty alleviation, such as asset redistribution, employment creation schemes and food security.
- Protective measures include specific actions (safety nets) for the protection against deprivation.

Arab countries are a heterogeneous group made of poor, low-income countries such as Mauritania, Yemen and Sudan; middle-income countries such as Egypt, Algeria and Tunisia; and rich oil-exporting countries (the Gulf States).   The poverty profiles of these groups are also heterogeneous. For the low-income group, the formal social security system would be limited for poverty alleviation, given low coverage and limited contingencies. The experiences of India and Bangladesh in poverty alleviation would be relevant for these countries.

In the middle-income countries, the formal social security system plays a major role in poverty alleviation, given the predominance of the public sector, high levels of urbanization and extensive formal labor markets. However, coverage is still limited and not all contingencies are provided. The national insurance system is operational, and these countries do not suffer from acute structural absolute poverty. Nevertheless, given limited public resources and the economic malaise of these countries, social security system performance is unlikely to meet poverty alleviation needs of the unemployed, the aged, the homeless, and provision for education and health care. Given the imbalance between the benefits provision and the poverty alleviation needs, the formal social security system needs major reforms to increase its efficiency and insure its financial solvency. The array of policies to be applied includes increasing the role of the private sector in providing private health insurance and private pension schemes. Privatizing social security systems may also help achieve efficiency and solvency. The experience of Chile and other Latin American Countries in this respect could prove helpful for Arab policy makers in this domain. The efficiency could also improved by abolishing universal subsidy and benefit provision and replacing it with tested targeting procedures. Rich Arab states have made considerable efforts in social policy and actually run a social security system based on a generous package. However, given their near absolute reliance on oil exports, the long-run financial soundness of this system is put into question. Most countries are engaged in a process of reforms to insure their soundness by changing the financial rules of this system.

In the forefront of combating poverty lies the role of the health care system of any nation. Access to health care constitutes a major element in the fight against human misery, suffering and morbidity. Health care systems are of two types: (a) curative; and (b) preventive. In industrialized countries and some developing countries, health problems are related to longitivity, lifestyle and the environment. The challenge to this system is basically the financial burden, given the problem of population aging and the increased dependency ratio. In middle-income countries, considerable progress has been made in building health care systems based on primary health care. Despite the improvements in the health of the population, traditional causes of mortality, i.e. infectious and parasitic diseases, are still widespread. These countries also witness the spread of new health problems such as chronic non-communicable diseases associated with aging and modern lifestyle. Therefore, these countries face old and new health problems. Given limited public resources and the need to extend health care systems to provide services to excluded rural communities and the urban poor, reforms are essential for the soundness and efficiency of the health care system.

For poor countries which witness difficult socio-economic conditions and limited financial and human resources to develop their health sector the immediate task is to combat deplorable conditions of hygiene and health and combat malnutrition and communicable diseases. Health care systems are usually based on three elements:

- Public systems: Universally available, and have preventive orientation and used in most LDCs for basic health care provision. These are usually financed by public funds through a wide varieties of health insurance and social insurance provisions.
- Private health systems: Oriented to curative medicine with limited access for those who can afford.
- Health insurance for workers and their families in modern, formal sectors: The health insurance is organized as part of the social security scheme.

Access to health care in the ACs is unevenly distributed. Health expenditure per capita in the MENA region was US$77 in 1990 compared to US$1860 for advanced countries and the world average of US$323. The ratio of health care expenditure to GDP in the ACs was half of the world level of 8.0 %, and the life expectancy at birth was 61 years below the world average of 65 and far below the level of advanced countries of 76 years. The infant mortality rate was 11.1 per 1000 compared to just 1.1 per 1000 for developed countries. These figures show that health performance of the ACs is below world average and much more effort needs to be done. The picture of health care at the country level reveals more disparities and suggests acute health problems for Arab low-income countries such as Yemen, Sudan and Mauritania. The fight against poverty requires modernizing the health systems and upgrading the health standards of the population.

Book Overview

The book is divided into four parts reflecting the importance of the issues discussed in the workshop.

Part I – Social Development

The first paper by Estes examines the trends of social development in the Middle East between 1970 and 1995. Nations of the Middle East are undergoing a dramatic transformation in an effort to realign their social, political, and economic systems to better meet the realities of increasing globalization and internationalization. However, the transformational efforts of many of the region's countries are impeded by recurrent problems of poverty, non-competitive public sector employment, uneven educational opportunities, inadequate human service infrastructure, eroding urban centers, and marginalization of the region's women and other historically disadvantaged population groups. The region's efforts directed at accelerating its pace of social development are further confounded by the comparatively high rate of population growth, environmental degradation, political tensions, and diversity-related social conflicts.

Viewed within the context of contemporary social policy challenges facing the region this paper assesses the extent of social progress in 22 West Asian and North African countries. More specifically, the paper reports the results obtained through the application of the author's previously developed Index of Social Progress (WISP) to an analysis of the region's socio-economic development since 1970. It identifies the region's major 25-year social development successes and failures and contrasts the region's social development achievements with those of other regions. It identifies the region's current social development leaders and socially least developing countries. It also delves into the major social, political, and economic forces that are likely to influence the region's future development beyond the year 2000. It also looks into the region's major social policy dilemmas especially in the areas of population, poverty, income security, health care, education, housing, and the provision of human services to women, the aged, and other vulnerable groups of the population.

Overall, the focus of Estes' paper is to provide a comparative perspective within which the region's recent and future social development efforts may be assessed. The paper also pinpoints the major social policy lessons, both positive and negative, that may be learned from the recent social development accomplishments of other countries located both within and outside the Middle Eastern region.

Arimah's paper investigates the link between poverty and social development using cross-national data drawn from African countries. In so doing, it seeks to achieve two objectives. The first is to construct measures of poverty for these countries. The second is to account for inter-country variations in the different measures of poverty while paying specific attention to various aspects of social development. Four measures of poverty are obtained. The first two are income-based measures which are derived using the poverty lines of the individual countries in relation to that of the continent as a whole. The second set of poverty measures is based on the explicit recognition of the multifaceted nature of poverty. Following from this, composite measures of poverty are obtained from a factor analysis of nine socio-economic variables, which reveal that poverty may be measured in terms of two distinct dimensions. These are the dimensions of poor health and high levels of mortality on the one hand, and that of inadequate housing on the other. Factor scores are then used to show inter-country variations in these two dimensions.

Further empirical analysis based on both the logit and ordinary least squares regression models reveals that inter-country variations in the various measures of poverty may be accounted for by variables indicative of different facets of social development. These include: (a) education-related variables such as adult literacy rate, public expenditure on education and female enrolment rate; (b) health-related variables which include expenditure on health and number of physicians per one thousand people; (c) increasing levels of democratization and good governance; and (d) the extent of military spending. Other variables apart from those pertaining to social development found to be significant in explaining variations in poverty measures include foreign aid, rate of economic growth, the physical disadvantage of being a landlocked country and the geographical region in which the country is located.

Part II – Poverty Measurement

The second part of the book deals with issues related to poverty measurement in the Arab countries and Africa. The paper by de Haan and Yaqub looks at the information that lies at the base of the debates during the 1990s about poverty. Their main argument is that particularly in Africa, too little is known about poverty, and that governments and donor agencies pay too little attention to this. This forms crucial limits on effective and timely action against poverty. They recognize that knowledge of poverty in Africa and the Middle East has increased during the last decade. To illustrate this, the paper discusses information on trends and profiles of poverty. However, they argue that the process of providing decision makers with sufficient and timely poverty information is merely beginning. The information available is often too scarce to rigorously cross-check, evaluate and answer significant questions which exist. Specifically, two questions are posited in the paper about the available poverty information: firstly, data availability, timeliness and quality; and secondly, its usefulness for the kinds of questions policy makers face.

The paper by Korayam assesses and compares the expenditure priorities of low-income people and the government in order to study the compatibility of their spending priorities. The problem arises from the fact that social policy measures are important means to reduce poverty and raise the standard of living of the low-income people in general. However, since there are budget constraints for the government, priorities have to be set in allocating government expenditure to different social policy measures. These priorities may be set by the government according to its own criteria, or may be set according to the interest of the low-income people as revealed by their expenditure patterns; i.e., giving higher priorities to those social services which represent higher relative shares in the budget of the low-income people. Alternatively, the government may set a scale of priorities that serve the interest of the low-income people, including the poor as a subgroup. Thus, the objective of her study is to assess the social policy priorities set by the government with respect to the needs of the low-income people in Egypt. The social policy measures examined in this context are government expenditures on food subsidy, on education, and on health services.

The core components of the Korayem's study is the identification of the low-income people in Egypt and the evolution of the size of this group in 1990/91 through 1995/96, this period covering the implementation of the Economic Reform and Structural Adjustment Program (ERSAP) in Egypt; and investigates the consumption pattern of the low-income households with respect to their expenditures on subsidized food commodities, education and health services. The study also examines per capita government expenditure on food subsidy, education and health and their relative share in government budget over the period 1990/91 - 1995/96. It assesses the efficiency of the social policy priorities set by the government in meeting the needs of the low-income people in Egypt. This is done by comparing the scale of priorities of social policy measures deduced from the expenditure patterns of the low-income people with the scale of priorities of these measures set by the government to determine whether or not the government is applying the appropriate right social policy measures for the low-income people.

The third paper on poverty measurement by Kimenyi investigates the psychological and biological deprivation in Angola. Despite its enormous natural resources, Angola remains one of the poorest countries in the world. A primary reason for this phenomenon has been a prolonged civil war that in addition to claiming thousands of lives, has led to the government's deplorable neglect of services such as health, education and infrastructure. The quality of life in this country has been further complicated by prevalence of land mines which have greatly handicapped food production. The consequence has been extremely low quality of life, high infant and maternal mortality, extremely high illiteracy rates and other malaises. Unfortunately, due to the civil war, reliable data have not been available to quantify accurately the extent of deprivation in this country and to evaluate the effectiveness of poverty alleviation policies that are now being put in place.

Under the sponsorship of the World Bank, a household consumption survey was conducted in 1995 in Angola by the National

Institute of Statistics (generally referred to as the Priority Survey). The data from this survey, though not perfect, is the best available and may be used to evaluate poverty status in the country. Kimenyi's paper seeks to establish a poverty line based on accepted international standards of caloric intake. Using the poverty line so established, the paper then computes various weighted poverty gap measures such as the Sen Index, Kakwani family of Poverty Indices, Thon Index, Takayama Index, and the GTF family of Indices. Sensitivity analysis is conducted to evaluate the adequacy of each of these indices and an alternative index developed by the author is presented. It is argued that for very poor societies such as those of Sub-Saharan Africa, a different weighting scheme is necessary to adequately capture psychological deprivation. The paper also presents a profile of the poor in Angola.

Part III – Social Reforms and Social Security

The third part of the book deals with social reforms and social security in the ACs and Africa. The paper by Bibi on the effects of the price system reforms on poverty in Tunisia proposes a methodology consistent with consumer theory that would permit to evaluate the impact of the price system reform on the poor population's welfare. Poverty line is estimated through the utilitarian approach and poverty measures based on the equivalent income approach which is an exact monetary measure of the households' welfare and which may be estimated using data on households' expenditures. Estimated parameters are then used to simulate the impact on poverty of the price system reform, which proposes to eliminate food subsidies. Furthermore, using a wide range of poverty lines and poverty measures, Bibi checks whether the budget saved as a result of this hypothetical reform, would allow the government to eradicate poverty in Tunisia, if a perfect targeting procedure could be used to identify the needy among the population at no cost. Results indicate that the reform would also allow saving 35 to 76% of the budget allocated to food subsidies. Targeting indicators such as the area of residence and the education level of the households head seem to be the most appropriate for channeling direct transfers in replacement of food subsidies to those poor households.

Sturm's paper focuses on the conditions to be met for a social security system to be efficient and sustainable. He discusses the rationale for government intervention through the operation of a social security system, pertinent market failures, distribution objectives and merit good considerations. Thereafter, he analyzes why and how government failure may limit the government's ability to achieve declared objectives and how the scope for such government failure may be limited in the design of the social security system. The major challenge to the efficiency of a social security system is its impact on the incentives of economic agents. The paper pinpoints the most damaging distortions of incentive structures which social security systems may introduce and possible ways of avoiding, or at least minimizing them. Questions of sustainability are discussed thereafter. The paper spells out the theoretical principles and illustrates the arguments with examples from existing social security systems, concentrating on the key areas of health care, old age pensions, unemployment insurance and welfare programs.

In the study of Fahm, the pension systems in Nigeria, Tunisia and Zambia are examined against the background of the experiences of OECD and Latin American countries. The main finding is that due to poor institutional framework, limited scope of financial markets, and macroeconomic instability, the pension systems are not able to meet the goal of income replacement and redistribution. It is argued that the challenge that faces African countries is how to build and sustain the institutional capacity necessary to make pension reforms successful. A gradual approach starting from the building of fiscal and macroeconomic viability, technical, institutional and administrative capacity, while at the same time reforming existing system along the line of multi-pillar, defined contribution and funded system, is recommended.

Part IV – Basic Health Services

The fourth part of the book addresses questions pertinent to basic health care and poverty alleviation in Africa and the ACs. The paper by Dorros, Robinson and Jensen of the WHO outlines primary health care reforms, drawing on experiences conducted at the WHO. Primary health care was begun twenty years ago with great hope and promise. It has not fulfilled this promise however, for many reasons. Major reasons have been the lack of policy deployment by the national government, and limited involvement of the community. A new model is proposed grounded on health care at the community level and more importantly, human capacity to be stewards of this important area.

The team of Odeyemi, Lilwall and Wilson discusses the gains associated with optimal spatial allocations of health ressources in a sparse rural Africa. Persistent economic constraints in most developing countries result in their inability to adequately fund a health care delivery system. Social and health care reforms which include the introduction of market-led economy and the policy of privatization of the hitherto government-delivered services, have been proposed as means of improving services in such countries. Studies however suggest that the adoption of such policy reforms   further adversely affect access to services especially by rural households, in   some cases resulting in poverty and destitution.   The development of a framework for the planning monitoring and evaluating of social and health care policies so as to avoid such adverse effect is the subject of their paper. The concept of Precision Service Delivery (PSD) in the planning and implementation of social and health care policies is introduced.   It involves the use of geo-spatial and econometric models in accurately   profiling the   socio-economic and   other demographic characterstics of the population within the delivery system. This ensures that social as weill as health care reforms are area-specific and introduced policy initiatives are appropriate and targeted at the right segment of the society.   It provides a means of ensuring equity and preventing further marginalization of the poor. The delivery of health care services in the livestock industry of Zimbabwe provides the case study for this paper.

Notes

1   Published research on poverty in Arab countries include: Morrison (1991) for Morroco; World Bank studies on the Social Safety Net Support Project in Algeria (1996); World Bank Project on Poverty Assessment in Yemen (1996); Zinelabidin (1996) for a sample of Islamic countries; ESCWA (1995) on policies to alleviate poverty in Egypt, Jordan and Yemen; Abdelkader (1994) on poverty and SAP in Sudan; Kanan (1996) on social policies and safety nets in selected Arabic countries; Baker (1996), an ESCWA study on poverty in the region; Aissa (1995) on poverty in Arab countries, to name some prominent studies.

2 The estimated the poverty line for Mauritania is 31% , and 20% for Yemen.

3 The definition of poverty by the UNDP (1997) from the point view of human development gives rise to high values of the HPI, especially affected by the high value of adult illiteracy rate .

4 The IFAD also developed a rural poverty index for styling its pattern worldwide.

5   Expenditure surveys are usually conducted on irregular basis, mostly every 10 years and data are not collected in a homogeneous single source and therefore unviable for comparison. The ILO source on expenditure surveys lists only eight surveys for the ACs, all of them conducted in the 1970s and the first half of the 1980s. World Bank sources on income distribution typically excludes Arab States, and incorporates only few data. Clearly, more efforts on data collection have to be done from original sources.

References

Abdelkader, A. (1994) 'SAP and Poverty in Sudan' (in Arabic). The Arab Institute of Research.
Aissa, N. (1995) 'Poverty in the Arab World'. Paper presented to the EGM on the Arab declaration in Amman on social development (in Arabic). ALO publication.

Baker, H. (1996) 'Poverty measurement in ESCWA region'. ESCWA Publication, Amman.

ESCWA (1995) 'Impact of selected macroeconomic and social policies on poverty: the case of Egypt, Jordan and Yemen'. ESCWA Publication, Amman.

ESCWA (1997) 'Database on poverty in the ESCWA region', Eradicating Poverty Studies No6. ESCWA Publication, Amman.

Gunan, S (1994) 'Social security options for developing countries', *International Labor Review*, 133 (1).

Jazairy, I., Alamgir, M. and Panuccio, T. (1992), 'The State of World Rural Poverty', IT publications, U.K

Kanan, T. (1996) 'The social impacts of economic reforms in ACs. Arab Monetary Fund', Arab United Emirates.

Morrison, C. (1991). 'Adjustment, Incomes and poverty in Morocco' *World Development* 19(11), pp. 1633-1651.

UNDP (1997) 'Human Development Report'. UNDP

WDR (1990) 'Poverty'. World Bank Report.

World Bank (1996) Yemen - Poverty Assessment. Report ID: 15158

World Bank (1996) Algeria - Social Safety Net Support Project Report ID:15392

World Bank (1997) 'World Development Indicators'.

Zinelabdin, R. (1996) 'Poverty in OIC: Status, Determinist, and agenda for action'. *Journal of Economic Cooperation among Islamic countries*. 17 (1), pp.1-40.

PART I:
SOCIAL DEVELOPMENT

2   Social Development Trends in the Middle East, 1970-95

Richard J. Estes[1]

Introduction

The countries of the Middle East have arrived at a critical crossroad in their transition toward modernization.   Anchored in centuries-old political and economic systems (Lapidus, 1996; Sonn, 1996), bitter ethnic rivalries (Goldschmidt,   1998;   Michel,   1997), recurrent   intra-regional   warfare (Mallat, 1998; Massoulie, 1998; Savir, 1998; Sayigh,   1998), and rising fundamentalism (Esposito, 1998; Kramer, 1996; Viorst, 1998), the majority of the region's countries have remained largely apart from the transformative processes that   are shaping development in other world regions (Estes, 1998a; UNDP, 1998; World Bank, 1998). Indeed, the impression exists that no economic or political miracles are occurring in the Middle East and that, to a very great extent, many of the region's countries are seeking to remain on the ·sidelines of modern history (Hunter, 1998; Sadiki, 1996; Sick and Potter, 1998; Zoubir, 1996).   And, yet, if the countries of the Middle East (ME or also referred to as "the region") are to flourish in the next century they, too, must deal more effectively with the same social realities that confront leaders of other countries and regions (Galal, 1997; Tessler, 1995).

At the outset of the new century, one of the most painful realities confronting   the   region's governments   is   a   legacy of inadequate and incomplete social policy initiatives. Apart from the poorest nations of Sub-Saharan Africa, no other major region enters the new century so ill prepared for the demands of increasing globalization as are the nations of the ME. The region's most urgent needs are reflected in its increasing population pressures (ESCWA, 1996c; Gilbar, 1997); continuing widespread poverty and income inequality (ESCWA, 1995b; UNDP, 1998); environmental degradation (Jabbra and Jabbra, 1997; Sexton, 1992; Starr, 1991); eroding urban infrastructures (ESCWA, 1996f; WRI, 1997); weak social welfare and other systems of formal social support (ESCWA, 1996b; 1996d; 1996e; USDHHS, 1997); recurrent human rights violations (Amnesty International, 1998; Monshipouri, 1998); as well as the continued marginalization of women (Abu-Lughod, 1998; Lobban, 1998) and other historically disadvantaged population groups (ESCWA, 1995a; UNICEF, 1998). Clearly, the region's governments must develop more proactive social policies if they are to complete their transformation toward modernization.

The research report assesses the social development successes and failures of 22 ME countries over the period 1970-1997. To this end, this paper:

- Reports the results obtained through application of the author's previously developed Index of Social Progress (WISP) to an analysis of the region's social and economic development between 1970 and 1995 (Estes, 1984; 1988; 1998a);
- Identifies the region's major social development successes and failures for the period 1970-1997, including its major social policy successes and failures;
- Contrasts the region's social development achievements with those of other regions (Estes, 1995; 1996a; 1996b; 1997; 1998b);
- Identifies the region's social development leaders (SLs) and socially least developing countries (SLDCs); and,
- Identifies and discusses the major forces that are likely to influence the region's future development at the outset of the new century.

Methodology

The present study is the third in a series of analyses of worldwide social development trends (Estes, 1984; 1988; 1998a). The objectives of all three studies are to: (a) identify significant changes in the adequacy of social provision[2] occurring throughout the world; and (b) assess national and international progress in providing more adequately for the basic social and material needs of the world's growing population.

Index of Social Progress (ISP)

The primary instrument used in this study is the author's extensively pre-tested Index of Social Progress (ISP). In its present form, the ISP consists of 45 social indicators that have been subdivided into 10 subindexes: Education (N=6); Health Status (N=7); Women Status (N=6); Defense Effort (N=1);

Economic (N=6); Demographic (N=6); Geography (N=3); Social Chaos (N=3); Cultural Diversity (N=3); and Welfare Effort (N=6). All ISP indicators are known to be valid indicators of social development. Indeed, the majority of the ISP indicators are employed regularly by other scholars of socio-economic development (Table 1).

Table 1 Index of Social Progress (ISP) Indicators

I.   EDUCATION SUBINDEX (N=6)
    Percent Age Group Enrolled, Primary Level (+)
    Percent Grade 1 Enrollment Completing Primary School (+)
    Percent Age Group Enrolled, Secondary Level (+)
    Percent Age Group Enrolled, Tertiary Level (+)
    Percent Adult Illiteracy (-)
    Percent GNP in Education (+)

II. HEALTH STATUS SUBINDEX (N=7)
    Life Expectation at 1 Year (+)
    Rate Infant Mortality Per 1000 Liveborn (-)
    Under 5 Years of Age Child Mortality Rate (-)
    Population in Thousands Per Physician (-)
    Per Capita Daily Calorie Supply as % of Requirement (+)
    Percent Children Fully Immunized at Age 1, DPT (+)
    Percent Children Fully Immunized at Age 1, Measles (+)

III. WOMEN STATUS SUBINDEX (N=6)
    Female Life Expectation At Birth (+)
    Female Adult Literacy Rate (+)
    Percent Married Women Using Contraception (+)
    Maternal Mortality Rate per 100,000 Live Births (-)
    Female Primary School Enrollment as Percent of Males (+)
    Female Secondary School Enrollment As Percent of Males (+)

IV. DEFENSE EFFORT SUBINDEX (N=1)
    Military Expenditures as Percent of GNP (-)

V. ECONOMIC SUBINDEX (N=6)
    Per Capita Gross National Product in Dollars (+)
    Real Gross Domestic Product Per Head (+)

Table 1 Cont

GNP Per Capita Annual Growth Rate (+)
Average Annual Rate of Inflation (-)
Per Capita Food Production Index (+)
External Public Debt as Percent of GNP (-)

VI. DEMOGRAPHY SUBINDEX (N=6)
    Total Population (Millions) (-)
    Crude Birth Rate Per 1000 Population (-)
    Crude Death Rate Per 1000 Population (-)
    Rate of Population Increase (-)
    Percent of Population Under 15 Years (-)
    Percent of Population Over 60 Years (+)

VII. GEOGRAPHY SUBINDEX (N=3)
    Percent Arable Land Mass (+)
    Natural Diaster Vulnerability Index (-)
    Average Annual Deaths From Natural Disasters Per Million Population (-)

VIII. SOCIAL CHAOS (N=3)
    Violations of Political Rights Index (-)
    Violations of Civil Liberties Index (-)
    Composite Human Suffering Index (-)

IX. CULTURAL DIVERSITY SUBINDEX (N=3)
    Largest Percent Sharing Same Mother Tongue (+)
    Largest Percent Sharing Same Basic Religious Beliefs (+)
    Largest Percent Sharing Same or Similar Racial/ Ethnic Origins (+)

X. WELFARE EFFORT SUBINDEX (N=5)
    Years Since First Law--Old Age, Invalidity, Death (+)
    Years Since First Law--Sickness & Maternity (+)
    Years Since First Law--Work Injury (+)
    Years Since First Law--Unemployment (+)
    Years Since First Law--Family Allowances (+)
    Subindex (N=46 Indicators, 10 Subindexes)

Weighted Index of Social Progress (WISP)

Owing to the volume of data gathered for this analysis, only statistically-weighted subindex and index scores are reported. Statistical weights were derived using a two-stage varimax factor analysis in which each indicator and, subsequently each subindex, was analyzed for its relative contribution in explaining changes in social progress over time. In doing so, the standardized values of individual indicators were averaged within the subindex and the resulting subindex averages were then multiplied by the factor loadings to create weighted subindex scores. Composite scores on the Weighted Index of Social Progress (WISP) were obtained through a summation of weighted subindex scores using a second system of statistical weights that took into account the differential importance of each subindex in explaining changes in social development over time[3].

The WISP Versus Other Measures of Social Progress

The ISP differs from other measures of social development in the number, range, and relevance of the indicators used in its construction. In all cases, the ISP is judged to be a more comprehensive instrument for assessing changes in social development over time than other indices of national and international progress (e.g., Gross National Product [GNP], Gross Domestic Product [GDP], the UNDP's "Human Development Index" [HDI], among others[4]).

Data Sources

The majority of the data used in the analysis were obtained from annual reports supplied by individual countries to the United Nations, the World Bank, the Organization for Economic Cooperation and Development, the Office of Policy Studies of the US Social Security Administration, and other international data collection organizations. Data for the Social Chaos, Cultural and Geographic subindexes were obtained from independent scholars and data gathering organizations (including Freedom House, Amnesty International, the Red Cross and Red Crescent Society, among others).

Country Selection

This study reports social development trends occurring in 22 Middle Eastern countries, i.e., 16 West Asian and 6 North African countries (Table 2). In addition to geographic location, two additional factors were used in selecting the 22 countries for inclusion in the present study: (a) all had populations of at least 600,000 people in 1970; and (b) timely, reliable, and valid social indicator data could be obtained for each country. For a few countries, statistical estimates were used to compensate for missing or incomplete data on fewer than three variables.

Time Frame

Index and subindex findings are reported separately for each of four time periods, i.e., 1970, 1980, 1990, and 1995. Thus, the study provides a cross-sectional analysis of the status of ME regional development at four discrete points in time. When available, supplemental social indicator data also are reported in selected tables for the period 1995-1997 (Tables 2 and 4).

Levels of Analysis

Data are reported for four levels of analysis: (a) worldwide development trends; (b) regional variations; (c) subregional variations and; (d) individual country performance on the WISP. Individual and aggregated scores are reported for all 22 countries included in the analysis.

World Social Development Trends

Figures 1 and 2 summarize the study's major findings on the WISP for all 160 countries included in the author's larger analysis of worldwide social development trends (Estes, 1998a). These time-series data cover the period 1970-1995 and reflect comparative WISP performance for the world's seven continental regions, i.e., North America, Australia-New Zealand, Europe, Latin America, Asia, Africa and, prior to its dissolution in 1991, the former Soviet Union.

Table 2 Selected Social Indicators for Near- & Middle Eastern Countries, 1995-97 (N=22)

SUB-REGION / Country	Pop. 1995 (Mil)	Average Annual Pop Growth 1990-97	Pop. Urban (%) 1997	Infant Mortality Rate/1k 1996	Child Mortality Rate/1k 1996	Maternal Mortality Rate/100k 1996	Life Expect. at Birth 1996	Primary School Enrollment 1995	Percent Adult Illiteracy 1995	PC GNP ($) 1997	PC GNP Avg. Ann. Growth (%) 1996-97	% Share Tot HH Inc Top 20% 1997
North Africa (N=6)	159.2	2.3	48.5	48.2	69.7	288.7	65.7	84.2	42.5	2138.3	2.5	44.1
Algeria	29.0	2.3	57.0	32.0	39.0	140.0	70.0	95.0	39.0	1490.0	-0.1	42.6
Egypt	60.0	2.0	45.0	53.0	66.0	170.0	66.0	89.0	49.0	1180.0	3.0	41.1
Libya	5.3	3.4	49.0	52.0	61.0	220.0	68.0	97.0	24.0	6510.0	⋮	⋮
Morocco	28.0	1.9	53.0	53.0	67.0	372.0	66.0	72.0	56.0	1250.0	-4.4	46.3
Sudan*	27.9	2.2	24.0	69.0	116.0	660.0	54.0	55.0	54.0	310.0	4.2	⋮
Tunisia	9.0	1.8	63.0	30.0	69.0	170.0	70.0	97.0	33.0	2090.0	9.7	46.3
West Asia (N=16)	173.6	2.0	72.8	28.0	36.3	194.1	70.5	79.2	22.3	6083.1	3.1	46.2
Armenia	4.0	0.9	69.0	16.0	20.0	21.0	73.0	⋮	0.0	530.0	5.4	⋮
Azerbijan	8.0	0.9	56.0	20.0	23.0	44.0	70.0	⋮	⋮	510.0	2.6	⋮
Bahrain	0.6	2.2	90.0	20.0	20.0	60.0	73.0	⋮	15.0	7820.0	⋮	⋮
Cyprus	0.7	1.3	54.0	9.0	10.0	5.0	77.0	⋮	6.0	14930.0	⋮	⋮
Georgia	5.0	-0.1	59.0	17.0	19.0	19.0	73.0	82.0	1.0	840.0	⋮	⋮
Iraq	22.0	2.7	74.0	57.0	112.0	310.0	62.0	91.0	42.0	2000.0	⋮	⋮
Israel	6.0	3.2	91.0	6.0	9.0	7.0	77.0	⋮	5.0	15810.0	⋮	42.5
Jordan	4.0	4.8	73.0	30.0	35.0	150.0	71.0	89.0	14.0	1570.0	1.5	50.1
Kuwait	1.6	-4.9	97.0	12.0	14.0	29.0	77.0	65.0	21.0	22110.0	⋮	⋮
Lebanon	4.0	1.9	88.0	31.0	36.0	300.0	70.0	97.0	15.0	3350.0	⋮	⋮
Oman	2.0	5.0	79.0	18.0	20.0	190.0	71.0	71.0	41.0	4950.0	⋮	⋮
Qatar	0.7	1.8	91.0	19.0	21.0	⋮	72.0	80.0	21.0	11570.0	⋮	⋮
Saudi Arabia	20.0	3.4	84.0	22.0	28.0	18.0	70.0	52.0	40.0	6790.0	⋮	⋮
Syria	15.0	2.9	53.0	31.0	36.0	179.0	69.0	91.0	29.0	1150.0	-0.6	⋮
Turkey	64.0	1.8	72.0	42.0	47.0	180.0	69.0	96.0	18.0	3130.0	6.4	⋮
Yemen*	16.0	4.5	35.0	98.0	130.0	1400.0	54.0	57.0	67.0	270.0	⋮	46.1
Total	332.8											
Average	15.1	2.1	66.2	33.5	45.4	221.1	69.2	80.9	28.1	5007.3	2.8	45.0

* Indicates countries officially classified by the United Nations as "Least Developing" (LDCs).

Data Sources: Unicef, 1998; World Bank, 1998.

The world's most socially developed regions are Australia-New Zealand, Europe, and North America (Figure 1). These regions had already attained the most favorable WISP ratings by 1970. Further improvements on the index continued to accumulate for these regions between 1970-1980 and 1980-1990.

Despite their past accomplishments, significant WISP losses occurred between 1990 and 1995 in three of the world's most socially advanced regions: North America (-14%), Europe (-9%), and Australia-New Zealand (-8%). The losses appear to be associated with the serious economic problems experienced by many countries in these regions. Most of these problems predate 1990 but continued on through 1995. Even so, comparatively few differences now characterize the development profiles of the highly advanced countries of North America (1995 WISP average = 79), Australia-New Zealand (1995 WISP average = 84), and Europe (1995 WISP average = 82).

The world's least developed regions are Africa (1995 WISP average = 21) and Asia (1995 WISP average = 46). Scores for the African region were consistently lower relative to those achieved by other world regions during the entire 25-year period studied, albeit some modest improvement in WISP performance occurred between 1990-1995, Africa's first positive WISP changes since 1970.

As reported in Figure 2, substantial 25-year gains occurred on the WISP for the Asian (+29%), Latin American (+11%), and African (+8%) regions. Important 25-year social gains also occurred for the North American (+7%), European (+5%) and Australia-New Zealand (+4%) regions.

Since 1980, Asia has emerged as the world's most rapidly developing region, especially its South Central (+56%), Western (+35%), and South East (+26%) subregions. Ironically, the world's slowest developing regions also are its already most socially advanced: Australia-New Zealand (+4%), Europe (+5%), and North America (+7%). The comparatively slow pace of development occurring in these regions reflects their already high level of development.

Figure 1   Average WISP scores by continent 1970-1995 (N=160)

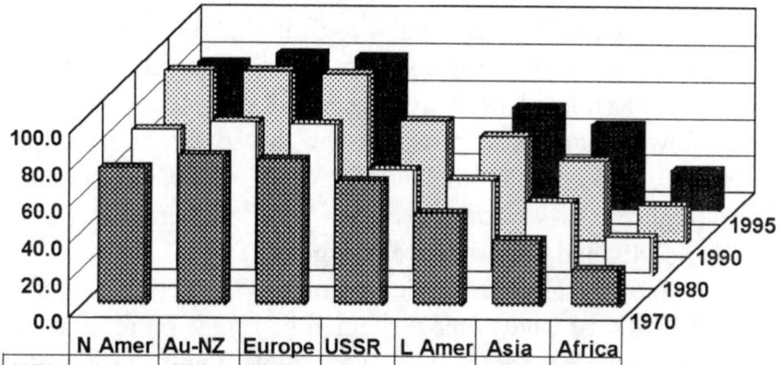

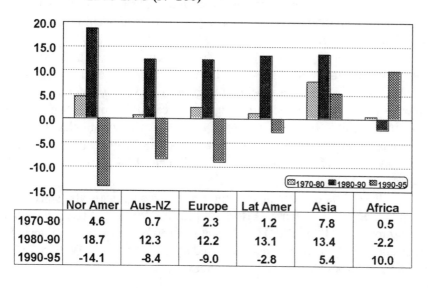

	N Amer	Au-NZ	Europe	USSR	L Amer	Asia	Africa
1970	73.9	81.0	78.6	66.9	49.8	35.7	19.8
1980	77.3	81.6	80.4	55.6	50.4	38.5	19.9
1990	91.8	91.6	90.2	65.3	57.0	43.7	19.5
1995	78.8	83.9	82.1	....	55.4	46.0	21.4

**Figure 2   Percent change in average WISP scores by continent
1970-1995 (N=160)**

	Nor Amer	Aus-NZ	Europe	Lat Amer	Asia	Africa
1970-80	4.6	0.7	2.3	1.2	7.8	0.5
1980-90	18.7	12.3	12.2	13.1	13.4	-2.2
1990-95	-14.1	-8.4	-9.0	-2.8	5.4	10.0

Development Trends in the Middle East

The data summarized in Figures 3 and 4 confirm that development trends in the ME differ in important respects from those observed for other world regions (Estes, 1998a). Until 1990, average WISP scores for the region were substantially lower than those observed for the world as a whole, i.e., regional scores of 36, 38, 41 and 49 for 1970, 1980, 1990, and 1995 respectively (Figure 3) vs. world average WISP scores for the same time periods of 45, 44, 49, and 49 respectively (Figure 1).

The pattern of less favorable average WISP scores for the region persisted until 1995 at which time the region's average score of 49 (Figure 3) equaled that observed for the world as a whole (Figure 1). The region's generally unfavorable performances on the WISP prior to 1995 are reflected on eight WISP's subindexes, especially on five West Asian subindexes for 1990: Defense Effort (M = -9), Welfare Effort (M = 4), Social Chaos (M = 6), Population (M = 8), and Women's Status (M = 7) subindexes (Figure 5)[5].   The North African region's poor performances on five subindexes in 1990 also contributed to region's overall lower development performance relative those of other world regions: Women's Status (M = 5), Social Chaos (M = 6), Population (M = 7), Economic (M = 8), and Welfare Effort (M = 9) subindexes (Figure 7).

The region's most substantial improvements on the WISP since 1990 occurred in West Asia which increased its subregional average score by 24% between 1990 and 1995, i.e. from 41 to 51. By contrast, average scores for the North African subregion increased by only 8% during the same time period, from 43 to 46.   North Africa's more modest five-year performance on the WISP are especially noteworthy given the subregion's earlier increases of 18% between 1970-1980 and 19% between 1980-1990 (Figures 3 and 4).

West Asia's most significant social accomplishments since 1990 occurred on its Defense Effort (+112%), Women Status (+42%), Demographic (+41%), and Health Status (+36%) subindexes (Figure 5). Important social advances also occurred on the subregion's Welfare Effort (+24%) and Social Chaos (+24%) subindexes.

Figure 3   Average WISP scores for the Middle East by
subregion, 1970-1995

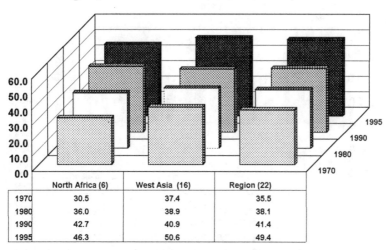

	North Africa (6)	West Asia (16)	Region (22)
1970	30.5	37.4	35.5
1980	36.0	38.9	38.1
1990	42.7	40.9	41.4
1995	46.3	50.6	49.4

Figure 4   Percent change in average WISP scores for the
Middle East (N=22), 1970-1995

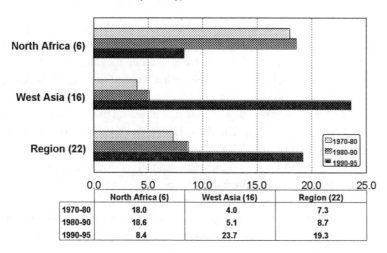

	North Africa (6)	West Asia (16)	Region (22)
1970-80	18.0	4.0	7.3
1980-90	18.6	5.1	8.7
1990-95	8.4	23.7	19.3

**Figure 5   Average WISP subindex scores for West Asia
(N=16), 1970-1995**

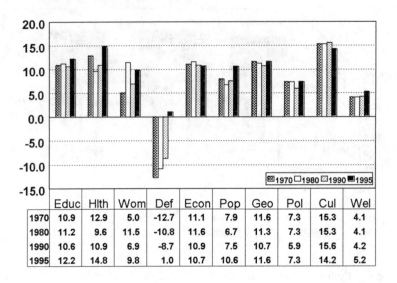

	Educ	Hlth	Wom	Def	Econ	Pop	Geo	Pol	Cul	Wel
1970	10.9	12.9	5.0	-12.7	11.1	7.9	11.6	7.3	15.3	4.1
1980	11.2	9.6	11.5	-10.8	11.6	6.7	11.3	7.3	15.3	4.1
1990	10.6	10.9	6.9	-8.7	10.9	7.5	10.7	5.9	15.6	4.2
1995	12.2	14.8	9.8	1.0	10.7	10.6	11.6	7.3	14.2	5.2

West Asia's losses on two subindexes, i.e. Cultural Diversity (-9%)
and Economic Status (-2%), did not appreciably reduce its 1995 composite
score on the WISP (Figure 6).   However, these negative trends on such
critical   dimensions of development are worrisome and need to be reversed if
the subregion is to sustain the gains reflected on other areas of the WISP.

North Africa's most significant recent social advances occurred on
the Women's Status (+35%), Cultural Diversity (+23%), Welfare Effort
(+14%), Health Status (+13%), and Demographic (+10%) subindexes
(Figure 7). These gains are significant and they are suggestive of the
potential for future positive changes in the same sectors. They also reinforce
North Africa's earlier accomplishments in these sectors.

North African countries,   however, did experience significant post-
1990 losses on four subindexes, i.e., Social Chaos (M = -17%), Geographic
(M = -16%), Defense Effort (M = -4%), and Economic (M = -4%)
subindexes (Figure 8). Losses of this magnitude are especially problematic
given the fragile nature of the subregion's earlier development
accomplishments and the persistence of widespread poverty in the region.

Figure 6 **Percent change in average WISP subindex scores for West Asia (N=16), 1970-1995**

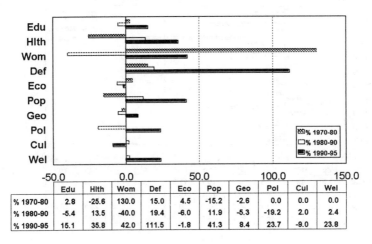

	Edu	Hlth	Wom	Def	Eco	Pop	Geo	Pol	Cul	Wel
% 1970-80	2.8	-25.6	130.0	15.0	4.5	-15.2	-2.6	0.0	0.0	0.0
% 1980-90	-5.4	13.5	-40.0	19.4	-6.0	11.9	-5.3	-19.2	2.0	2.4
% 1990-95	15.1	35.8	42.0	111.5	-1.8	41.3	8.4	23.7	-9.0	23.8

Figure 7 **Average WISP subindex scores for North Africa (N=6), 1970-1995**

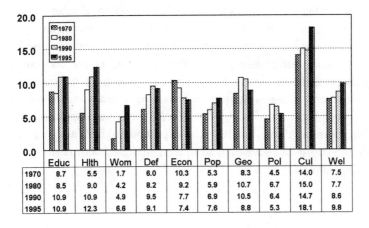

	Educ	Hlth	Wom	Def	Econ	Pop	Geo	Pol	Cul	Wel
1970	8.7	5.5	1.7	6.0	10.3	5.3	8.3	4.5	14.0	7.5
1980	8.5	9.0	4.2	8.2	9.2	5.9	10.7	6.7	15.0	7.7
1990	10.9	10.9	4.9	9.5	7.7	6.9	10.5	6.4	14.7	8.6
1995	10.9	12.3	6.6	9.1	7.4	7.6	8.8	5.3	18.1	9.8

Figure 8   Percent change in average WISP subindex scores for North Africa (N=6), 1970-1995

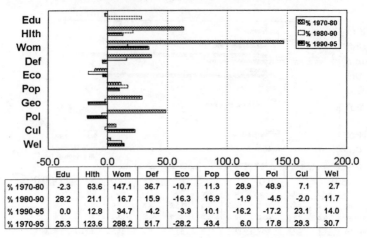

	Edu	Hlth	Wom	Def	Eco	Pop	Geo	Pol	Cul	Wel
% 1970-80	-2.3	63.6	147.1	36.7	-10.7	11.3	28.9	48.9	7.1	2.7
% 1980-90	28.2	21.1	16.7	15.9	-16.3	16.9	-1.9	-4.5	-2.0	11.7
% 1990-95	0.0	12.8	34.7	-4.2	-3.9	10.1	-16.2	-17.2	23.1	14.0
% 1970-95	25.3	123.6	288.2	51.7	-28.2	43.4	6.0	17.8	29.3	30.7

Recent dramatic increases in defense spending in combination with rising levels of Social Chaos within the North Africa subregion, are ominous and threaten many of the important social gains made by the subregion's countries since at least 1980 (Sadiki, 1996; Sayigh, 1998; Zoubir, 1996).

As revealed in the preceding data, dramatic social changes are occurring in the region. These changes are significant and they are broad-based. They also reflect substantial new investments on the part of the region's governments in social development. Overall, the region's positive social development changes suggest an increased capacity on the part of the region's government in providing for at least the basic social and material needs of their growing populations. The data reported here also confirm the asynchronous nature of development in the Middle Eastern region *vis-à-vis* other world regions.

The recent social development gains of the West Asia subregion, in particular, are of considerable significance given: (a) West Asia's slower pace of development prior to 1995; (b) West Asia's serious problems of poverty; (c) the decision reached by a majority of the subregion's governments to reduce previously excessive levels of defense spending; (d) West Asia's new commitments to invest in broad-based development initiatives; and (e) the reality that somewhat more than half of the region's population resides in West Asia, i.e. approximately 174 million people.

On the other hand, concern does exist regarding the recent negative development trends observed for the North Africa subregion. These trends are generally negative and undermine North Africa's significant accomplishments of earlier decades. Should these trends continue they could prove troublesome for the region-as a whole given North Africa's: (a) persistently high levels of social chaos (Amnesty International, 1998; Sayigh, 1998); (b) rising expenditures for defense and military purposes (UNDP, 1998); (c) weakening economic condition (World Bank, 1998); and (d) the subregion's extraordinary wealth gap (UNDP, 1998).

Subregional and Country Performances on Selected Social Indicators

The social indicator data reported in Table 2 provide further confirmation of the important differences existing in the development profiles of the region's countries and subregions. Population size in the region, for example, ranges from approximately 64 million people in Turkey to fewer than 700,000 persons in Cyprus, Qatar, and Bahrain. The region's pattern of urbanization also varies substantially with the greatest concentrations of urbanization occurring in West Asia (73% vs. 49% for North Africa). Within West Asia, urbanization varies from a high of 97% for Kuwait to only 35% for Yemen. Literacy levels, especially those of women, economic growth rates, and per capita income also vary significantly both within and between the two subregions (ESCWA, 1996e; UNDP, 1998). Population growth rates differ somewhat for the two subregions with the results that population growth rates remain exceptionally high in three of the region's poorer countries, i.e. Oman with 5.0%, Jordan's 4.8% and 4.5% for Yemen.

Though improved in comparison with earlier years, infant and child mortality remain high in the Middle East, especially in North Africa where 48 infant and 70 child deaths occur each year per 1000 live-born children in the region (vs. 28 and 36, respectively for the West Asia subregion). Furthermore, North African children who survive into adulthood can expect to live five years less on the average than children born in West Asia, i.e., 66 vs. 71 years. Adult illiteracy levels also differ appreciably between the two subregions, i.e., 43% and 22% for North Africa and West Asia, respectively. Subregional primary school enrolment ratios in the two subregions also vary and significant income disparities exist, i.e., $2138 and $6083 for North Africa and West Asia, respectively. Intra-regional differences in income inequality at the country level are even more pronounced.

Overall, the development challenges facing leaders of the North Africa subregion are greater, more serious, and more perplexing than those which confront leaders of West Asia (UNDP, 1998). The reasons for this are two-fold: (a) the comparatively plentiful supply of natural resources in the West Asia subregion relative to those available in North Africa (WRI, 1997); and (b) West Asia's comparatively higher levels of human capacity development (ESCWA, 1995a). As a result of these advantages, the countries of West Asia are characterized by higher per capita income levels, lower inflation rates, greater opportunities for international trade, and substantially larger national economies. West Asian countries also have somewhat longer and more successful histories than do the countries of North Africa in using public social programs to distribute the benefits of economic development more equitably (ESCWA, 1996b; USDHHS, 1997).

Regional Social Leaders and Socially Least Developing Countries

WISP performances for the region's individual countries are reported in Table 3. These data, along with the selected social indicator data reported in Table 2, were used to group the region's countries into three social development groupings, i.e., regional Social Leaders (SLs), regional Middle Performing Countries (MPCs), and regional Socially Least Developing Countries (SLDCs). Figure 9 ranks the region's 22 countries by their 1995 WISP performances and net change in WISP ranks between 1980 and 1995.

Table 3   Country rankings on the Weighted Index of Social Progress (WISP) for the Middle East by 1995 rank (N=22)

COUNTRIES	WISP 1970 (Base=107)	WISP 1980 (Base=124)	WISP 1990 (Base=124)	WISP 1995 (Base=160)	RANK WISP70 (Base=107)	RANK WISP80 (Base=124)	RANK WISP90 (Base=124)	RANK WISP95 (Base=160)
Cyprus	...	...	...	74.8	...	...	...	35.3
Israel	55.5	63.0	73.3	73.7	37.0	32.0	32.0	38.2
Armenia	...	...	...	67.5	...	...	...	47.3
Tunisia	44.2	47.9	57.0	61.8	53.0	56.0	51.0	56.5
Jordan	28.7	39.2	50.2	55.6	70.0	65.0	60.0	68.5
Georgia	...	...	...	55.3	...	...	...	68.5
Lebanon	53.1	63.5	44.8	55.2	41.0	30.0	68.0	68.5
Kuwait	...	...	...	54.7	...	...	...	73.3
Algeria	35.6	35.8	50.3	54.3	61.0	74.0	59.0	73.3
Turkey	43.6	49.4	55.0	52.4	54.0	55.0	53.0	78.4
Azerbaijan	...	...	...	52.1	...	...	...	78.4
Libya	21.2	40.4	43.8	50.8	84.0	62.0	70.0	83.3
Bahrain	...	...	...	49.6	...	...	...	86.3
Egypt	35.2	37.2	47.3	49.2	62.0	68.0	65.0	86.3
Saudi Arabia	...	29.1	48.2	48.3	...	82.0	63.0	89.2
Syria	32.3	39.6	38.8	46.6	64.0	64.0	74.0	91.0
Qatar	...	...	...	45.6	...	...	...	92.3
Morocco	28.6	36.2	44.9	45.3	71.0	72.0	67.0	92.3
Oman	...	...	...	35.7	...	...	...	107.0
Iraq	31.8	34.8	35.3	32.5	66.0	76.0	80.0	110.2
Sudan*	18.0	18.4	12.9	16.3	88.0	100.0	105.0	134.2
Yemen*	...	...	...	10.6	...	...	...	141.2
Minimum Score	18	18	13	11	37.0	30.0	32.0	35.3
Maximum Score	55	64	73	75	88.0	100.0	105.0	141.2
Average Score	35.6	41.1	46.3	49.5	62.6	64.3	65.2	81.8

* Indicates countries officially classified by the United Nations as "Least Developing."

... Countries not included in the base line year indicated.

Figure 9   Rank ordered WISP scores and net changes in WISP ranks for Middle East countries, 1980-1995 (N=22)

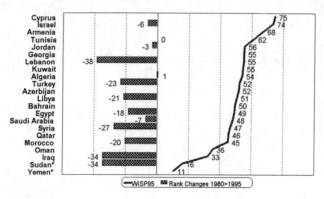

Regional Social Leaders (SLs)

The region's four SLs are identified in Table 4: Cyprus (WISP = 75), Israel (WISP = 74), Armenia (WISP = 68), and Tunisia (WISP = 62). All four of these countries attained WISP scores well above those achieved by the regionas a whole and, indeed, well above the average score of 49 reported elsewhere for the world as a whole (Estes, 1998a). In fact, WISP scores for the region's SLs averaged 70 in 1995, a score within reach of average score reported for all SLs worldwide (Average = 86).

In comparison with the region's other countries, Middle Eastern SLs are characterized by higher per capita income levels ($8340), faster rates of economic expansion, comparatively lower inflation levels, slower population growth (1.8%), more favorable infant (15/1000) and child (27/1000) mortality rates, and considerably longer average life expectation (74 years). As a group, the region's SLs also have in place a broader array of more fully established publicly financed social programs that absorb many of the predictable risks to income security to which people everywhere in the world are exposed, i.e., work injury, sickness and disability, old age, pregnancy, unemployment, premature death, and solitary survivorship (Table 5). As a consequence, per capita public sector investments in social welfare and social security are considerably higher in the SLs than elsewhere in the region (World Bank, 1998). Unfortunately, only about 6% of the region's population, 20 million people, reside in its SLs.

Table 4 Selected social and economic indicators for Near- and Middle Eastern countries by development grouping, 1995-97 (N=22)

SUB-REGION / Country	WISP 1995	Pop. 1995 (Mil)	Average Annual Pop Growth 1990-97	Pop. Urban (%) 1997.0	Infant Mortality Rate/1k 1996.0	Child Mortality Rate/1k 1996.0	Maternal Mortality Rate/100k 1996.0	Life Expect. at Birth 1996.0	Primary School Enrollment 1995.0	Percent Adult Illiteracy 1995.0	PC GNP ($)	PC GNP Avg. Ann. Growth (%)	% Share Tot HH Inc Top 20%
SOCIAL LEADER (N=4)	69.5	19.7	1.8	69.3	15.3	27.0	50.8	74.3	97.0	11.0	8340.00	7.6	44.4
Cyprus	75.0	0.7	1.3	54.0	9.0	10.0	5.0	77.0		6.0	14930.00		
Israel	74.0	6.0	3.2	91.0	6.0	9.0	7.0	77.0		5.0	15810.00		42.5
Armenia	68.0	4.0	0.9	69.0	16.0	20.0	21.0	73.0		0.0	530.00	5.4	
Tunisia	62.0	9.0	1.8	63.0	30.0	69.0	170.0	70.0	97.0	33.0	2090.00	9.7	46.3
MIDDLE (N=14)	51.1	245.2	1.7	69.1	31.0	36.6	144.7	70.3	83.8	26.3	4947.86	1.2	45.0
Jordan	56.0	4.0	4.8	73.0	30.0	35.0	150.0	71.0	89.0	14.0	1570.00	1.5	50.1
Georgia	55.0	5.0	-0.1	59.0	17.0	19.0	19.0	73.0	82.0	1.0	840.00		
Lebanon	55.0	4.0	1.9	88.0	31.0	36.0	300.0	70.0	97.0	15.0	3350.00		
Kuwait	55.0	1.6	-4.9	97.0	12.0	14.0	29.0	77.0	65.0	21.0	22110.00		
Algeria	54.0	29.0	2.3	57.0	32.0	39.0	140.0	70.0	95.0	39.0	1490.00	-0.1	42.6
Turkey	52.0	64.0	1.8	72.0	42.0	47.0	180.0	69.0	96.0	18.0	3130.00	6.4	
Azerbijan	52.0	8.0	0.9	56.0	20.0	23.0	44.0	70.0			510.00	2.6	
Libya	51.0	5.3	3.4	49.0	52.0	61.0	220.0	68.0	97.0	24.0	6510.00		
Bahrain	50.0	0.6	2.2	90.0	20.0	20.0	60.0	73.0		15.0	7820.00		
Egypt	49.0	60.0	2.0	45.0	53.0	66.0	170.0	66.0	89.0	49.0	1180.00	3.0	41.1
Saudi Arabia	48.0	20.0	3.4	84.0	22.0	28.0	18.0	70.0	52.0	40.0	6790.00		
Syria	47.0	15.0	2.9	53.0	31.0	36.0	179.0	69.0	91.0	29.0	1150.00	-0.6	
Qatar	46.0	0.7	1.8	91.0	19.0	21.0		72.0	80.0	21.0	11570.00		
Morocco	45.0	28.0	1.9	53.0	53.0	67.0	372.0	66.0	72.0	56.0	1250.00	-4.4	46.3
SOCIAL LDCs (N=4)	23.8	67.9	3.6	53.0	60.5	94.5	640.0	60.3	68.5	51.0	1882.50	4.2	46.1
Oman	36.0	2.0	5.0	79.0	18.0	20.0	190.0	71.0	71.0	41.0	4950.00		
Iraq	33.0	22.0	2.7	74.0	57.0	112.0	310.0	62.0	91.0	42.0	2000.00		
Sudan*	16.0	27.9	2.2	24.0	69.0	116.0	660.0	54.0	55.0	54.0	310.00	4.2	
Yemen*	11.0	16.0	4.5	35.0	98.0	130.0	1400.0	54.0	57.0	67.0	270.00		46.1
Total		332.8											
Average	49.5	15.1	2.1	66.2	33.5	45.4	221.1	69.2	80.9	28.1	5007.27	2.8	45.0

* Indicates countries officially classified by the United Nations as "Least Developing" (LDCs).

Data Sources: Unicef, 1998; World Bank, 1998.

Table 5   Age of publicly financed social security welfare programs for selected Middle Eastern countries, 1880-1997 (N=22)

Country	Old Age, Invalidity,& Disability	Sickness & Maternity	Work Injury	Unemploy- ment	Family Allowance	All Programs
Social Leaders (N=4)	47.3	49.8	52.3	37.8	36.5	44.7
Cyprus	39.0	39.0	53.0	39.0	8.0	35.6
Israel	42.0	42.0	42.0	25.0	36.0	37.4
Armenia	73.0	83.0	40.0	74.0	51.0	64.2
Tunisia	35.0	35.0	74.0	13.0	51.0	41.6
Mid Performing Countries (N=14)	29.0	21.7	38.2	4.7	11.4	21.0
Jordan	17.0	0.0	17.0	0.0	0.0	6.8
Georgia	39.0	40.0	40.0	4.0	0.0	24.6
Lebanon	32.0	32.0	52.0	0.0	52.0	33.6
Kuwait	19.0	0.0	19.0	0.0	0.0	7.6
Algeria	46.0	46.0	76.0	0.0	54.0	44.4
Turkey	46.0	50.0	50.0	0.0	0.0	29.2
Azerbaijan	0.0	0.0	0.0	4.0	0.0	0.8
Libya	38.0	38.0	38.0	22.0	0.0	27.2
Bahrain	19.0	0.0	19.0	0.0	0.0	7.6
Egypt, U.A.R.	45.0	36.0	59.0	36.0	0.0	35.2
Saudi Arabia	33.0	26.0	48.0	0.0	0.0	21.4
Syrian Arab	36.0	0.0	49.0	0.0	0.0	17.0
Qatar	0.0	0.0	0.0	0.0	0.0	0.0
Morocco	36.0	36.0	68.0	0.0	53.0	38.6
Social LDCs (N=4)	22.0	9.8	32.3	7.8	0.0	14.4
Oman	20.0	0.0	18.0	0.0	0.0	7.6
Iraq	39.0	39.0	59.0	31.0	0.0	33.6
Sudan*	21.0	0.0	48.0	0.0	0.0	13.8
Yemen*	8.0	0.0	4.0	0.0	0.0	2.4
Averages (N=22)	31.0	24.6	39.7	11.3	13.9	24.1

Source: USDHHS, 1997: Social Security Programs Throughout the World.

The   development trends observed for Israel (Figures 10 and 11) are typical of those observed for all four SLs, i.e., a pattern of steady, sustained, growth across a broad range of sectors for each of the study periods. Particularly noticeable are Israel's high levels of public investment in the Health, Education, and Economic sectors.   In recent years, investments in these sectors, though declining, have remained high in response to reduced public expenditures for defense and military purposes combined with manageable increases in population size.   The absence of major natural disasters, high levels of cultural homogeneity, and favorable Welfare Effort trends also work to Israel's advantage in accelerating its pace of social development.   These positive social development trends resulted in a net increase of 34% in Israel's WISP scores between 1970 and 1995 (Table 3).

Figure 10   WISP subindex scores for Israel, 1970-1995

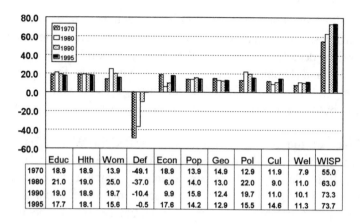

	Educ	Hlth	Wom	Def	Econ	Pop	Geo	Pol	Cul	Wel	WISP
1970	18.9	18.9	13.9	-49.1	18.9	13.9	14.9	12.9	11.9	7.9	55.0
1980	21.0	19.0	25.0	-37.0	6.0	14.0	13.0	22.0	9.0	11.0	63.0
1990	19.0	18.9	19.7	-10.4	9.9	15.8	12.4	19.7	11.0	10.1	73.3
1995	17.7	18.1	15.6	-0.5	17.6	14.2	12.9	15.5	14.6	11.3	73.7

Figure 11   Percent change in WISP subindex scores for Israel, 1970-1995

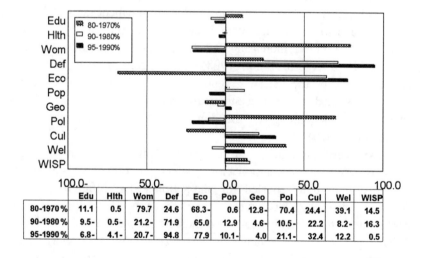

	Edu	Hlth	Wom	Def	Eco	Pop	Geo	Pol	Cul	Wel	WISP
80-1970 %	11.1	0.5	79.7	24.6	68.3-	0.6	12.8-	70.4	24.4-	39.1	14.5
90-1980 %	9.5-	0.5-	21.2-	71.9	65.0	12.9	4.6-	10.5-	22.2	8.2-	16.3
95-1990 %	6.8-	4.1-	20.7-	94.8	77.9	10.1-	4.0	21.1-	32.4	12.2	0.5

Regional Socially Least Developing Countries (SLDCs)

The ME region also contains four SLDCs, i.e., countries in which the pace of social progress either has stagnated or has deteriorated to levels below those of earlier decades: Yemen (WISP = 11), Sudan (WISP = 16), Iraq (WISP = 33), and Oman (WISP = 36). WISP scores for the SLDCs averaged only 24 in 1995 (Table 4), an average score well below that achieved by both the region and the world as a whole for the same year (Figure 1).

Three of the region's SLDCs are located in West Asia. Three SLDCs are also currently experiencing unprecedented levels of social turmoil, i.e. Iraq, Sudan, and Yemen, much of which is associated with chronic poverty in combination with weak economies, high unemployment, and high levels of income inequality. Approximately 20% of the region's populations, 68 million people, reside in its SLDCs (Table 4).

SLDC per capita income levels averages only $1883 with a low of $270 for Yemen and a high of $4950 for Oman (Table 4). While the majority of these countries are experiencing low-moderate rates of economic expansion, the benefits normally associated with even modest levels of growth are offset by higher inflation and unemployment rates. Most of the SLDCs are also confronted with declining markets for their dwindling exports and rapidly increasing levels of public sector indebtedness (ESCWA, 1998; World Bank, 1998). As a consequence of both trends, unemployment in the SLDCs tends to be high while effective social programs designed to assist economically displaced persons, are either non-existent or inadequate given the dimensions of the country's economic difficulties (Table 5).

Another consequence of recurrent social failures in the region's SLDCs is that life expectation averages less than 60 years, 14 years lower on average than that reported for the region's SLs. Infant (61/1000) and child mortality (95/1000) rates are high as is adult illiteracy (51%). Unfortunately, these highly negative trends are among the worst in the world and have not improved much over 1980 levels (UNICEF, 1998). In every case, increasing levels of social chaos in the region's SLDCs have contributed to human rights violations of a magnitude sufficient to warrant condemnation by leading international human rights groups (Amnesty International, 1998).

The social development trends summarized in Figures 12 and 13 for Sudan are typical of those observed for all four of the region's SLDCs, i.e., a pattern of development under-performance combined with steady social deterioration across a broad range of social sectors and time periods.

Figure 12 WISP subindex scores for Sudan, 1970-1995

	Educ	Hlth	Wom	Def	Econ	Pop	Geo	Pol	Cul	Wel	WISP
1970	-0.1	5.9	-0.1	9.9	12.9	4.9	7.9	-1.1	1.9	4.9	18.0
1980	4.0	4.0	3.0	13.0	4.0	3.0	10.0	9.0	5.0	-1.0	18.0
1990	1.7	1.0	-0.7	15.8	3.6	3.1	9.0	5.9	1.9	0.1	12.9
1995	5.1	4.1	1.8	10.2	3.5	2.8	-2.0	1.9	4.3	2.8	16.3

Figure 13   Percent change in WISP subindex scores for Sudan, 1970-1995

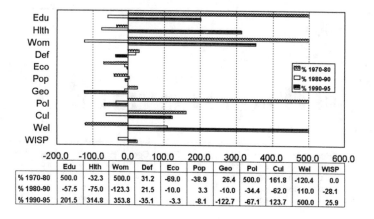

	Edu	Hlth	Wom	Def	Eco	Pop	Geo	Pol	Cul	Wel	WISP
% 1970-80	500.0	-32.3	500.0	31.2	-69.0	-38.9	26.4	500.0	161.8	-120.4	0.0
% 1980-90	-57.5	-75.0	-123.3	21.5	-10.0	3.3	-10.0	-34.4	-62.0	110.0	-28.1
% 1990-95	201.5	314.8	353.8	-35.1	-3.3	-8.1	-122.7	-67.1	123.7	500.0	25.9

Middle Performing Countries (MPCs)

Fourteen of ME's countries are classified as MPCs: Jordan (WISP = 56), Georgia (WISP = 55), Lebanon (WISP = 55), Kuwait (WISP = 55), Algeria (WISP = 54), Turkey (WISP = 52), Azerbaijan (WISP =52), Libya (WISP = 51), Bahrain (WISP = 50), Egypt (WISP = 49), Saudi Arabia (WISP = 48), Syria (WISP = 48), Qatar (WISP = 46), and Morocco (WISP = 45). WISP scores for the MPCs average 51. Approximately 245 million people, 74% of the region's total population, reside in these MPCs (Table 4).

Development patterns are more variable, and fluctuate more rapidly in the region's MPCs than in either the SLs or SLDCs (Table 4). The social development trends reported for Egypt (Figures 14 and 15) and Turkey (Figures 16 and 17) are typical of the asynchronous nature of development characteristic of the region's MPCs, i.e., steady, but unremarkable, time-limited progress across selected sectors and time periods. The data also reveal the forward and backward nature of social development in the MPCs, i.e., a pattern in which recent social development accomplishments fail to achieve the degree of integration required to sustain these changes over the long term.

Figure 14 WISP subindex scores for Egypt, 1970-1995

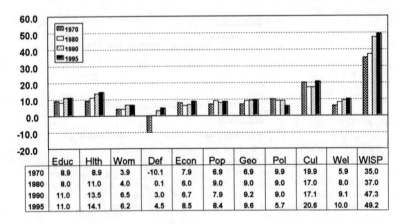

	Educ	Hlth	Wom	Def	Econ	Pop	Geo	Pol	Cul	Wel	WISP
1970	8.9	8.9	3.9	-10.1	7.9	6.9	6.9	9.9	19.9	5.9	35.0
1980	8.0	11.0	4.0	0.1	6.0	9.0	9.0	9.0	17.0	8.0	37.0
1990	11.0	13.5	6.5	3.0	6.7	7.9	9.2	9.0	17.1	9.1	47.3
1995	11.0	14.1	6.2	4.5	8.5	8.4	9.6	5.7	20.6	10.0	49.2

Figure 15 **Percent change in WISP subindex scores for Egypt, 1970-1995**

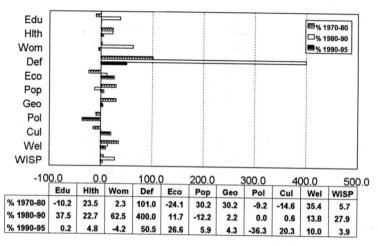

	Edu	Hlth	Wom	Def	Eco	Pop	Geo	Pol	Cul	Wel	WISP
% 1970-80	-10.2	23.5	2.3	101.0	-24.1	30.2	30.2	-9.2	-14.6	35.4	5.7
% 1980-90	37.5	22.7	62.5	400.0	11.7	-12.2	2.2	0.0	0.6	13.8	27.9
% 1990-95	0.2	4.8	-4.2	50.5	26.6	5.9	4.3	-36.3	20.3	10.0	3.9

Figure 16 WISP subindex scores for Turkey, 1970-1995

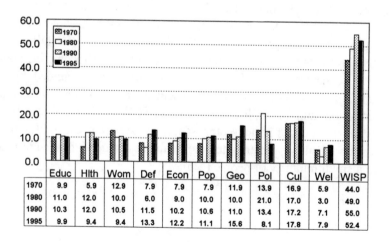

	Educ	Hlth	Wom	Def	Econ	Pop	Geo	Pol	Cul	Wel	WISP
1970	9.9	5.9	12.9	7.9	7.9	7.9	11.9	13.9	16.9	5.9	44.0
1980	11.0	12.0	10.0	6.0	9.0	10.0	10.0	21.0	17.0	3.0	49.0
1990	10.3	12.0	10.5	11.5	10.2	10.6	11.0	13.4	17.2	7.1	55.0
1995	9.9	9.4	9.4	13.3	12.2	11.1	15.6	8.1	17.8	7.9	52.4

Figure 17　Percent change in WISP subindex scores for Turkey, 1970-1995

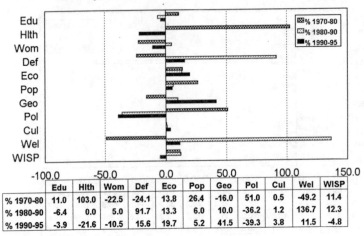

	Edu	Hlth	Wom	Def	Eco	Pop	Geo	Pol	Cul	Wel	WISP
% 1970-80	11.0	103.0	-22.5	-24.1	13.8	26.4	-16.0	51.0	0.5	-49.2	11.4
% 1980-90	-6.4	0.0	5.0	91.7	13.3	6.0	10.0	-36.2	1.2	136.7	12.3
% 1990-95	-3.9	-21.6	-10.5	15.6	19.7	5.2	41.5	-39.3	3.8	11.5	-4.8

Today, life expectation in the region's MPCs averages 70 years whereas infant (31/1000) and child (37/1000) mortality rates remain high. Adult illiteracy (26%) and primary school enrolment levels (84%) are also high in the MPCs. Income inequality is more problematic than in the region's MPCs where, on the average, 45% of total household income is concentrated among the group's top 20% of income earners (UNDP, 1998). The pattern reflects the group's long-standing patterns of income inequality and wealth concentration. The situation is further compounded by the slower pace of MPC economic development in combination with higher average inflation and unemployment rates (ESCWA, 1998; World Bank, 1998). Unfortunately, public sector social programs in the MPCs are of comparatively recent origin and lack the financial resources needed to reach other than a small minority of people (Table 5).

Discussion

Indeed, the ME countries have arrived at a critical social policy crossroad. The region's traditional political and economic systems have proven to be largely ineffectual in solving increasingly more complex problems. The situation is especially precarious in the region's four SLDCs in which some 20% of its population, i.e. 68 million people, reside. Chronic poverty, urban deterioration, environmental erosion, and income inequality are only some of the profound challenges confronting the region's leaders at the outset of the new century.

The data reported in this analysis suggest that the majority of the ME governments are committed to the modernization of their societies. The necessary preconditions needed for transformation into modern nation-states already is far along in the region's four SLs (Abukhalil, 1997; Handoussa, 1998). Other countries in the region, however, continue to struggle with problems of limited or declining natural resources (e.g., Egypt, Jordan), rapidly expanding populations (e.g., Jordan, Saudi Arabia, Yemen), and oppositional political voices (e.g., Algeria, Iraq, Kuwait, Morocco, Syria). Still, other countries are continuing the search for more efficacious approaches for integrating deeply felt religious traditions with the requirements of modern, mostly secular, nation-states (e.g., Egypt, Saudi Arabia, Turkey). And still, other countries in the region do not appear to have yet made the commitment to modernizing their macro economic and political environments (e.g., Iraq, Sudan).

The social development trends reported in this study for the region's 14 MPCs, reveal less optimistic patterns than those identified for the SLs (UNDP, 1998; World Bank, 1998). Even so, the social changes taking place in the majority of MPCs are moving generally in a positive direction. Over time, some MPCs are likely to attain development profiles comparable to those of the SLs. Development trends in the lower performing MPCs, however, are more mixed and the possibility exists that several of these countries may be reclassified as SLDCs in future surveys.

Finally, the social conditions reported in this study for the region's four SLDCs, i.e. Yemen, Sudan, Iraq, and Oman, are deplorable and require urgent attention both within the region and on the part of the larger international community. At a minimum, preferential development assistance needs to be extended to the 65 million people, nearly 20% of the region's total population that reside in its SLDCs. Failure to act decisively on the special development needs of the SLDCs will undermine the region's capacity in achieving its broader based development objectives for the next century. It also will continue to undermine the region's peace and security, an issue of considerable concern to the larger community of nations. Certainly, careful consideration needs to be given to establishing more effective political and economic systems within the SLDCs (ESCWA, 1998; Moghadam, 1991; Zoubir, 1996) along with the establishment of viable civil society institutions that have proven invaluable in accelerating the pace of development for other countries in the region (Ahmida, 1997; Norton, 1996).

Notes

1 The author expresses his appreciation to Prof. Dr. Frans Lammerty, Dean of the Faculty of Social Sciences at Katholieke Universiteit von Leuven, Belgium, for providing him with the opportunity to complete work on this manuscript while a Visiting Professor in the Faculty.

2 Adequacy of social provision refers to the changing capacity of governments to provide for the basic social and material needs of the people living within their borders, e.g. food, clothing, shelter and access to at least basic health, education and social services (Estes, 1984: 199-209).

3 The following factor loadings and formulae were used as statistical weights in calculating composite WISP scores for individual countries:

WISP95 = {[(Factor 1)*.697)]+[(Factor 2)*.163)]+[(Factor 3)*.140]} where:

Factor 1 = [(Hlth*.93) + (Educ*.91) + (Welfare*.92) + (Woman*.91) + (Political*.84) + (Econ*.71) + (Diversity*.64) + (Demographic *.93)]

Factor 2 = [(Defense Effort * .93)]

Factor 3 = [(Geographic *.98)]

4 See Estes, 1999 for a more complete discussion of alternative approaches to the measurement and assessment of social development.

5 Worldwide performance on all the WISP's subindexes was set statistically at 10.0. Thus, subindex scores with a value below 10 reflect less favorable development trends vis-à-vis the world as a whole, while scores greater than 10 reflect more favorable development trends.

References

Abukhalil, As'ad. (1997), 'Change and Democratization in the Arab World: The Role of Political Parties', *Third World Quarterly*, 18(1), pp 149-163.

Abu-Lughod, Lila. (1998), *Remaking Women: Feminism and Modernity in the Middle East*, Princeton University Press, Princeton.

Ahmida, Ali Abdullatif. (1997), 'Inventing or Recovering "Civil Society" in the Middle East', *Critique*, 10 (Spring), pp 127-134.

Amnesty International. (1998), Country Reports, (series)., London: Amnesty International.

Esposito, John L. (1998), *Islam and Politics*, Syracuse University Press, Syracuse.

Estes, Richard J. (1984), *The Social Progress of Nations*, Praeger, New York.

_____. (1988), *Trends in World Social Development*, Praeger, New York.

_____. (1995), 'Social Development Trends in Africa: The Need for a New Development Paradigm', *Social Development Issues*, 17(1), pp 18-47.

_____. (1996a), 'Social Development Trends in Latin America, 1970-1994: In the Shadows of the 21st Century', *Social Development Issues*, 18(1), pp 25-52.

_____. (1996b), 'Social Development Trends in Asia', *Social Indicators Research*, 37(2), pp 119-148.

_____. (1997) 'Trends in European Social Development: Development Prospects For the New Europe', *Social Indicators Research*, 42, pp 1-19.

_____. (1998a), 'Trends in World Social Development, 1970-95: Development Prospects for a New Century', *Journal of Developing Societies*, 14(1), pp 1-29.

_____. (1998b) 'Social Development Trends In The Successor States To The Former Soviet Union: The Search For A New Paradigm', in Kempe R. Hope, Jr., *Challenges of Transformation and Transition From Centrally Planned to Market Economies*, UNCRD Research Report Series No. 26. (Nagoya: United Nations Centre for Regional Development), pp. 13-30.

_____. (1999), 'The 'Poverties': Competing Definitions and Alternative Approaches to Measurement', *Social Development Issues*, (forthcoming).

Galal, Mohamed Noman. (1997), 'Global Interdependence and the Middle East', *Philosophy and Social Action* 23(1), pp 43-49.

Gilbar, Gad G. (1997),. *Population Dilemmas in the Middle East*, International Specialized Book Services, Portland.

Goldschmidt, Arthur Jr. (1998), *Concise History of the Middle East*, 6th Edition, Westview Press, Boulder, Colorado.

Handoussa, Heba. (1998), *Economic Transition in the Middle East: Global Challenges and Adjustment Strategies*, Columbia University Press, New York.

Hunter, Shireen T. (1998), *The Future of Islam and the West: Clash of Civilizations or Peaceful Coexistence?* Greenwood Publishing Group, Westport CT.

Jabbra, Joseph G; and Jabbra, Nancy W. (1997), 'Challenging Environmental Issues: Middle Eastern Perspectives', *Journal of Developing Societies* 13(1), pp 1-17.

Kramer, Martin. (1996), *Arab Awakening and Islamic Revival: The Politics of Ideas in the Middle East.*, Transaction Publishers, New Brunswick.

Lapidus, Ira M. (1996), 'State and Religion in Islamic Societies', *Past & Present*, 151, pp 3-27.

Lobban, Richard (ed). (1998), *Middle Eastern Women and the Invisible Economy*, University Press of Florida, Gainesville.

Mallat, Chibli. (1998). *Middle East into the Twenty-First Century: Studies on the Arab-Israeli Conflict, the Gulf Crisis*, L P C/InBook.

Massoulie, Francois. (1998), *Middle East Conflicts*, Interlink Publishing Group, Northampton.

Michel, Thomas. (1997), 'Social and Religious Factors Affecting Muslim-Christian Relations', *Islam and Christian-Muslim Relations* (8)1, pp 53-66.

Moghadam, Valentine M. (1991), 'The Neo-Patriarchal State in the Middle East: Development, Authoritarianism and Crisis', *Socialism and Democracy*, 7(3), pp 125-140.

Monshipouri, Mahmood. (1998), *Islamism, Secularism, and Human Rights in the Middle East*, Lynne Rienner Publishers, Boulder.

Norton, Augustus R. (ed), (1996), *Civil Society in the Middle East*, Volumes I & II, Brill Academic Publishers, Boston.

Sadiki, Larbi. (1996), 'The New World (Dis)Order: Between Occident and Orient', *Political Expressions*, 1(2), pp 127-149.

Savir, Uri. (1998), *The Process: 1,100 Days That Changed the Middle East*, Random House, New York.

Sayigh, Yezid. (1998), *Armed Struggle and the Search for State*, Oxford University Press, New York.

Sexton, Richard. (1992) ' The Middle East Water Crisis: Is It the Making of a New Middle East Regional Order?', *Capitalism, Nature, Socialism*, 3(4), pp 65-77.

Sick, Gary and Lawrence Potter. (1998), *The Persian Gulf at the Millennium*, St. Martin's Press, New York.

Sonn, Tamara. (1996), 'Islam and the Political Process in the Arab World: A Post Gulf War Update', *Journal of Developing Societies*, 12(2), pp 191-204.

Starr, Joyce R. (1991) 'Water Security: The Missing Link in Our Mideast Strategy', *Current World Leaders* 34(4), pp 571-588.

Tessler, Mark. (ed), (1995), *Democracy, War and Peace in the Middle East*, Indiana University Press, Bloomington, Indiana.

United Nations Children's Fund (UNICEF). (1998), *The State of the World's Children, 1998*, Oxford University Press, New York.

United Nations Development Programme (UNDP). (1998), *Human Development Report, 1998*, Oxford University Press, New York.

United Nations Economic and Social Commission for Western Asia (ESCWA). (1995a). (Human Development in the Arab World: Cultural and Social Dimensions, ESCWA, Beirut, Sales # E/ ESCWA/SD/1995/7 (Arabic).

_____. (1995b) Measuring Poverty in the Countries of the Economic and Social Commission for Western Asia, ESCWA, Beirut, Sales # E/ESCWA/SD/1995/8/Add.1/Rev.1 (Arabic).

_____. (1996b), Financing Human Development in the Arab World, ESCWA, Beirut, Sales # E/ ESCWA/SD/1996/4 (Arabic).

_____ (1996c), Population Growth and Economic Development, ESCWA, Beirut, Sales # E/ ESCWA/POP/1996/WG.2/6.

_____ (1996d), Population Growth and Health, ESCWA, Beirut, Sales # E/ ESCWA/POP/1996/WG.2/7.

_____. (1996e), Population Growth and Education, ESCWA, Beirut, Sales # E/ ESCWA/POP/1996/WG.2/8.

_____. (1996f), Population Growth and Housing, ESCWA, Beirut, Sales # E/ ESCWA/POP/1996/WG.2/9.

_____. (1998), (Survey of Economic and Social Developments, 1997-1998, ESCWA, , Beirut.

United States Department of Health and Human Services (USDHHS). (1997), Social Security Programs Throughout the World, 1997, Social Security Administration, Washington.

Viorst, Milton. (1998), *In the Shadow of the Prophet*, Anchor Books, London.

World Bank. (1998), *World Development Report*, 1998, World Bank, Washington.

World Resources Institute (WRI). (1997), *World Resources, 1996-97*, Oxford University Press, New York.

Zoubir, Yahia H. (1996), 'The Failure of the Authoritarian Developmentalist Regimes and the Emergence of Radical Protest Movements in the Middle East and Africa: The Case of Algeria', *Journal of Third World Studies*, 13(1), pp 127-184.

3 Poverty and Social Development in Africa

Arimah Benedict Chukuwka

Introduction

Poverty has increasingly become a global phenomenon threatening the survival of humanity particularly in developing countries. Given that over 20% of the world's five billion people live in abject poverty, it is accepted that the dangers posed by poverty must be addressed and alleviated in the short term and eventually eradicated in the long run. In this respect, the United Nations declared 1996 the *International Year for the Eradication of Poverty*. What constitutes poverty has evolved over time and has varied considerably across societies and cultures. Although universally accepted definitions and criteria have emerged, there are nonetheless country-specific poverty lines and criteria for distinguishing the poor from the non-poor. These reflect normative concepts on well being, welfare, rights, as well as national priorities.

Poverty as defined by the World Bank (1990) is the inability to attain a minimum standard of living. Poverty is also understood to mean the inability of families to meet basic needs such as food, adequate housing, health care and educational expenses. The manifestations of poverty are multidimensional. These include starvation and child malnutrition; infant and maternal mortality; illiteracy; poor health; vulnerability to events and circumstances which place lives and livelihood in jeopardy; overcrowded and poorly ventilated habitation; absence of basic facilities; proliferation of slums and squatter settlements; breakdown of waste disposal arrangements; inadequate water and power supply; and squalid conditions of environmental sanitation, among many others.

Poverty remains a major problem in Africa. Not only has it become increasingly entrenched and multifaceted over the years, it has continued to defy efforts at its eradication. In this regard, the World Bank (1992) notes that the number of poor people in sub-Saharan Africa increased from 185 million in 1985 to 216 million in 1990. Further estimates provided by the World Bank (1997) reveal that about 45% of Africa's population subsist on less than one US dollar a day. When compared to other regions in the developing world, Africa has experienced severe decline in most of its socio-economic indicators. In the 1980s, per capita income in Africa fell by

2.5% per annum. This is in contrast to other regions that witnessed positive growth rates varying from 1.9% in Latin America to 6.8% in East Asia. Since the 1980s, Africa's poverty situation has been compounded by the outbreak of civil wars, political instability, droughts, high external debts and a high population growth rate of about 3.1%.

The persistence of poverty in Africa has led to the proliferation of studies designed to gain further insights into the nature of this problem and proffer ameliorative solutions. Most of these studies have focused on assessing the various impacts of the Structural Adjustment Programs (SAP) adopted by most African countries in the 1980s, as well as investigating coping mechanisms adopted by households. The major conclusion reached by most of these studies (UNICEF, (1987); Seregeldin, 1989; Van der Hoeven, 1991; Kayizzi-Mugerwa and Levin, 1994; Kayizzi-Mugerwa and Lufumpa, 1995) is that apart from leading to an intensification of poverty, the adjustment programs have had negative social consequences on low income and vulnerable families. It is perhaps in recognition of these negative social repercussions that the African Development Bank (ADB) in conjunction with the UNDP and the World Bank in 1988, launched the Social Dimensions of Adjustment (SDA) initiative. The SDA projects sought to mitigate hardships encountered by poor and vulnerable families by focusing on four key areas. These include: (a) improved management of macro and sectoral policies; (b) social action programs and projects to assist vulnerable socioeconomic groups; (c) improved national information systems to enhance policy and program formulation; and (d) institution building and training to integrate social dimensions as part of the current policy and implementation process (ABD, *et al.* 1990).

Few studies however, exist that seek to examine the link between poverty alleviation and social development in Africa. This is rather surprising, given the fact that in an attempt to reduce poverty levels, many African countries have embarked on various forms of social development. These include good governance, democratization, improving literacy levels, increased investment in education, health and other infrastructure and services, reduction in military spending, increased access to various forms of micro credit and a general increase in human capital investment among others. Since these aspects of social development have been adopted to improve the quality of life and reduce the level of poverty in the respective African countries, there is the need to investigate in a systematic and rigorous manner, their impacts on poverty reduction. Such an undertaking will further enhance the understanding on the role social development plays in poverty alleviation.

The main purpose of this study is to investigate in a systematic manner the link between poverty and social development using cross-national data drawn from 54 African countries. In order to achieve this, the paper has two objectives. The first is to provide poverty profiles for these countries using at least two sets of such measures. The first set is a series of poverty lines based on income, while the second is a composite measure to be derived from an amalgam of socio-economic indicators. This will enable the determination of the extent of poverty among African countries and group these countries on the basis of their poverty profiles. Such an undertaking will also show if there are any discernible differences when poverty is defined on the basis of income on the one hand, and when defined on the basis of composite measures derived from an amalgam of socio-economic indicators, on the other.

The second objective of the paper is to account for variations in the extant levels of poverty among African countries, while paying specific attention to various aspects of social development. Specifically, answers are sought for the following questions:

- What roles do increasing levels of investment in education, health and in other aspects of human development play in accounting for the level of poverty between African countries?
- Do countries with significantly higher levels of investment in health, education as well as in other aspects of human development have lower levels of poverty?
- What is the link between poverty and good governance in Africa?
- Are reductions in military expenditure associated with a reduction in poverty levels within the African continent?

Answers to these questions will be of immense benefit, as they will strengthen the information base upon which decisions on poverty alleviation may be made in Africa.

Development Strategies and Poverty Alleviation

Following the United Nations (1986) view, development may be seen as a comprehensive, economic, social, cultural and political process, aimed at the constant improvement of the well-being of the entire population and all its individuals on the basis of their active, free and meaningful participation in development and in the fair distribution of the ensuing benefits. Yet, development strategies adopted in Third World countries have been narrowly conceived and often seen as synonymous with economic growth. It is therefore not surprising that there are instances in which increases in economic growth indicators have been associated with increasing levels of unemployment and poverty (Adelman and Morris, 1973; Lisk, 1983). This section sketches a brief overview of the key development strategies as they relate to poverty alleviation in developing countries. In so doing, some of the weaknesses of these strategies are identified. Given the differences and similarities in objectives, policy emphases and underlying philosophies, four dominant approaches to development in Third World countries may be identified. These are commonly referred to as: (a) growth-oriented; (b) employment-oriented; (c) anti-poverty-oriented; and (d) social development-oriented approaches of which the last incorporates the basic needs approach.

Growth-Oriented Approach

The main objective of the growth-oriented approach is to increase the rate of output within a country over a period of time by increasing the rate of capital formation (Lisk, 1983). In this case, growth is a function of increase in capital stock, and emphasis is placed on the mobilization of savings. Rapid growth in GNP and its components are seen as the sole objectives of development (Dower, 1992). The basic thinking is that increases in GNP would result in higher standards of living through its positive impacts on other economic and social parameters.

Two variants of growth-oriented strategies may be identified. These are balanced and unbalanced growth. Balanced growth entails the simultaneous massive investment in all fronts with the object of reaching the point where an increased rate of aggregate growth may be generated. According to Lisk (1983), this implies the need to overcome the various encumbrances that may impede the rapid growth of output, and often results in a bias for capital-intensive projects and a desire for rapid industrialization. Rather than an investment approach, the unbalanced growth strategy entails a selective approach that involves concentrating on key industries or sectors where linkage effects or complementaries are deemed to be strongest. In essence, growth-oriented approaches to development focus on investment projects. This entails the general introduction and increase in industrialization, advanced technology, as well as modern bureaucratic and economic mechanisms into the modern sector where commercial and technical linkages are supposed to be greatest.

A number of weaknesses have been associated with the growth-oriented approach to development. Firstly, Lisk (1983) observes that the policies, which will make the attainment of a more equitable distribution of income, are hardly taken into consideration. This is because it is thought that such policies would adversely affect capital accumulation, which is required for investment and rapid growth of the GNP. Secondly, in growth-oriented approaches, employment creation and promotion policies are rarely given the attention they require. This is because in the modern sector, production is dependent on capital-intensive technology. The bias for high technology and capital-intensive methods of production has provided little or no scope for the much anticipated trickle-down process. Lisk (*op. cit.*) further notes that the consequences of this are the withholding of gains of the modern sector from the traditional or informal sector which invariably provides subsistence for majority of the population. Thirdly, the role that current consumption can play in fostering development, is not given adequate consideration. This perhaps follows from the view that redistribution of purchasing power in favor of low-income groups, may negatively affect growth by reducing investment and savings. According to Lardy (1975), this view barely takes cognizance of the possibility of the simultaneous increase in both consumption and investment that may result from the redistribution of purchasing power, provided that some of the country's investible resources are channeled towards providing the goods and services consumers require. Fourthly, the main preoccupation with growth in GNP by the growth-oriented strategy may also be questioned. This is because instances are rife where increase in GNP occurs, but certain things such as poverty, unemployment and gross inequality in the distribution of resources remain widespread.

The foregoing criticisms point to the inadequacy of growth-oriented approaches as means of coping with problems of poverty that so often beset African countries. In this respect, Lisk (*op. cit.*) outlines the need for broad-based development objectives, which take due cognizance of a wide-range of socio-political and institutional factors that determine and are determined by the process of economic and social development.

Employment-Oriented Approach

In addition to economic growth, the objective of the employment-oriented approach encompasses a broader notion of development, which includes improvements in living conditions of individuals. In other words, the employment-oriented approach seeks to reconcile economic development with the broader distribution of incomes via increases in productive employment. In this regard, employment creation and promotion are seen as the major means of bringing about a more even distribution of the benefits of economic growth. The thrust of this approach is that simultaneous increases in both output and employment may be attained by the direct substitution of labor for capital in the production process. This in turn, has often led to the setting of employment targets contingent upon higher levels of GNP growth than may be feasible. If high levels of employment are to be attained in relation to output, a key requirement is the restructuring of domestic demand and production towards relatively higher levels of labor-intensive output. Basically, this may be achieved by reducing the capital intensity required for production in the modern sector and by providing a supply of capital that is commensurate with the need for increased rates of labor absorption and output growth in the traditional or informal sector (Lisk, *op. cit.*).

In developing countries, certain conditions have to be met before the gains in both output and employment can be achieved. The first of these according to Leibenstein (1966), is the possibility of substituting labor for capital. This in turn, implies a relatively high degree of administrative, managerial and technical efficiency. Secondly, Lisk (*op. cit.*) reminds us that the price of factors needs to be established at realistic levels in relation to their costs so as to avoid the adoption and utilization of inefficient and inappropriate technology. The main snag however, is that these are not readily present in many developing countries. In this respect, Lisk cautions that productivity and employment objectives should be reconciled on the basis of what GNP growth rate is required to attain a substantial increase in employment levels.

Anti-Poverty Approach

Based on the realization that previous approaches which seek to effect a redistribution of income via greater access to paid employment have failed to include low-income/vulnerable groups, the anti-poverty approach development seeks to increase per capita income above a predetermined poverty line, as well as reduce income and social inequalities (Lisk, *op. cit.*). This range of objectives is extended to include the transformation of social structures, including a progressive redistribution of income in favor of the poor.

This approach may be seen to represent a major reorientation of development towards the poor as it seeks to redistribute wealth, assets and output mainly through the reallocation of productive resources in their favor. Ameliorative measures are mainly directed towards overcoming certain institutional bottlenecks that are thought to be responsible for keeping the incomes of the poor at low levels. Such institutional bottlenecks may include lack of or insufficient access to productive assets such as land and appropriate technology, as well as educational and health facilities. Following the explicit identification of various poverty groups, a common practice is to design separate action-oriented programs for each. Each program consists of policy packages designed to rectify specific causes of poverty. According to Lisk (*op. cit.*), such anti-poverty packages often include measures designed to change the pattern and tenure of land ownership; improve access to basic education, vocational training, health facilities, development finance, as well as other productive assets; enhance the development of small scale businesses; and reduce birth rates.

The implied assumption of the anti-poverty approach is that following the initial redistribution of productive assets in favor of the poor, it is possible to achieve an increase in their per capita income faster than those of the more prosperous sections of the population. Lisk (*op. cit.*) however, cautions that this may not be possible for two reasons. Firstly, in the case of paid employment, any attempts at improving the earning capacity of the unskilled and semi-skilled unemployed and underemployed will first require the services of technical and managerial personnel earning above-average incomes. In this regard, some of the benefits are likely to accrue to the well-off sections of the population. Secondly, given that institutional arrangements in most developing countries are mainly in favor of middle- and high-income groups, it may not be possible to exclude these groups from benefiting from the anti-poverty policy packages designed exclusively for poor households. For instance, in developing countries, housing programs designed specifically for low-income families have been hijacked by the more affluent groups on account of the inability of the former to pay for such houses. This in part, may be attributed to the inability of planners and policy makers to adequately integrate the concerns of low-income households into such housing-related programs. The bottom line however, is that anti-poverty policies can only be effectual after adequate consideration has been given to socio-institutional consequences for different groups within the economy.

Social Development

The emergence of social development as an alternative strategy may be attributed to the failure of previous development approaches to solve the problem of poverty affecting most developing countries. The main goal of social development is to improve the social and material well-being of people everywhere and, in so doing, promote the highest possible level of human development. The more specific objectives of social development include the following: (a) the realization of more balanced approaches to social and economic development; (b) the elimination of the various barriers to development; (c) the realization of new social arrangements that accelerate the pace of development and guarantee the satisfaction of basic needs of people everywhere in the world; and (d) the transformation of societies toward more humanistic values based on social justice, the promotion of peace and the attainment of the fullest possible level of human development (Estes, 1998).

From the foregoing, social development incorporates the basic needs approach which entails satisfying the essential requirements of a country's population within a given time horizon. In this regard, two sets of targets are identified. The first relates to meeting personal consumption needs such as food, shelter and clothing. The second pertains to basic public services such as education, health, sanitation, access to potable water, as well as cultural and transportation facilities. It is also seen that social development further seeks to reduce and eventually eliminate poverty by focusing attention on the development and improvement in human capital. Following from this, Lisk (1983, pp.47-48) notes that "... the basic needs targets are not restricted to the eradication of absolute poverty, but extend to the satisfaction of needs over and above the subsistence levels as a means of eliminating relative poverty through a continuous process of economic development and social progress."

Social progress in this respect includes such aspects as: improvements in literacy levels; increased investment in education, health, nutrition, family planning and other infrastructure and social services; a general increase in human capital investment; good governance; increasing levels of democratization and mass participation in socio-economic and political decisions; and a reduction in military spending, among others. Access to adequate health and education for instance are regarded as basic needs for social development in the sense that they are directly related to an individual's well-being and chances of obtaining adequately paid employment. The attainment of relatively high levels of social development especially in the areas enumerated above, will ultimately foster productivity and hence reduce the level of poverty. This is in line with Green's (1990) assertion that only a labor force that is literate, healthy, and well fed can constantly and increasingly be efficient, productive and innovative. Conversely, inadequate access to education, ill health and malnutrition can severely constrain the ability of individuals to work long, hard and productively, thereby leading to rising levels of poverty.

Since the social development approach seeks to satisfy basic needs and eliminate poverty, it may be regarded as being identical to the conventional anti-poverty approach. A number of conceptual differences may be identified. Firstly, conventional anti-poverty approaches focus on specific groups within a country, while the social development approach sees poverty as being widespread and as such, is concerned with the entire population. Secondly, apart from increasing the supply of basic goods and services, the social development approach is also preoccupied with increasing the level of aggregate demand. This is unlike the conventional anti-poverty approach, which is merely concerned with raising incomes of the poor to a minimum subsistence level.

Social development as an alternative approach to poverty alleviation, has a number of advantages over other development strategies. Firstly, social development is concerned with the attainment of ends rather than means. This is unlike growth-oriented strategies where emphasis is placed on GNP as a means of development. In this respect, Hicks and Streeten (1981) point out that social development covers aspects of human, social, economic and cultural development which are not covered in most growth-oriented approaches. Secondly, the social development approach may be seen as a people-centered and people-oriented strategy to development. Here the focus is essentially on human beings. This perhaps is because human beings are the source of ideas, decisions and actions on investment, as well as innovation and other opportunities (World Bank, 1983). Thirdly, the social development approach is able to specify certain minimum levels of personal consumption and access to public and social services that are desirable for decent living. This in turn, makes it possible to define minimum targets on a global basis. For instance, minimum targets for food, housing and education may be defined with respect to daily calories intake, square meters of space per person and the minimum educational requirement for adequately paid employment respectively. Apart from facilitating the identification of those whose basic needs are not being met, such an approach avoids the weakness of relating the diversity of human needs to a relatively abstract index such as the GNP (Lisk, 1983). These advantages which are by no means exhaustive, are perhaps indications that the social development approach may be a veritable strategy for poverty alleviation in Africa.

It may be relevant to note that as in the case of the basic needs approach, there is the possibility that social development approach may also run the risk of being a top-down approach. One of the major criticisms of the conventional basic needs approach that was dominant in the 1970's, was that it started with a predefined set of basic needs and left little room for participation. However, Estes (1998) points out that the goals of social development are pursued through the fullest possible participation of people in determining both the means and objectives of development. Social development therefore stresses effective mass mobilization and participation in the formulation and eventual execution of programs. Apart from being crucial for the support of program or project objectives, mass participation adds a political dimension to the social development approach. This has basically been absent from previous development strategies.

Extent and Variations in Poverty Levels in Africa

Measuring the Extent of Poverty

The measurement of poverty adopted in this section focuses on both its economic and social dimensions. Poverty itself may be measured in a variety of ways. The most conventional of these is the poverty line (PL) which is commonly seen as the starting point for assessing the extent of poverty and separating the poor from the non-poor (World Bank, 1993; Rakodi, 1995). The PL is an income-based approach, which is indicative of the budget restrictions within which a household can choose its consumption goods (Hagenaars, 1991). In this regard, people or households are regarded as poor if their income or expenditure is below an acceptable minimum. The PL can therefore be defined as the income or expenditure required to sustain a minimum standard of living. This income or expenditure is seen in terms of the basic (food and non-food) needs considered adequate for meeting levels of decent living in the affected society. Households whose incomes fall below this minimum level are deemed to be poor.

Although the PL has been used extensively in analyzing the extent, nature, determinants and symptoms of poverty in developing countries (Rani and Salleh, 1991; Minhas *et. al.*, 1992; Mohan and Thottan, 1992; Mason, 1994), it is not without certain methodological drawbacks. For instance, Rakodi (1995) notes that problems do arise with respect to variations in the composition and size of households, estimating income levels in a partly monetized society, the consumption of own production and the fact that actual consumption often exceeds income, and the selection of appropriate deflators. Similarly, Ariffin (1994) points to the fact that being an income-based approach, the PL cannot adequately capture the true welfare or standard of living of the household; neither can it reflect the differential poverty situation that may arise from costs of living that can be defrayed by non-monetary means. Finally, Tolosa (1978) observes that focusing solely on the PL presupposes that low levels of income are reflections of deficiencies in education, health, housing and nutrition. This may not always be the case, as many countries have high GNP per capita but low socio-economic and human development indicators. The enumerated weaknesses are indications that the PL may be a necessary but not sufficient means for the analysis of poverty levels. It is therefore necessary to obtain measures of poverty, which reflect the social and related conditions prevailing in a given area.

Variations in Poverty Levels on the Basis of Income

In this section, PLs are presented for the various African countries. The purpose is to determine the extent and variations in poverty levels when defined on the basis of income. The main problem however, is that PLs do not exist for all countries. Even if such national PLs did exist, they are likely to be country-specific and inherently arbitrary, thereby making cross-country comparison difficult. In this respect, the World Bank (1985) has devised a way for obtaining PLs for countries where they do not exist or those with insufficient data. This may be obtained as follows:

PL = GNP per capita x 0.35 x 1.25 x average household size   (1)

While Equation 1 is intuitively appealing, no justification is provided for the constants 0.35 and 1.25. However, the equation implies that PL per capita (or per household member) is equal to 0.438 GNP per capita (0.35 x 1.25 in the equation). Thus, Equation 1 simply means that the PL of the average household is equal to the relative PL per capita (set arbitrarily at 0.4338 of GNP per capita) multiplied by the average household size. Equation 1 may then be rewritten as:

PL = relative poverty line per capita x average household size   (2)

where the relative PL is equal to 0.438 of GNP per capita. This equation explicitly shows the assumed relative poverty line which one may agree with or disagree. Moreover, putting the equation directly in this way no longer necessitates the justification for the constants 0.35 and 1.25 as noted earlier.

Although the above equations provide crude estimates of PL, they are nonetheless useful guides in the absence of reliable data which is often the case in Africa. The estimated PLs for the different African countries are presented in Table 1. They pertain to the annual income required to sustain the minimum standard of living in terms of basic needs for the average household size in the country in question. Table 1 which presents a snapshot of the general pattern of poverty within the continent, shows that the PL varies from as low as US$128 for Somalia to as high as about US$15940 for Libya.[1] Countries with high PLs include Seychelles, Botswana, South Africa, Gabon and Mauritius, while those with the lowest set of PLs include Mozambique, Ethiopia, Eritrea, Congo Democratic Republic and Burundi. Countries with PL values that lie in between these two extremes include Algeria, Morocco, Tunisia, Swaziland and Cape Verde.

The PLs as shown in Table 1, only reveal what annual income is required to sustain the basic needs of the average household in the country in question. In order to meaningfully group these into different levels of poverty, their PLS may be compared with those of the continent as a whole. For this purpose, the World Bank's suggestion is followed i.e., that good practice is to consider two PLs – the upper and the lower PLs. The former is two-thirds of the average per capita consumption, which captures the poor, while the latter is one-third of the average consumption being indicative of the very poor. Since the PL for the continent as a whole may be regarded as the average, countries whose PL fall below two-thirds of this mean may be regarded as being poor, while those falling below one-third are deemed to be very poor. The PL obtained for the continent is US$2402. Two-thirds of this is $1601, while one-third is $801. On the basis of the foregoing, three categories of countries may be derived. Firstly, countries with PL greater than $1601 are considered not poor. Secondly, those in which PLs fall between $801 and $1601 are seen as poor. Finally, those in which the PL falls below $801 are deemed to be very poor.

Table 1 Estimated poverty lines for African countries (1996)*

Country	Poverty line (US$)	Country	Poverty line (US$)
Algeria	5180	Angola	967
Egypt	2249	Cameroon	1716
Libya	15939	Central African Republic	811
Morocco	3550	Chad	564
Sudan	1063	Congo	1999
Tunisia	4678	Equatorial Guinea	1043
Botswana	8294	Gabon	6913
Lesotho	1686	Sao Tome and Principe	650
Namibia	5719	Congo Democratic Republic	330
South Africa	8285	Burundi	367
Swaziland	3017	Comoros	1103
Burkina Faso	720	Djibouti	2430
Cape Verde	2253	Ethiopia	246
Benin	1084	Eritrea	295
Gambia	1381	Kenya	703
Ghana	907	Madagascar	522
Guinea	2065	Malawi	399
Guinea Bissau	491	Mauritius	6898
Cote d'Ivoire	1995	Zimbabwe	1289
Liberia	1385	Rwanda	394
Mali	868	Reunion	1608
Mauritania	1524	Seychelles	14385
Niger	642	Somalia	128
Nigeria	761	Tanzania	379

Table 1 Cont

Country	Poverty line (US$)	Country	Poverty line (US$)
Senegal	1773	Uganda	710
Sierra Leone	618	Zambia	765
Togo	1152	Mozambique	238
Africa			**2402**

*The PL is the annual income required to sustain the minimum standard of living in terms of basic (food and non-food) needs for the average household size in the country in question.
Source: Author's own Calculation

The categorizations of these countries on the basis of their PLs are presented in Table 2. Countries in the not-poor category include Algeria, Botswana, Cote'd Ivoire, Libya, Mauritius, South Africa and Tunisia. Collectively, this group of countries accounts for about 39% of the countries in Africa. Examples of countries, which may be described as poor, are Angola, Benin, Gambia, Ghana, Mali, Sudan and Zimbabwe. A total of thirteen countries make up this group, thereby, accounting for about 24% of countries within the continent. Countries in the very poor category include Burkina Faso, Chad, Ethiopia, Malawi, Niger, Rwanda, Sierra Leone and Somalia. This group of countries constitutes about 37% of all African countries. When the two categories of the poor and very poor countries are taken as one group, the conclusion reached is that about 61% of African countries are poor.

Table 2 Categorization of countries on the basis of their poverty lines

Category	Country
Not poor*	Algeria, Botswana, Cameroon, Cape Verde, Congo Republic, Cote d' Ivoire, Djibouti, Egypt, Gabon, Guinea, Lesotho, Libya, Mauritius, Morocco, Namibia, Reunion, Senegal, Seychelles, South Africa, Swaziland, Tunisia
Poor**	Angola, Benin, Central African Republic, Comoros, Equatorial Guinea, Gambia, Ghana, Liberia, Mali, Mauritania, Sudan Togo, Zimbabwe
Very poor***	Burkina Faso, Burundi, Chad, Congo Democratic Republic, Ethiopia, Eritrea, Guinea Bissau, Kenya, Madagascar, Malawi, Mozambique, Niger, Nigeria, Rwanda, Sierra Leone, Somalia, Tanzania, Uganda, Zambia

* Countries in which PLs are greater than two-thirds that of the African continent (greater than US$1601).
** Countries in which PLs fall between one-thirds and two-third that of the African continent (US$801-US$1600).
*** Countries in which their PLs fall below one-third that of the African continent (less than US$801).

While Table 2 provides an indication of the relative levels of poverty among countries in Africa, it tells nothing about the incidence of poverty within each of these countries. For instance, Table 2 shows that Angola is a poor country, but it does not reveal anything about the extent of poverty within Angola. Similarly, the Table points to the fact the Sierra Leone is a very poor country, but gives no indication of the level of poverty within the country. To determine the extent or incidence of poverty within the various countries, it is necessary to have an idea of the proportion of those living below the PL in each country. Two sets of such data are obtained from the *World Development Indicators* (World Bank, 1998). The first pertains to the percentage of a country's population living below the national or official PL as deemed appropriate for the country in question by its relevant authorities. Given that national PLs are country-specific and inherently arbitrary, this makes cross-country comparison difficult. The second data set relates to the proportion of a country's population living on less than US$1 per day. Such a measure permits cross-country comparison, as it suggests that a person on say, living on $1 per day in South Africa has the same income as a person on $1 a day in Tunisia. Data on the percentage of people living below the national PL and those below $1 a day are respectively available for 22 and 21 of the 54 countries under consideration. These are presented in Tables 3 and 4 respectively.

With respect to the percentage of the population living below the national PL, four discernible patterns of poverty may be identified. These are very high, high, medium and low levels of poverty. The countries with a very high incidence of poverty include Zambia, Gambia, Sierra Leone and Uganda. Within this group of countries, the proportion of the population living below the PL varies between 55% and 86%. Examples of countries in which the incidence of poverty is high include Lesotho, Guinea-Bissau, Kenya and Cameroon. Among these countries, the proportion of those living below the PL is at least 40%. Countries with medium levels of poverty include Nigeria, Togo, Benin, Burundi and Ghana, where at least 30% of the population is estimated to be living below the PL. Finally, countries with the least levels of poverty are those such as Mauritius, Tunisia, Morocco, and Algeria in which less than one-quarter of the population is deemed to be poor.

In the case of the proportion of those living on less than $1 per day, Table 4 shows that approximately four levels of poverty may be identified. The countries having very high levels of poverty are Guinea-Bissau, Zambia, Uganda and Niger where between 62% and 88% of the population survive on less than $1 a day. Examples of countries with high levels of poverty are Senegal, Kenya, Lesotho and Zimbabwe where more than 40% of the population subsist on less than $1 a day. Countries with moderate levels of poverty include Botswana, Guinea and South Africa. Among these countries, the proportion of their population living on less than $1 a day varies between 24% and 33%. Finally, countries experiencing the lowest levels of poverty are Algeria, Egypt, Morocco and Tunisia, in which those living on less than $1 per range from less than 2% to 7.6%. Although there is some degree of overlap in the list of countries falling into the four groups when the two measures of poverty are considered independently, a clear picture that emerges when both measures are taken into consideration is that countries in North Africa have the lowest levels of poverty.

Table 3   Percentage of population in African countries living below their national poverty line

Country	Population below the Poverty Line (%)*	Survey year
Algeria	22.6	1995
Benin	33.0	1995
Burundi	36.2	1990
Cameroon	40.0	1984
Gambia	64.0	1992
Ghana	31.4	1992
Guinea-Bissau	48.8	1991
Kenya	42.0	1992
Lesotho	49.2	1993
Malawi	54.0	1990-1991
Mauritania	57.0	1990
Mauritius	10.6	1992
Morocco	13.1	1990-91
Nigeria	34.1	1992-93
Rwanda	51.2	1993
Sierra Leone	68.0	1989
Tanzania	51.1	1991
Togo	32.3	1987-89
Tunisia	14.1	1990
Uganda	55.0	1993
Zambia	86.0	1993
Zimbabwe	25.5	1990-91

* Percentage of population living below the poverty line deemed appropriate for the country by its authorities.
Source: World Bank (1998) World Development Indicators, pp.64-66

Table 4 International poverty line – population below US$1 per day

Country	Population below US $1 per day (%)*	Survey year
Algeria	< 2.0	1995
Botswana	33.0	1985-86
Cote d' Ivoire	17.7	1988
Egypt	7.6	1990-91
Ethiopia	46.0	1981-82
Guinea	26.3	1991
Guinea Bissau	88.2	1991
Kenya	50.2	1992
Lesotho	48.8	1986-87
Mauritania	31.4	1988
Morocco	<2.0	1990-91
Niger	61.5	1992
Nigeria	31.1	1992-93
Rwanda	45.7	1983-85
Senegal	54.0	1991-92
South Africa	23.7	1993
Tanzania	10.5	1993
Tunisia	3.9	1990
Uganda	69.3	1989-90
Zambia	84.6	1993
Zimbabwe	41.0	1990-91

*Percentage of population living on less than US$1 per day at 1985 international prices.
Source: World Bank (1998) *World Development Indicators*, pp.64-66

Although the preceding discussion roughly reinforces the established patterns of well-being and prosperity within the continent, it has only focused on variations in poverty levels from the income perspective, thus painting only a partial picture of the nature and extent of poverty. This is because as observed earlier, the income-based approach is bedevilled by a number of methodological weaknesses. Furthermore, poverty transcends the lack of or insufficiency of income and extends to various aspects of socio-economic deprivation.

Variations in Poverty Levels on the Basis of Socio-economic Indicators

Given the multidimensional manifestations of poverty, a discussion of poverty profiles on the basis of socio-economic indicators involves two distinct steps. The first is the choice of indicators to describe the socio-economic profile of each country. A combination of factors is crucial in the choice of poverty indicators. These include: indicators in which there exists an easily interpretable theoretical relationship with the phenomenon of poverty: indicators which cover health, nutrition housing and other aspects of social development; indicators which in part reflect access to social services; and indicators which have previously been used to characterize poverty. Collectively, these considerations give rise to the set of indicators presented in Table 5. The choice of these nine indicators ensures that the multifaceted nature of poverty is adequately taken into consideration.

The second step pertains to the method of aggregating these indicators to obtain composite measures of poverty. In order to meaningfully analyze, as well as achieve a more parsimonious and efficient characterization of poverty, the nine indicators in Table 5 are collapsed into fewer numbers of composite factors. This is achieved by using the factor analysis, which is a statistical procedure for transforming a set of inter-correlated variables into a small number of uncorrelated orthogonal dimensions. These results are summarized in Tables 6 and 7.

Table 5 Definition of socio-economic indicators of poverty

Variable	Definition	Mean	Standard deviation	Source
Life expectancy at birth (1996)	Number of years a new born infant would live if prevailing patterns of mortality at the time of its birth were to stay the same throughout its life	54.42	8.68	World Bank (1998) *World Development Indicators*
Infant mortality rate (1996)	Number of infants who die before reaching one year of age, per 1,000 live births in a given year	83.63	34.68	World Bank (1998) *World Development Indicators*
Under five years- mortality rate (1996)	Probability that a newborn baby will die before reaching age 5, per thousand live births, if subject to current age-specific mortality rates	141.91	60.08	World Bank (1998) *World Development Indicators*
Maternal mortality ratio (1990-1996)	Number of women who die during pregnancy and childbirth, per 100,000 live births	673.15	440.47	World Bank (1998) *World Development Indicators*

Table 5 Cont

Variable	Definition	Mean	Standard deviation	Source
Prevalence of child malnutrition (1990-1996)	Percentage of children under 5 whose weight by age is less than minus two standard deviations from the median of the reference population	24.96	10.95	World Bank (1998) *World Development Indicators*
Incidence of tuberculosis (1995)	Number of new tuberculosis cases per 100,000 population	191.78	92.01	World Bank (1998) *World Development Indicators*
Access to safe water (1995)	Percentage of the population with reasonable access to an adequate amount of safe water	54.90	19.87	World Bank (1998) *World Development Indicators*
Access to sanitation (1995)	Percentage of the population with excreta disposal facilities	41.96	26.63	World Bank (1998) *World Development Indicators*
Level of overcrowding (1993)	Number of persons per room	2.37	1.03	Shelter-Afrique (1996) *Continental Shelter Atlas for Africa*

Table 6 shows that the nine socio-economic indicators may be reduced to two main factors or dimensions. This implies that two independent dimensions of poverty may be identified. Collectively, the two factors account for 61% of the information contained in the original data set. To label these dimensions, indicators that load highly on each factor need to be examined. An examination of Table 6 shows that the first factor which accounts for 53% of the variance in the original data set, may be regarded as a health-related dimension with high levels of mortality. This factor is characterized by high rates of infant and under five mortality, high rates of maternal deaths, a high prevalence of child malnutrition and low levels of life expectancy at birth. In effect, this dimension may be seen to measure poverty from the health perspective.

Table 6 Factor loadings of poverty indicators

Indicator	Factor I	Factor II
Life expectancy at birth	-0.9234	-0.2332
Infant mortality rate	0.8804	0.3097
Under five mortality rate	0.8419	0.2053
Maternal mortality ratio	0.6798	0.3466
Prevalence of child malnutrition	0.5616	0.3928
Incidence of tuberculosis	0.4999	0.1788
Access to safe water	-0.4086	-0.7096
Access to sanitation	-0.4283	-0.6012
Level of overcrowding	0.0748	0.6269
Eigenvalue	4.7895	0.6875
Variance (%)	53.2	7.6
Cumulative variance (%)	53.2	60.9

The factor scores presented in Table 7 are indicative of the performance or how well each country fares with respect to each dimension. Variations in the performance of the different countries with respect to the first dimension reveal that Sierra Leone with a factor score of 2.28 experiences the worst health and mortality levels. This is followed by Rwanda, Malawi, Niger, and Burkina Faso. Other poor countries in terms of poor health and high mortality levels include Liberia, Burundi, Guinea, Zambia and Angola. On the other hand, countries such as Algeria, Reunion, Tunisia, Seychelles, Morocco, Cape Verde, Libya, Mauritius, Egypt and South Africa may be seen as the best ten countries with the opposite health conditions. In other words, these countries experience low levels of infant and under five mortality, low rates of maternal deaths, a relatively low level of child malnutrition, as well as relatively high levels of life expectancy at birth. With the exception of Cape Verde, a noticeable feature of the ten well-off countries is that they are either located in northern or southern Africa. The poverty rankings of other countries with respect to the health dimension may be gleaned from Table 7.

Table 7 Factor scores of poverty levels for individual African countries

Country	Factor I	Factor II
Algeria	-1.86064(54)	-0.11343(32)
Egypt	-1.26933(46)	-0.40597(37)
Libya	-1.40198(48)	-1.10809(52)
Morocco	-1.42411(50)	0.42189(13)
Sudan	-0.17747(34)	0.45762(12)
Tunisia	-1.73237(52)	-0.06011(28)
Botswana	0.00096(29)	-0.83628(46)
Lesotho	-0.46039(40)	0.40639(14)
Namibia	-0.26995(35)	-0.15136(34)

Table 7 Cont

Country	Factor I	Factor II
South Africa	-1.12464(45)	-0.42708(39)
Swaziland	-0.29161(37)	0.30593(18)
Burkina Faso	1.16923(5)	-0.59342(42)
Cape Verde	-1.41302(49)	-0.09063(29)
Benin	-0.02783(31)	0.29680(19)
Gambia	0.28572(22)	-0.70208(43)
Ghana	-0.54437(41)	0.56776(11)
Guinea	1.04457(8)	-0.78306(45)
Guinea Bissau	0.82882(12)	1.14714(6)
Cote d'Ivoire	0.24814(23)	-0.71176(44)
Liberia	1.13158(6)	-0.11032(31)
Mali	0.61048(16)	0.38562(15)
Mauritania	0.40513(20)	0.08442(23)
Niger	1.27453(4)	-0.10394(30)
Nigeria	-0.13921(33)	0.85128(7)
Senegal	-0.05807(32)	-0.39052(35)
Sierra Leone	2.27800(1)	0.24200(21)
Togo	0.31133(21)	-0.03093(27)
Angola	0.92907(10)	0.76228(8)
Cameroon	-0.40846(38)	-0.14508(33)
Central African Republic	-0.00334(30)	1.20988(5)
Chad	0.52731(18)	0.70054(9)
Congo	0.19952(24)	0.31945(16)
Equatorial Guinea	0.64615(15)	-0.54870(41)
Gabon	0.12926(26)	-1.07835(49)
Sao Tome and Principe	-1.08362(44)	-0.41891(38)
Congo Democratic Republic	0.41910(19)	0.26502(20)
Burundi	1.08584(7)	-0.97709(48)
Comoros	-0.43713(39)	0.02340(25)
Djibouti	0.06370(28)	2.56387(1)
Ethiopia	0.53949(17)	1.30017(3)
Eritrea	0.09616(27)	1.27316(4)
Kenya	-0.83635(42)	0.31398(17)
Madagascar	-0.90173(43)	2.30688(2)
Malawi	1.37408(3)	-0.53099(40)
Mauritius	-1.35336(47)	-1.70743(54)
Zimbabwe	-0.28929(36)	-0.90306(47)
Rwanda	1.67608(2)	-1.07951(50)
Reunion	-1.75832(53)	-1.09287(51)
Seychelles	-1.47623(51)	-1.57266(53)
Somalia	0.76593(13)	0.63518(10)
Tanzania	0.16405(25)	-0.40350(36)
Uganda	0.66757(14)	0.03473(24)
Zambia	0.95613(9)	-0.00425(26)
Mozambique	0.91490(11)	0.20599(22)

The rank of each country with respect to a given factor is indicated in parentheses.

The question that arises at this juncture is: To what extent are variations in the health and mortality dimension of poverty reflections of the level of social development and human capital investment in these countries? Put differently, have countries such as Algeria, Reunion, Tunisia, Seychelles and Morocco with low rates of mortality and improved health conditions, paid greater attention to meeting basic social and human development concerns than countries such as Sierra Leone, Rwanda, Malawi, Niger and Burkina Faso that are deemed to be the poorest in terms of the health and mortality dimension? A general statement that can be made is that the five countries with the lowest poverty rankings with respect to the health and mortality dimension, are generally more prosperous than the five countries with the highest poverty rankings. Whether or not this difference in prosperity is transformed into greater emphasis in social and human development concerns, is the object of investigation in subsequent discussion.

The second factor, which accounts for 7.6% of the variance in the original data, may be referred to as a dimension of inadequate housing. This is because as indicated by the factor loadings, this dimension is associated with high levels of overcrowding, as well as inadequate access to safe water and sanitation. Overcrowded habitation and the absence of potable water and sanitation, characterize slum and squatter settlements in Africa and are also symptomatic of high levels of poverty (Hardoy *et. al.*, 1995). The pattern of factor scores in Table 7 shows that the poorest countries in terms of inadequate housing are Djibouti, Madagascar, Ethiopia, Eritrea, Central African Republic and Guinea-Bissau. On the other hand, examples of countries with low levels of inadequate housing include Mauritius, Seychelles, Libya, Reunion and Rwanda. With the exception of Rwanda, the other four countries that fall into the group are those with the least poverty rankings in terms of the health and mortality dimension. To some extent, it would then appear that countries that are well off with respect to the health dimension, are also those with low levels of inadequate housing. Perhaps it is this group of countries that has been able to articulate social development programs to improve their housing conditions.

This section is concluded with a brief note on the similarities and differences in the various measures of poverty utilized in this paper. If differences exist among the different measures of poverty adopted, then this further strengthens the case for the need to go beyond investigating poverty from the income approach. In order to establish whether or not differences exist, the correlation coefficients for the different poverty measures are obtained. This requires a slight reclassification of countries in Table 2 to obtain a dummy variable indicative of the level of poverty. In this case, the poor and very poor countries are classified as a single group and each country given a value of one, while the not-poor group constitutes a different category with each country taking on a value of zero. In essence, this means that countries in which the PLs fall below two-thirds of the African mean ($1601) are regarded as poor and assigned values of one, while those with PLs greater than $1601 are seen as not poor and are given values of zero. This newly created variable may then be indicative of the probability of a country being poor. The correlation coefficients of the different poverty measures are presented in Table 8. A high positive pairwise correlation may be taken to imply a high degree of similarity between the two measures in question. Conversely, a low positive pairwise correlation means that the two measures are dissimilar.

A point of interest lies in the inter-correlation of the income-based measures with those based on socio-economic indicators. Table 8 shows that the correlation coefficients are generally low. The exceptions are the pairwise correlations between the percentage of the country's population living below the national PL and the factor scores of the first dimension on the one hand, and the percentage of living on less than $1 on the other. The pairwise correlations are 0.76 and 0.73 respectively. However, following Hauser's (1974) rule of thumb, these pairwise correlations do not exceed 0.80, and as such, cannot be deemed to be highly similar. The conclusion then is that the various measures of poverty are highly dissimilar and as such, warrant separate investigation.

Table 8   Correlation matrix of poverty measures

Poverty measures	Probability of country being poor*	% of population living below the PL*	% of population living on less than $1 a day*	Factor I¶	Factor II¶
Probability of country being poor*	1.00	0.56	0.58	0.57	0.28
% of population living below the PL*	0.56	1.00	0.73	0.76	0.13
% of population living on less than $1 a day*	0.58	0.73	1.0	0.67	0.29
Factor I¶	0.57	0.76	0.67	1.00	0.08
Factor II¶	0.28	0.76	0.29	0.08	1.00

Note: The correlation coefficients obtained for the percent of population living below the PL are based on 22 observations
*Income-based poverty measures
¶Poverty measures derived from socio-economic indicators

Explanatory Framework for Variations in Poverty Levels

The model outlined seeks to explain variations in poverty levels from the social development perspective. Consequently, it is hypothesized that variations in poverty levels among African countries can be accounted for by differences in basic social and human development concerns. These concerns are in part reflected in varying literacy levels and governments' commitment to education; state of health infrastructure and government's commitment to the health sector; type of government in power; and the level of military expenditure. In addition to these, it is also hypothesized that other external, economic, environmental and locational factors partly account for variations in the level of poverty among African countries. Linking these variables lead to the following equation:

$$POV_i = f(EDUC_i, HEALTH_i, GOVT_i, MILEXP_i, OTHERS_i) \qquad (3)$$

where: POV_i denotes the various measures of poverty; $EDUC_i$ is a row vector of variables indicative of the current state of literacy and education in country i; $HEALTH_i$ is a row vector of variables representative of health infrastructure and government's commitment to health in country i; $GOVT_i$ is a dummy variable which indicates whether the government in country i is democratically elected; $MILEXP_i$ is the level of military expenditure in country i; and $OTHERS_i$ is a row vector of other (non-human and social) variables that can affect the level of poverty in country i. A further breakdown and definition of these variables are presented in Table 9.

Table 9 Definition of variables used in explaining poverty levels

Variable	Definition	Source
Adult literacy rate (1995)	Percentage of adults aged 15 and above who can, with understanding, read and write a short, simple statement about their everyday life	UNESCO (1996) *Statistical Yearbook*
Public expenditure on education (1995)	Percentage of GNP accounted for by public spending on public education plus subsidies to private education at all levels	UNESCO (1996) *Statistical Yearbook*
Primary school enrolment ratio (1995)	Primary school enrolment as percentage of relevant age group	UNESCO (1996) *Statistical Yearbook*
Female educational enrolment (1994)	Female pupils as a percentage of total enrolment in primary education	UNESCO (1996) *Statistical Yearbook*

Table 9 Cont

Variable	Definition	Source
Expenditure on health (1990-94)	Sum of public and private health expenditure as a percentage of GDP	World Bank (1998) *World Development Indicators*
Physicians per thousand people (1994)	Number of graduates of medicine / total population x 1000	World Bank (1998) *World Development Indicators*
Expenditure on housing (1993)	Percentage of total government expenditure allocated to housing and related activities	Shelter-Afrique (1996) *Continental Shelter Atlas for Africa*
SHAF*	Equals 1, if country is a member of Shelter-Afrique	Shelter-Afrique (1996) *Continental Shelter Atlas for Africa*
Type of government*	Equals 1, if government in power was democratically elected	
Military expenditure (1995)	Military expenditure as a percentage of GNP	World Bank (1998) *World Development Indicators*
Foreign aid (1996)	Official development assistance and official aid per capita	World Bank (1998) *World Development Indicators*
Economic growth (1995-96)	Average annual growth in GNP between 1995 and 1996	World Bank (1998) *World Development Indicators*
Landlocked*	Equals 1, if country is landlocked	
Region*	Equals 1, if country is located in either North or Southern Africa	

* Otherwise equals zero

As a basis for the empirical analysis, the specification, rationale and justification of these choice of variables are discussed. Five measures of poverty constitute the dependent variables. Three of these are income-based measures, while the other two are factor scores (composite measures) derived from a factor analysis of nine socio-economic indicators. The first of the income-based measures is defined as the probability of a country being poor. This variable takes on a value of one if a country's PL is below two-thirds of the African mean ($1601) and zero if greater than $1601. The second income-based measure is the percentage of a country's population living below the national PL, and the third is the percentage of a country living on less than $1 a day. The factor scores are indicative of poverty levels in terms of poor health and inadequate housing conditions.

A main emphasis of social development is education, as it is seen as a key instrument for social empowerment, improving the productivity of the poor and combating absolute poverty (Deng, 1995). In this study, the impact of education in explaining variations in poverty levels is assessed by using four variables. These are adult literacy rates, public expenditure on education, primary school enrolment and female education enrolment. It is hypothesized that countries which perform well on these four education-related variables, will have relatively low levels of poverty. This is because previous studies (Glewwe, 1990; Schultz, 1993, 1998; Vijverberg, 1993; Ojo and Oshikoya, 1994) have clearly shown that investment and improvement in education yield high returns to both individuals and the society at large, thereby, increasing overall levels of productivity. Furthermore, education is likely to make individuals more innovative as it inculcates in them newer and better ways of doing things. The overall effect of this is to reduce the level of poverty.

Another area of emphasis in social development pertains to improved health status of the general populace. Just as in the case of education, improvements in health will ultimately lead to increased productivity, which in turn, contributes to a better life. Furthermore, improvements in health status will lead to reductions in the levels of both mortality and morbidity. Two input measures are used in analyzing the impact of various African governments' commitment to health on poverty reduction. These are health expenditure and the number of physicians per thousand people. While the former may be seen in terms of the financial resources committed to the health sector, the number of physicians per thousand people may be regarded as a proxy measure of the state of health infrastructure in the country. It is posited that countries which allocate more financial resources to the health sector as well as those with more physicians per thousand population will, other things being equal, have lower poverty levels.

Social development in part, implies good governance and an increasing trend towards democratization. The dummy variable - type of government - is indicative of democratically elected governments. It is meant to examine the extent to which variations in poverty levels, can be attributed to whether or not a government is democratically elected. A democratically elected government is an indication of effective mass participation in governance unlike authoritarian or totalitarian regimes. A popularly elected government is likely to be more humane in outlook and have the welfare of its citizenry at heart. Furthermore, democratically elected governments have a moral obligation to provide for the basic social and human development concerns of its citizens, unlike most authoritarian regimes whose main preoccupation is to continue to perpetuate itself in power even at the expense of the general populace. Following from this, it is hypothesized that with democratically elected governments, countries are more likely to have lower levels of poverty.

Social development further emphasizes a less demilitarized society especially among African countries. This implies a reduction in both military personnel and overall military spending. Genuine reductions in military expenditure offer considerable scope for reorienting budget priorities since such reductions can be channeled towards meeting basic social and human development concerns. Furthermore, the UNDP (1994) notes that there are serious educational and health implications of increased military expenditure in developing countries, since spending on arms, eats up scarce resources that could have been used to improve various aspects of social and human development. It is therefore hypothesized that African countries with high military expenditure will, other things being equal, experience high incidence of poverty.

There are likely to be instances where certain measures of poverty would require specific explanatory variables to account for inter-country variations. This is the case of the dimension of inadequate housing. In addition to the type of government and military expenditure, governments' expenditure on housing and its commitment to provide decent housing are additional social development-related factors that will account for variations in the dimension of inadequate housing conditions. Housing expenditure is measured by the percentage of the central government's expenditure allocated to housing and related activities, while commitment to providing decent housing is measured by a binary variable (SHAF) which indicates a country's membership of the African-based housing organization, Shelter-Afrique, which is owned by a consortium of African governments. Shelter-Afrique among others seeks to alleviate the problems of housing in member countries. Membership of this organization would therefore signify seriousness on the part of governments to improve housing conditions in their countries.

Apart from social development-related factors, there are other variables that may in part, account for variations in the level of poverty between African countries. The exclusion of these variables may imply that estimates obtained only on the basis of the social development-related variables, are biased. For this reason, a number of external, economic, physical and locational variables are included in the analysis. The first of these is foreign aid. This may be viewed as an external factor and is measured by the amount of official development assistance and official aid per capita. Although the motives for foreign aid have varied from idealism, international solidarity, political expediency, ideological confrontation to commercial self-interest (UNDP, 1994), a key objective for the flow of aid from donor (rich) countries to recipient (poor) countries is to alleviate poverty (White, 1994; Oxfam, 1995). Whether aid flows have been able to reduce poverty in Africa, remains contentious for a variety of reasons. However, given the altruistic motive for foreign aid, it is hypothesized that aid flow will be greater among poorer countries.

An economic factor likely to account for the variation in poverty levels is the rate of economic growth. This is measured by the average annual growth in GNP between 1995 and 1996. Ideally, an increase in economic growth should reduce poverty levels. However, this depends on a number of conditions. The first of these pertains to how the increase in economic growth is distributed, particularly what share of this increase goes to the poor. The second is the use to which this increase is put. If the increase in economic growth is used to support public services, particularly in terms of education, health and poverty alleviation programs, then economic growth will undoubtedly bring about reductions in poverty levels. These conditions notwithstanding, it is posited that an increase in economic growth, will have a negative impact on poverty levels.

A physical variable that may account for inter-country differences in poverty levels, is whether or not a country is landlocked. Landlocked countries are disadvantaged in the following respects. Firstly, they lack seaports or natural harbors which are considered crucial for the economy. Secondly, in landlocked countries, points of contact with the outside world during the pre-colonial and colonial periods, were limited. Consequently, this reduced the scope for development at that time, and the effect of this is still evident in many landlocked African countries. Thirdly, many landlocked countries in Africa lack the head-start gained by other countries within the continent in the development process. Since port towns which are absent in landlocked countries, were the passages of entrance into the country by the colonialists, these towns flourished and so to some extent, did the country itself. Given the foregoing, it is therefore hypothesized that landlocked countries will have high levels of poverty.

Finally, a variable that pertains to the region in which the country is located, is included in the analysis to account for differences in poverty levels due to country location. A cursory look at the different measures of poverty clearly shows a lower incidence of poverty for countries located in northern and southern Africa *vis-à-vis* other regions of the continent. This regional variable may then be seen as capturing a number of immeasurable inter-country differences that can affect the level of poverty. It is hypothesized that this variable will have a negative impact on poverty levels.

Determinants of Poverty Levels in Africa

This section seeks to account for observed variations in poverty levels between African countries. Specifically, the effects of the various social and human development-related factors on the different measures of poverty are analyzed. Such an undertaking is necessary, given that very few studies explicitly investigate the link between poverty and social development.

Statistical Analysis

Given that the dependent variables (poverty measures) are both dichotomous and continuous, two different multivariate statistical techniques – the logit and ordinary least squares (OLS) regression models - are employed. In general, the logit regression model estimates the probability of a dependent variable being above or below a specified threshold value, given a set of independent variables (Mason, 1994). In this paper, the logit regression model is used in estimating the probability of an African country being poor, i.e. the probability that a country's PL is below that of the African mean, given its different social and human development-related factors. The logit regression model is of the form:

$$\text{Log } \frac{P}{1-P} = b_0 + b_i X_i \qquad (4)$$

Solving for P,

$$P = \frac{1}{1 + e^{-(b0 + biXi)}} \qquad (5)$$

which is the logistic probability function, where P is the probability of a country being poor; X_i is a row vector of social and human development-related factors; and e is the natural logarithm. On the other hand, the OLS involves the specification and identification of the type and nature of the dependence of a continuous variable on more than one independent variable. For our purpose, the OLS is used in estimating the effects of social and human development variables on the following four measures of poverty – percentage of a country's population living below its national PL;

percentage of a country's population living on less than $1 a day; factor scores of poor health and high mortality levels; and factor scores of inadequate housing conditions. The OLS regression model used is of the form:

$$Y_i = b_0 + b_i X_i \qquad (6)$$

where Y_i pertains to various measures of poverty; X_i is a row vector of social and human development factors; b_0 and b_i are the respective intercept and coefficients of the regression model. The estimates of the logit regression model obtained through an iterative maximum likelihood procedure, as well as those of the OLS are presented in Tables 10 and 11 respectively. In the case of the logit regression model, the reported coefficients are the partial derivatives of the expected probability of a country being poor with respect to the variable in question.

Probability of a Country Being Poor

One of the most important social development variables affecting the probability of a country being poor is the female educational enrolment rate. Table 10 shows that the coefficient is negative, thereby indicating that 1% increase in female primary school enrolment will, other things being equal, reduce the probability of a country being poor by about 0.003. This finding points to the importance of universal primary education as an effective tool for economic and social empowerment, especially among girls. It is noteworty that the returns to female education are quite high (Herz, et. al., 1991). Similarly, increased female education can reduce fertility levels, improve the productivity of women and contribute to national growth (World Bank, 1983; 1997). The ameliorative effect of increased female primary school enrolment on poverty levels, points to the need to correct imbalances in gender education that often characterize African countries, as such imbalances can hamper women's responses to economic incentives and poverty alleviation.

Adult literacy rate on the other hand, appears to have a counter-intuitive positive impact on the probability of a country being poor. This implies that African countries with increasing levels of adult literacy rates, are more likely to be poor. This anomalous finding may be an indication of the fact that occasionally, educational and skill acquisition programs adopted in many Third World countries, are not adequately designed to reduce unemployment and poverty levels. Shedding more light on this, Lisk (1983) notes that while many developing countries have expanded their educational system, they have failed to achieve significant improvements in the living conditions of the general populace. This in part, may be attributed to the mismatch between acquired skills and employment opportunities. While it is important to improve literacy levels, such programs should be seen within the overall framework of national macro-planning for socio-economic development. In this way, the entire educational system would be in consonance with the needs of the country's employment requirements.

The state of health infrastructure as measured by the number of physicians per thousand people, is a major determinant of poverty levels among African countries. Specifically, the coefficient indicates that an increase of one physician per thousand people will, *ceteris paribus,* reduce the probability of a country being poor by 6.883. This finding conforms to expectation, and further supports the notion that improvements in health-related infrastructures, are accompanied with benefits that accrue to the masses.

The logit regression model further shows that the type of government significantly influences the likelihood of an African country being poor. Specifically, the coefficient indicates that the probability of a country being poor decreases by 2.323 if the government in power is democratically elected. The size of the coefficient is an indication of the relative importance of this variable in accounting for the probability of a country being poor. It is also an indication that increasing levels of democratization, political stability and good governance are compatible with, and are prerequisites, for poverty reduction. This finding provides important lessons for the African continent, which has a history of authoritarian rule, political instability and is currently the most poverty-stricken region in the world.

Closely related to the type of government is the issue of military expenditure. The percentage of a country's GNP that is devoted to military spending, has a positive and significant impact on its probability of being poor. The coefficient reveals that a 1% increase in the proportion of the GNP allocated as military expenditure will, other things being equal, increase the probability of a country being poor by 0.2492. This in effect, implies that African countries with high military expenditure *vis-à-vis* those with low expenditures, are more likely to be poor. This finding further highlights the irony of high military spending in the face of intensifying levels of poverty in Africa. Poor and extremely poor countries like Ethiopia, Mozambique, Rwanda, Sierra Leone, Sudan and Somalia devote at least 5% of their GNP to military spending. In fact, in 1992, Ethiopia and Sudan respectively allocated 20.1% and 15.8% of their GNP to military-related expenditure. These proportions are a far cry from what each of these countries devoted to education and health in the same year. On the other hand, military expenditure takes up tiny fractions of the GNP of prosperous African countries such as Mauritius, Morocco, Seychelles and Tunisia. For instance in 1995, Mauritius and Tunisia respectively devoted 0.4% and 2.0% of their GNP to military spending. While high military expenditure has been justified on the grounds that it provides a deterrent against external invasion and aggression, it is seen that these countries with high military expenditure experience greater internal turmoil and civil strife than those with low military spending. From the preceding, there is the need for African countries particularly those with high military expenditure and moderate to high levels of poverty to reorder their budget priorities in favor of basic social and human development concerns.

The region in which the country is located is the last significant determinant of the probability of an African country being poor. The coefficient reveals that countries located in northern and southern Africa are less likely to be poor than those located in other regions of the continent. This coefficient may best be seen to reflect the impact of climatic, cultural, historical and other immeasurable region-specific factors that may in one way or the other, affect the probability of a country being poor.

Table 10   Logit regression results of the determinants of poverty in Africa

Variable	Regression coefficient
Adult literacy rate	0.0016(1.97)**
Public expenditure on education	-0.0267(0.86)
Female educational enrolment	-0.0029(1.97)**
Physicians per thousand people	-6.8834(1.99)**
Type of government	-2.3248(1.67)**
Military expenditure	0.24924(1.83)**
Foreign aid	-6.58e-05(0.97)
Economic growth	-0.0100(0.66)
Landlocked	0.0381(0.11)
Region	-5.1972(1.37)***
Constant	8.1354(1.41)***
Loglikelihood estimate	-12.42
N	53

Note: In the case of the logit regression, the first number is either the partial derivative of the expected probability of a country being poor with respect to the variable in question, or the difference in the expected probability attributable to the variable taking on alternative values of one and zero, depending on whether the variable is continuous or discrete.
*Significant at the 0.01 level and above (one-tail test)
**Significant at the 0.05 level (one-tail test)
***Significant at the 0.1 level (one-tail test)
Absolute t-values are in parentheses.

Percentage of Population Living Below the PL

When poverty is measured as the percentage of a country's population living below the national PL, the regression model in Table 11 shows that 67.2% of the variation in this measure of poverty is accounted for by the nine variables that enter the model. There are however three significant variables that explain inter-country differences in percent of those living below the PL. The first of these is public expenditure on education. The coefficient indicates that a 1% increase in the proportion of GNP allocated to education will, other things being equal, bring about a 4.5% reduction in the proportion of a country's population living below its official PL. This finding further points to the possible role that adequate investment in education can play in alleviating the level of poverty in Africa. A possible conclusion that may be drawn from this is that increasing the expenditure on education can be seen as a means of providing the poor with affordable services. Similarly, Jimenez (1994) notes that investment in basic social infrastructure such as education constitutes sound development strategy.

Access to health services as measured by the number of physicians per one thousand people, emerges as the most important variable accounting for variations in the percentage of those living below the national PL. Specifically, the coefficient reveals that an increase of one physician to one thousand people will result in a 40.33% reduction in the proportion of a country's population living below its official PL. The relatively large size of the coefficient is an indication of the importance of improved access to health services in reducing the level of poverty. In Africa, access to health services is abysmally low. Apart from Egypt and Libya with 1.8 and 1.1 physicians per thousand people in 1994 respectively, there is hardly any African country having a physician-population ratio that exceeds 0.3 per thousand people. If the poverty reduction benefits associated with improved health services are to be reaped by African countries, it then implies that there is the need for various governments to allocate more resources towards improving the current state of health infrastructure.

The last significant variable explaining variations in the percentage of a country's population living below its official PL is the type of government in power. The coefficient indicates that having a democratically elected government in power will, other things being equal, reduce the proportion of the country's population living below the PL by 19.45%. A plausible interpretation that may be given to this finding is that, democratically elected governments are more likely to initiate and implement programs capable of alleviating poverty. This is because genuine democracy entails mass participation in governance, whereby, people have a say in the critical decisions affecting their every day lives through open and accountable political structures right from the grassroots to the national level.

Percentage of Population Living on Less Than $1 a Day

In the case of poverty being measured as the percentage of a country's population living on less than $1 a day, Table 11 shows that the only significant variable that explains inter-country variations in this measure is access to health care services as indicated by the number of physicians per one thousand people. The coefficient implies that an increase of one physician to one thousand people will, other things being equal, occasion a 22.4% reduction in the percentage of a country's population surviving on less than $1 a day. As in the case of the proportion living below the national PL, the size of the health care coefficient is an indication of the importance that improved access to health services can play in reducing poverty levels in Africa.

Factor I: Dimension of Poor Health and High Mortality Levels

When poverty is measured as a composite dimension of poor health and high levels of mortality, the multiple regression model in Table 11 shows that 75% of the variation in this measure of poverty is accounted for by the twelve variables that enter the model. Adult literacy rate and public expenditure on education are key education-related variables that explain inter-country variations in the factor scores measuring the health and mortality dimensions of poverty. The coefficient measuring the impact of adult literacy rate indicates that a 1% increase in the proportion of a country's literate adult population will bring about a 0.242 reduction in the dimension of poor health and mortality. Similarly, an increase of 1% in the proportion of GNP allocated to education will, other things being equal, result in a 0.1882 decrease in the same dimension. A fact that emerges from these findings is that improvements in different facets of education will increase the awareness of, and prevention against health-related problems.

As with other measures of poverty, the state of the health infrastructure/access to health services as measured by the number of physicians per one thousand people, emerges as the most important determinant of inter-country variations in the dimension of poor health and high levels of mortality. The coefficient reveals that an increase of one medical doctor per one thousand people will, *ceteris paribus*, result in a 0.352 decrease in the dimension of poor health and high levels of mortality. The negative impact of improved access to health services on poor health and high mortality levels conforms to expectation and further lends credence to the ameliorative influence of improved health services on levels of poverty.

Military expenditure has a positive impact on the dimension of poor health and high levels of mortality. The coefficient implies that a 1% increase in the proportion of the GNP devoted to military spending will result in a 0.272 increase in poor health and high levels of mortality. A conclusion that may be drawn from this finding is that part of the financial resources that African governments could have used to reduce the existing state of poor health and high mortality levels in their various countries, are currently being spent on defense and other military-related purposes. This is a rather worrisome situation because as pointed out by the UNDP (1994, p. 50), the chances of an individual dying from preventable health-related problems are 33 times greater than the chances of dying from a war due to external aggression. While some developing countries, notably those in Latin America and the Middle East are cutting down on military expenditure, the same cannot be said of African countries, as military spending has continued to increase in the face of widespread impoverishment. All these call for radical changes in the pattern of military spending among African countries.

The impact of foreign aid on the dimension on poor health and high levels of mortality appears counter-intuitive. Specifically, the coefficient reveals that $1 increase in aid per capita will result in a 0.123 increase in poor health and high levels of mortality. This finding conveys the impression that foreign aid is not adequately channeled to countries where they are most needed, or when properly directed, they are not utilized in alleviating the condition of the poor in terms of improving their overall health status and reducing the high levels of mortality. This is in line with the conclusions reached by the UNDP (1994) and Oxfam (1995). Firstly, foreign aid is not necessarily targeted at poor countries but at strategic allies, and as such, may not be an antidote for poverty. For instance, less than one-third of foreign aid goes to 67% of the world's poorest countries. Secondly, social and human development concerns are rarely given the priority they deserve by bilateral and multilateral donors who respectively direct 7% and 16% of their aid to primary health care, rural water supplies, nutrition programs, basic education and such related areas. The UNDP (1994) further observes that even the African Development Bank which exists to cater for the needs of the continent, allocates just 4% of its aid to social and human development concerns. Finally, even if there were to be an adequate flow of foreign aid, its effectiveness would be reduced if it becomes a mechanism of effecting debt repayments. The Oxfam (1995) notes that this has been the case of sub-Saharan African countries, which in

1993, received $18 billion in foreign aid and spent half of it on debt servicing. In such situations, aid becomes a means of debt repayment rather than that of poverty alleviation.

The coefficient measuring the impact of economic growth suggests that a 1% increase in the average annual growth of a country's GNP, will be associated with a 0.156 increase in the dimension of poor health and high levels of mortality. This finding implies that improvements in economic growth have not been translated into corresponding improvement in basic health and mortality conditions. It would then appear that governments in African countries put the income accruing from economic growth to uses other than those that pertain to poverty alleviation. On the other hand, this anomalous finding may be attributed to the way in which the economic growth variable has been calibrated. Perhaps if the growth period covered more than the 1995-96 time frame, a more plausible result may have been obtained.

The regression model further shows that the physical disadvantage of the country and its geographical region can affect the dimension of health and mortality. More specifically, being landlocked increases the dimension of poor health and high levels of mortality of a country by 0.195. In the case of geographical region, the coefficient implies that being located in northern or southern Africa decreases the country's dimension of poor health and high levels of mortality by 0.247. As in the case of the first measure of poverty, this coefficient may also be seen to reflect the effect of other immeasurable region-specific factors that may affect this dimension of poverty. The effects of these two variables conform to expectation and indicate that other factors apart from those that pertain to social development, can significantly account for variations in poverty levels.

Table 11   OLS regression results of the determinants of poverty levels in Africa

Variable	% living below poverty line	% living on less than $1 a day	Factor I (dimension of health and mortality)	Factor II (dimension of inadequate housing)
Adult literacy rate	-	-	-0.242(2.47)*	-
Public expendi-ture on education	-4.508(2.10)**	0.286(0.81)	-0.182(1.71)**	-
Primary school enrolment ratio	-	-	0.000(0.01)	-
Female educ enrolment	0.635(0.88)	0.002(0.02)	-0.134(1.15)	-

Table 11 Cont

Variable	% living below poverty line	% living on less than $1 a day	Factor I (dimension of health and mortality)	Factor II (dimension of inadequate housing)
Expenditure on health	3.06(1.12)	-3.123(0.22)	0.107(0.97)	-
Physicians per thousand people	-40.331(2.74)*	22.409(1.53)* **	-0.352(3.65)*	-
Type of govt	-19.450(1.60)***	-4.536(0.07)	0.018(0.19)	0.104(0.65)
Military expenditure	1.945(0.83)	0.231(0.15)	0.272(3.05)*	-0.093(0.64)
Foreign aid	0.112(1.11)	0.616(1.22)	0.123(1.42)***	0.116(0.75)
Economic growth	0.290(0.44)	-0.604(0.24)	0.156(1.92)**	0.030(.021)
Landlocked	-	-	0.195(2.15)**	0.025(0.17)
Region	-	-	-0.247(2.02)**	-0.156(0.82)
Expenditure on housing	-	-	-	-0134(0.78)
SHAF	-	-	-	-0.298(1.78)**
Constant	39.41(1.18)	31.82(0.48)	1.584(2.10)**	0.874(2.08)**
R^2	0.672	0.506	0.750	0.143
F-ratio	3.330	1.539	11.19	0.92
N	22	21	53	53

*Significant at the 0.01 level and above (one-tail test)
**Significant at the 0.05 level (one-tail test)
***Significant at the 0.1 level (one-tail test)
Absolute t-values are in parentheses.
- Not included in the model

Factor II: Dimension of Inadequate Housing

The multiple regression model explaining inter-country variations in the dimension of inadequate housing has a low R^2 of 14.3%. This may partly be attributed to the fact that this factor contains just 7.6% of the variance in the original data set from which it was obtained. The only significant variable is governments' commitment to providing decent housing as measured by membership of the African-based housing organization – Shelter-Afrique (SHAF). The regression model reveals that countries that are members of SHAF are less likely to have inadequate housing conditions than those of non-member countries. This finding implies that commitment to providing decent accommodation on the part of the relevant authorities which in turn reduces the level of inadequate housing, may be seen as a means of alleviating poverty.

Conclusion: Summary and Policy Implications

This paper has sought to investigate the link between poverty and different facets of social development using cross-national data drawn from African countries. In so doing, an attempt was made to achieve two objectives. The first was to provide measures of poverty for these countries. The second sought to account for inter-country variations in the different measures of poverty while paying attention to various aspects of social development. Five measures of poverty were obtained. The first three are income-based measures. The first of these pertains to the identification of countries with PLs below two-thirds that of the continent's mean. This makes it possible to determine the poor and non-poor countries within the context of the whole continent. The second income-based measure relates to the proportion of a country's population that is living below the official PL , and the third pertains to the percentage of a country's population living on less than $1 a day. On the basis of these two measures, the incidence of poverty within each country is determined. The second set of poverty measures is based on the explicit recognition of the multifaceted nature of poverty. Following from this, composite measures of poverty were obtained from a factor analysis of nine socio-economic variables. The factor analysis showed that poverty may be measured in terms of two distinct dimensions. These are the dimension of poor health and high levels of mortality on the one hand, and that of inadequate housing one the other. Factor scores were then used to show inter-country variations in these two dimensions.

The analysis further revealed that inter-country variations in the different measures of poverty may be accounted for by variables indicative of different aspects of social development. These include:
- Education-related variables such as adult literacy rate, public expenditure on education and female enrolment rate;
- Health-related variables which include expenditure on health and number of physicians per one thousand people;
- Increasing levels of democratization and good governance; and
- The extent of military spending.
- Other variables apart from those pertaining to social development found to be significant in explaining variations in poverty measures include the flow of foreign aid, level of economic growth, the physical disadvantage of being a landlocked country and the geographical region in which the country is located.

Policy Implications

What then are the policy implications of some of the findings obtained in this paper? Findings have consistently shown that improvements in education and health will invariably lead to reduction in poverty levels. The policy recommendation here is for African governments to commit more resources to improve all aspects of their educational and health sectors. Increased investment in these sectors is one of the best uses to which a country may put its resources. Improvements in the educational sector should seek to increase female enrolment. This is because apart from alleviating poverty, increased female education will reduce fertility levels and infant mortality, as well as enhance maternal health. Furthermore, improvement in education should seek to increase overall enrolment in primary education. Apart from yielding very high returns and improving the level of basic education, increased investment in primary education offers one of the greatest possibilities of reducing poverty. It is also crucial that these improvements in the educational sector be in consonance with the overall framework of the national microeconomic planning of the country in question. This will prevent a situation in which there is a mismatch between acquired skills and the employment needs of the country.

Findings have further shown that democratically elected governments are more likely to bring about a reduction in the extent of poverty within a country. A policy recommendation arising from this finding is the need for more African countries to embrace the ideals and principles of democracy and good governance. This should, among others, involve effective mass participation whereby, people have a voice in the formulation and implementation of programs that affect their every day lives. In fact, the United Nations (1997, p. 2) notes that many cases, poverty is perpetuated by exclusion from decision making and lack of participation in the policy making process. A positive step being taken in this direction is that certain African countries reputed for having some of the worst authoritarian and most repressive governments, have begun to embark upon political reforms expected to lead to a democratization of the civil society.

To effectively reduce widespread levels of poverty in Africa, there is the pressing need for various governments to reorder their budget priorities to the extent that it reduces and de-emphasizes high levels of military spending. Findings from this paper have consistently shown that high levels of military expenditure are associated with high levels of poverty. Too often, African countries, particularly the poor ones, spend more than what is necessary on military-related purposes. For cuts in military expenditure to be meaningful, these have to be genuinely channeled to meet the needs of the poor especially in providing for their basic social and human development needs.

Finally, the international community can play a more proactive role in eradicating poverty in Africa. Findings have revealed that the flow of foreign aid to African countries has not been associated with the improvements in health and reduction in mortality levels. A number of reasons may account for this, one of the most important being that both bilateral and multilateral donors accord little priority to social development concerns. The policy imperative here is the need for donors to increase their current aid allocation for basic social and human development concerns. This increase in aid allocation can then be tied to conditions such as increasing levels of democratization and good governance, reduction in military spending and a sincere commitment to poverty alleviation on the part of the various governments. Such considerations are likely to make foreign aid a more effective poverty alleviation tool.

Note

1   The GNP per capita used in estimating the poverty lines for the various countries were obtained from the *World Development Indicators*, (World Bank, 1998). Average household data were taken from the *Habitat Atlas*, (United Nations Center for Human Settlements, 1996).

For a number of countries, there were a few empty cells (missing values). These were replaced with the mean values for the poverty category to which a particular country belongs.

References

Adelman, I. and Morris, C. T. (1973), *Economic Growth and Social Equity in Developing Countries*, Stanford University Press, California.

African Development Bank, UNDP and World Bank. (1990*)*, *The Social Dimensions of Adjustment in Africa: A Policy Agenda*, World Bank, Washington. D. C.

Ariffin, J. (1994), 'Poverty: Conceptual Underpinning, Trends and Patterns in Malaysia and a Literature Review', in J. Ariffin (ed.), *Poverty Amidst Plenty*, Pelanduk Publications, Malaysia.

Deng, L. A. (1995), *Poverty Reduction: Lessons and Experiences from Sub-Saharan Africa, Environment and Social Development*, Working Paper, No. 6, African Development Bank, Abidjan.

Dower, N. (1992), 'Sustainability and the Right to Development', in R. Attfield and B. Wilkins (eds.), *International Justice and the Third World*, Routledge, London.

Estes, R. J. (1998), *Resources for Social and Economic Development: A Guide to Scholarly Literature*, School of Social Work, University of Pennsylvania.

Glewwe, P. (1990), *Schooling, Skills and Returns to Education, Living Standards Measurement Survey*, Working Paper, No. 84, World Bank, Washington, D. C.

Green, R. H. (1990), 'The Human Dimension of the Test of, and Means of Achieving Africa's Economic Recovery and Development: Reawaking the Social Fabric, Restoring the Broken Pot', in A. Adedeji, R. Rasheed and M. Morrison (eds.), *The Human Dimension of Africa's Persistent Economic Crisis*, Hans Zell Publishers, London.

Hardoy, J. E., Mitlin, D. and Satterthwaite, D. (1995), *Environmental Problems in Third World Countries*, Earthscan Publications, London.

Hagenaars, A. J. M. (1991), 'The Definition and Measurement of Poverty', in L. Osberg (ed.), *Economic Inequality and Poverty: International Perspective*, M.E. Inc, New York.

Hauser, P. D. (1974), 'Some Problems in the Use of Stepwise Regression Techniques in Geographical Research', *Canadian Geographer*, Vol. 18, pp. 148-158.

Hicks, N. and Streeten, P. (1981), 'Indicators of Development: The Search for a Basic Needs Yardstick', in P. Streeten, P. and R. Jolly (eds.), *Recent Issues in World Development: A Collection Survey Articles*, Pergamon Press, New York.

Herz, B. K., Subbarao, M. H. and Raney, L. (1991), *Letting Girls Learn: Promising Approaches in Primary and Secondary Education*, World Bank Discussion Paper 133, World Bank, Washington, D.C.

Jimenez, E. (1994), *Human and Physical Infrastructure: Public Investment and Pricing Policies in Developing Countries*, World Bank, Washington, D.C.

Kayizzi-Mugerwa, S. and Levin, J. (1994), 'Adjustment and Poverty: A Review of the African Experience', *African Development Review*, Vol 6, pp. 24-36.

_____ and Lufumpa, C. (1995), *Poverty Alleviation in Africa: Putting the Challenge in Perspective, Environment and Social Development*, Working Paper, No. 9, African Development Bank, Abidjan.

Lardy, N. R. (1975), *Regional Growth and Income Distribution: The Chinese Experience*, Yale University, New Haven.

Lisk, F. (1983), 'Conventional Development Strategies and Basic-Needs Fulfillment', in M. Todaro (ed.), *The Struggle for Economic Development*, Longman, New York.

Mason, A. D. (1994), 'Targeting the Poor in Rural Java', *IDS Bulletin*, Vol. 27, pp. 67-82.

Minhas, B. S., Kansal, S. M. and Jain, L. R. (1992), 'The Incidence of Poverty in States (1970-71 to 1983)', in B. Hariss, S. Guhon and R.H. Casser (eds.), *Poverty in India: Research and Policy*, Oxford University Press, Bombay.

Mohan, R. and Thottan, P. (1992), 'The Regional Spread of Urbanization, Industrialization and Poverty', in B. Hariss, S. Guhon and R.H. Casser (eds.), *Poverty in India: Research and Policy*, Oxford University Press, Bombay.

Ojo, O. and Oshikoya, T. (1994), *Determinants of Long Term Growth: Some African Results*, Economic Research Paper, No. 19, African Development Bank, Abidjan.

Oxfam. (1995), *The Oxfam Poverty Report*, Oxfam, United Kingdom and Ireland.

Rakodi, C. (1995), 'Poverty Lines or Household Strategy? A Review of Conceptual Issues in the Study of Urban Poverty', *Habitat International*, Vol. 19, pp. 407-426.

Rani, O. and Salleh, A. M. (1991), 'Malays in the Reserve Areas of Kuala Lumpur: How Poor Are They?', in M.Y.H. Johan (ed.), *Urban Poverty in Malaysia*, Institute for Development Studies, Subbah.

Seregeldin, I. (1989), *Poverty, Adjustment and Growth in Africa*, World Bank, Washington, D.C.

Shultz, T. P. (1993), 'Investment in Schooling and Health in Men and Women', *Journal of Human Resources*, Vol. 28, pp. 337-342.

_____. (1998), *The Formation of Human Capital and the Economic Development of Africa: Returns to Health and Schooling Investment*, Economic Research Paper, No. 37, African Development Bank, Abidjan.

Tolosa, H. C. (1978), 'Causes of Poverty in Brazil', *World Development*, Vol. 6, pp. 1087-1101.

UNDP. (1994), *Human Development Report 1994*, Oxford University Press, New York.

UNICEF. (1987), *Adjustment with a Human Face*, Oxford University Press, New York.

United Nations. (1986), *Declaration on the Right to Development*, United Nations, New York.

_____. (1997), *1997 Report on the World Social Situation*, Oxford University Press, New York.

Van der Hoeven, R. (1991), 'Adjustment with a Human Face: Still Relevant of Overtaken by Recent Events', *World Development*, Vol. 19,1835-45.

Vijverberg, W. P.M. (1993), 'Educational Investments and Returns for Women and Men in Cote d' Ivoire', *Journal of Human Resources*, Vol. 28, pp. 933-974.

White, H. (1994), 'How Much Aid Flow is used in Poverty Reduction', *IDS Bulletin*, Vol. 27, pp. 83-99.

World Bank. (1983), 'Poverty, Growth and Human Development', in M. Todaro (ed.), *The Struggle for Economic Development*, Longman, New York.

_____. (1985), *Zimbabwe Urban Sector Review*, East Africa Projects Department, Water Resources Division, World Bank, Nairobi.

_____. (1990), *World Development Report 1990: Poverty*, Oxford University Press, New York.

_____. (1992), *World Development Report 1992: Development and the Environment*, Oxford University Press, New York.

_____. (1993), *Poverty Reduction Handbook*, World Bank, Washington, D.C.

_____. (1997), *Taking Action to Reduce Poverty in Sub-Saharan Africa*, World Bank, Washington, D.C.

_____. (1998), *World Development Indicators*, World Bank, Washington, D.C.

PART II:
POVERTY MEASUREMENT

4 What is Known about Identifying the Poor in Africa and the Middle East?

Arjan de Haan and Shahin Yaqub

Introduction

This paper discusses the usefulness of currently available information on the poor, for designing public action against poverty in Africa and the Middle East. This issue is raised against the background of recent arguments that emphasize economic growth as a means of alleviating poverty. There is little debate that a link between growth and poverty exists. It is to be emphasized however that growth is not all that matters for poverty reduction. Firstly, even if economic growth rates explain 50% of the variation in poverty incidences as some recent research suggests, 50% is still unexplained, indicating a large margin for poverty-reducing policy. Secondly, studies reveal that the growth-poverty elasticity varies across regions and is the lowest in Africa. Thirdly, the "poor" cannot be regarded as a homogeneous group. In Kenya and Nigeria for example, extreme poverty increased while "moderate" poverty decreased, suggesting that the poorest profited less from economic growth. Overall in Africa, as to be discussed later, the poverty gap (average shortfall below the poverty line [PL] of the poor) worsened faster than the headcount index (share of population below the PL). This indicates that not only did more people slip below the PL, but that even among those already poor, many got even poorer. In the Ivory Coast for example, even in the context of a rapidly contracting economy, many of the poor were no longer poor a year later. [1] Therefore, anti-poverty policies have a role to play.

     For anti-poverty interventions, policy-makers and program designers require accurate information on the poor. Without accurate and timely information, it is difficult to know whom to target with anti-poverty measures, and know who benefits from specific policies. Different anti-poverty interventions involve different levels of targeting. This results in different demands   for information on the poor. Sectoral targeting, i.e. spending in sectors which are relatively more important to the poor (e.g. primary health care), is the least demanding in terms of specific information about the poor. Self-targeting, by definition, does not need such detailed information. Nevertheless, key information is still essential to know where to implement these programs for example, and to properly evaluate them. Several anti-poverty policies rely on administered targeting, which requires detailed information on the poor, to determine indicators or socio-economic categories highly correlated with poverty. Often, the record of administered targeting has not been good. In Burkina Faso during the mid-1980s, famine early warning systems were used to target food aid to the arid northern Sahelian zone. Yet, Sahelian households had higher and more diversified incomes than households in the more favorable agro-ecological zones in the south. As a result, better-off households living in the Sahel, received ten times more food aid than more vulnerable households in the south (Reardon et al. cited by Lundberg and Diskin 1995: 16). Examples like this illustrate that fairly detailed knowledge is essential for avoiding targeting errors, such as leakage to the non-poor and imperfect coverage of the poor.

This paper discusses the information commonly available on poverty in Africa and the Middle East. Conclusions about trends in poverty and socio-economic profiles of the poor depend on the definition of poverty used. Some definitions have centered around broader notions of human capabilities combining health, education and income indicators (e.g. UNDP's Human Development Index). Other definitions have been narrower, focussing on single yardsticks of welfare. Other approaches have attempted to leave definitions of welfare to local communities themselves, rather than adopt externally imposed criteria. Each definition presents a degree of uncertainty whether some "justifiably deprived" people may have been ignored. Quite often, differences emerge in the groups identified as poor, and sometimes the differences are irreconcilable. Also, poverty definitions may be used to alter purposefully the recognized constituency of the poor (e.g. Ukraine Human Development Report 1996: 28).

The importance of definitional choice in poverty analysis is not underestimated which is later discussed. However, the focus is on inadequate consumption as a key element of poverty, supported by a few other indicators. In choosing other indicators, "output indicators" (e.g. life expectancy) are highlighted rather than what may be regarded as "input indicators" (e.g. access to health care). Such data are even less available than data on consumption-poverty. For practical reasons, the authors had to rely on international sources for information. This means that this report on poverty information is not as comprehensive as it should be. It is assumed however, that international efforts to gather information, specifically in Africa, would have uncovered significant sources of poverty information of high quality.

Poverty Trends

Sub-Saharan Africa (SSA) has become the world's poorest region since 1988 when its GDP per capita fell below that of South Asia's. Africa has been falling behind, as inequality between countries has risen substantially. While global average per capita GDP grew at 1.0% during 1975-1985, SSA contracted by –0.3% (Barro 1997:21). In 1996, GNP per capita adjusted for purchasing power which in SSA was $1450, whereas in South Asia, it was $1520. In the Middle East and North Africa, it was much higher at $4530 (World Development Indicators Report 1998).

Recently, most African countries have exhibited positive economic growth with the exception of Angola, Cameroon, Zambia, Madagascar, Libya and Congo. Average annual growth in the Middle East and North Africa during 1980-1990 was 0.4% and 2.6% during 1990-1996. In 1997, SSA registered 3.7% growth in real GDP and 0.9% growth in GDP per capita (African Development Report (1997). However, growth in SSA has been too low to make a real impact on poverty. To achieve a reduction in the number of poor of 2% per year in SSA, the World Bank estimates that growth of 6 to 7% is necessary.[2]

Table 1 shows recent trends in poverty in Africa and the Middle East compared to other parts of the world. The World Bank's estimates of purchasing power parity (PPP) consumption poverty shown in the Table, are generally accepted as being reasonably, though by no means perfectly, comparable across countries and time.[3] The figures indicate that the number of "poor", defined as those living on less than $1 per person per day at internationally comparable prices, increased between 1987 and 1993 in SSA from 180 million to almost 220 million. The headcount index in SSA increased slightly until 1990, then fell slightly, but was in 1993 still higher than in 1987. Most striking in SSA perhaps, is the relatively rapid increase in the poverty gap after 1990, which measures how far below the PL the poor fell on the average. In contrast, in North Africa and the Middle East, poverty by all three indicators is much lower, with both poverty incidence and poverty gap falling. The absolute number of people in poverty has remained static at about 10 million.

These regional trends mask divergent country-level trends. Appendix B shows poverty estimates which are not based on the $1 per capita per day poverty line of Table 1, but on nationally determined PLs. This Table stresses that there are very few countries for which trend data are available, and usually only for two points in time. The definitions of poverty underlying these estimates differ across countries, and so the trend in one country cannot be compared against the trend in another. Therefore, the comparison of trends across countries should be limited only to the direction of change, and should exclude the discussion on levels. In summary, the trends are:

- Tanzania - Poverty declined between 1983 and 1991.
- Rural Ethiopia - In the six villages for which panel data are available, poverty declined during 1989-1994/95.
- Kenya - Poverty declined slightly between 1981/82 and 1992.
- Ghana and Nigeria - Poverty declined sharply as both exhibited economic growth.
- Morocco - Poverty declined between 1970 and 1985.
- Sudan - Extremely rapid increase in poverty and inequality during the 1980s. There are doubts about the quality of the data (Hassan 1997). This was after an increase during the 1970s according to another data set (Farah and Sampath 1995).
- Côte d'Ivoire - Rapid increase in the poverty headcount between 1985 and 1988 (Grootaert and Kanbur 1995). Data for 1996 are not comparable to those of earlier years.
- Egypt - A steady increase in poverty between 1981/2 and 1995/6 (El-laithy 1998).

Table 1   Population living below US$1 per day, 1987-1993
(1985 PPP exchange rates)

	Number of poor (millions)			Poverty incidence (%)			Poverty gap (%)		
	1987	1990	1993	1987	1990	1993	1987	1990	1993
Sub-Saharan Africa	179.6	201.2	218.6	38.5	39.3	39.1	14.4	14.5	15.3
Middle East & North Africa	10.3	10.4	10.7	4.7	4.3	4.1	0.9	0.7	0.6
South Asia	479.9	480.4	514.7	45.4	43.0	43.1	14.1	12.3	12.6
East Asia & Pacific	464.0	468.2	445.8	28.2	28.5	26.0	8.3	8.0	7.8
Eastern Europe & Central Asia	2.2	n.a.	14.5	0.6	n.a.	3.5	0.2	n.a.	1.1
Latin America & Caribbean	91.2	101.0	109.6	22.0	23.0	23.5	8.2	9.0	9.1
TOTAL	1,277.1	n.a.	1,313.9	30.1	n.a.	29.4	9.5	n.a.	9.2

N.B.   Poverty incidence is the proportion of the population below the PL. The poverty gap is the mean distance of the poor below the PL, expressed as a percentage of the PL.

Source: World Bank, Poverty Reduction, 1996: 4

These   estimates define poverty in terms of a lack of purchasing power over goods and services, e.g., below $1 per capita per day. Another way of understanding poverty, especially relevant in the African context, is to look at food intakes.   Estimates of inadequate food intakes shown in Table 2, indicate that the proportion and number of people who are undernourished in terms of energy intakes, have increased in SSA since 1969-1971. In North Africa and Near East, while the proportion of undernourished has fallen, the absolute number of people who have inadequate food intakes has increased substantially during the 1980s from 27 million to 37 million. In terms of the intensity of food inadequacy, the average per capita energy consumption of the undernourished population, declined in SSA from 1490 kcal/day in 1969-1971 to 1470 kcal/day in 1990-1992. In the Middle East and North Africa, this figure rose from 1570 kcal/day to 1640 kcal/day (FAO 1996: Table 16). In other words, the hungry in SSA got even hungrier.

Table 2 Prevalence of food intake inadequacy

	Period	Total population (million)	Proportion undernourished %	Number undernourished (million)
Sub-Saharan Africa	1969/71	270	38	103
	1979/81	359	41	148
	1990/92	501	43	215
North Africa and	1969/71	180	27	48
Near East	1979/81	236	12	27
	1990/92	323	12	37
East and South East	1969/71	1166	41	476
Asia	1979/81	1417	27	379
	1990/92	1694	16	269
South Asia	1969/71	711	33	238
	1979/81	892	34	303
	1990/92	1138	22	255
Latin America	1969/71	279	19	53
	1979/81	354	14	48
	1990/92	443	15	64
Developing countries	1969/71	2608	35	918
	1979/81	3260	28	906
	1990/92	4104	20	841

Source: FAO (1996), Table 14.45

These inadequate food intakes are reflected in anthropometric measures. Trends in the prevalence of underweight children for the eighteen countries where they are available (usually two points in time only), are shown in Table 3. In some countries of Africa, over one in four children under 5 years are underweight. In most SSA countries, the trend appears to be stagnant or even worsening.

Adult body mass indices (BMI) are shown in Table 4 for available countries, about ten in total. Data on trends are not available from the same FAO source. The BMI measures a person's body mass standardized for the person's height. A value of under 18.5 is considered inadequate. In most countries, one in ten persons is found to have too low BMI. Notably, in each country, large proportions of the population have very high BMI. This phenomenon is being reported for more and more developing countries.

For other poverty-related indicators, data are reported over a much longer period. To provide an impression of these, data are presented at a regional level in Table 5. However, this does not mean that these are available for all individual countries. As with the poverty data reported in Table 1, these imply "educated guesses" for the countries in the region for which data are not available. These data suggest slightly more positive trends. Infant mortality rates have continued to decrease throughout 1970-1993, and as expected, much more rapidly in the Middle East and North Africa than in SSA. A similar continuing positive trend is indicated by the data on life expectancy. Primary school enrolment rates, however, have been declining in SSA since the early 1980s.

This section has summarized the available information on trends in poverty and related indicators. This confirms that a number of these indicators are worsening in SSA, but it also serves to emphasize how little is actually known for many countries. The regional averages can be misleading since they often include "analytically-derived estimates" rather than "measured estimates" for many countries thereby involving considerably greater assumptions. Poverty trends are available for at best, only ten countries in the region, and for child weight, for less than 20 countries. Moreover, this is usually for only two points at a time, which is insufficient to talk about trends in the proper sense. The next section looks at the kind of data available at the meso-level regarding the characteristics of poverty.

Poverty Profile

This section illustrates the kinds of information available on the characteristics of the poor commonly used for administered targeting of benefits and for analyses of effects on policies on specific groups. It also illustrates some commonalities, from which rules of thumb for targeting may be developed. Significant differences exist which policymakers need to be informed about, when formulating anti-poverty interventions. Policies are likely to fail if for example, the heterogeneity among the poor is ignored such as circumstances, vulnerability, characteristics, etc. Differences and divergences among the poor, rural-urban differences, economic or employment characteristics, gender, age, education and ethnicity are discussed.[4]

Table 3   Trends in inadequate child weight, % of underweight under 5 year olds

	Survey Years				Prevalence, %			
Algeria	1987	1990	1992		8.6	9.2	9.2	
Egypt	1978	1990	1992	1995 [e]	16.6	10.4	9.4	16.8
Ethiopia	1982	1992 [a,d]			38.1	47.7		
Ghana	1988	1994 [b]			27.1	27.4		
Jordan	1975	1990			17.4	6.4		
Kenya	1982 [a]	1987 [a]	1993		22.0	18.0	22.3	
Lesotho	1976	1981	1992		17.3	13.3	15.8	
Madagascar	1984	1992			32.8	39.1		
Malawi	1981	1992			23.9	27.2		
Mauritania	1981	1991			31.0	47.6		
Morocco	1987 [d]	1992			11.8	9.0		
Rwanda	1976	1985	1992		27.8	27.5	29.2	
Senegal	1986 [d]	1993 [c]			17.5	20.1		
Sierra Leone	1975	1978	1990		31.0	23.2	28.7	
Togo	1977 [d]	1988			20.5	24.4		
Tunisia	1975	1988 [f]			20.2	10.4		
Zambia	1985	1988	1992		20.5	25.8	25.1	
Zimbabwe	1984	1988 [d]	1994		20.7	10.0	15.5	

N.B. [a] Rural areas; [b] Excludes some districts; [c] 0-35 months; [d] 6-36 months, adjusted 0-59 months; [e] 6-71 months; [f] 3-36 months.

Source: FAO (1996), Table 22: 72

Table 4   Adult body mass indices, % of adults in each BMI class

		<16.00	16.00-16.99	17.00-18.49	18.50-24.99	25.00-29.99	≥30.00
Ghana	1987-8	2.8	3.9	13.3	62.0	17.1	0.9
Mali	1991	1.9	3.2	11.2	76.5	6.4	0.8
Morocco	1984-5	0.5	1.1	5.4	69.1	18.7	5.2
Senegal	1992-3	1.4	2.0	10.2	70.4	12.2	3.7
Tunisia	1990	0.3	0.6	3.0	58.9	28.6	8.6
Women only:							
Congo	1986-7	0.6	1.8	8.7	73.7	11.8	3.4
Ghana	1993	0.8	1.7	8.7	75.9	9.7	3.2
Kenya	1993	0.5	1.3	7.4	76.8	11.5	2.4
Morocco	1992	0.3	0.5	2.8	62.0	23.3	11.1
Zambia	1992	0.0	1.1	6.0	70.3	16.9	5.7

N.B. BMI is the weight divided by the height squared $(kg/m)^2$.
Source: FAO (1996), Table 25: 77

Table 5   Infant mortality, life expectancy and primary school enrolment

	1970	1982	1987	1993
Infant mortality (per 1000 live births)				
Middle East and North Africa	135	90	67	53
Sub-Saharan Africa	132	112	103	93
Developing countries	97	71	63	54
Life expectancy				
Middle East and North Africa	53	59	63	66
Sub-Saharan Africa	44	48	50	52
Developing countries	56	61	63	65
Gross primary School enrolment ratios (%)				
Middle East and North Africa	68	91	94	96
Sub-Saharan Africa	50	74	69	67
Developing countries	78	95	105	107

N.B. Some of these figures do not correspond exactly to the years shown.

Source: World Bank, Poverty Reduction, 1996: 3

Economic Divergences among the Poor

The poor is not a homogeneous group, and neither are trends uniform. Not all the poor profit equally from economic growth, or suffer from decline. Table 1 shows that overall, the poverty gap decreases or increases in line with the headcount index. The average of the Middle East and North Africa conforms to this pattern. Also, in Ghana, both intensity of poverty and incidence of extreme poverty declined in line with the incidence of moderate poverty.[5] In Ethiopia, between 1989 and 1994, poverty depth declined even more rapidly than the poverty headcount.[6]

In SSA, between 1987 and 1993, the poverty gap increased faster than the headcount index, suggesting diverging patterns among the poor. Such a change is illustrated by Kenya between 1981/82 and 1992. While the incidence of rural poverty fell from 48 to 46% in 1992, the incidence of rural extreme poverty increased from 11% to 20%. For both poverty and extreme poverty, depth increased.[7] Conversely in Egypt, while the incidences of rural and urban poverty rose between 1990/1 and 1995/6, the incidence of rural extreme poverty fell; the same applies to poverty depth measures.   With the economic recovery of Nigeria, poverty decreased rapidly between 1985 and 1992. However, while the absolute number of the poor decreased from 36 million to 34.7 million, the number of extreme poor increased from 10 million to 13.9 million.[8]

The Ivory Coast illustrates some unexpected effects under economic contraction. The increasing poverty corresponds with the 28% GDP per capita fall between 1985-1990.   But poverty did not decline as fast as the economic contraction, and inequality actually decreased.   Furthermore, Grootaert and Kanbur (1995) conclude from panel data for three successive periods that despite the severe economic recession, there was heterogeneity among the poor, and that some of the poor were upwardly mobile in the short run. The proportion of the extreme poor who were not poor one year later is quite high at 27%, 23% and 6% in each of three successive one-year panels.

Spatial Location of Poverty

By far, the largest number of poor in Africa and the Middle East live in rural areas, though the balance is shifting towards the expanding cities. Rural poverty incidence, and often also the poverty gap, tend to be much higher than urban poverty. This is illustrated in Table 6 which shows for example that in South Africa in 1993, rural poverty was 73.7% and in urban areas, 40.5%. The picture however, is not uniform.

Firstly, within the urban category, smaller urban and peri-urban areas have much higher poverty than main cities. For example, in South Africa in 1993, urban poverty overall was 40.5%, but in the metropolitan areas, it was less than half of that at 19.7%. In Mauritania, poverty incidence in peri-urban areas in 1990 was 54%, much higher than the 18% in the main urban centres of Nouakchott, Nouadhibou and Zouerate, and much closer to the incidence in the rural centre of 62%. In Cameroon, in 1983/4 (the latest year for which a national household survey existed), the poverty incidence in Yaoundé was 1% with urban areas of the South registering 34% and in rural areas of the South at 47%. Data on Kenya suggest that there are pockets of extreme poverty in cities. In 1992, 46% of the rural population had a level of expenditure below the upper poverty line, and 20% below the extreme poverty line. In urban areas, the respective figures were 29 and 25%, i.e. extreme poverty incidence was higher in urban areas.

Secondly, trends in some of the countries show a relative worsening of urban poverty. In Ghana, rural poverty declined from 42% in 1988 to

34% in 1992. Though poverty remained worst in rural areas, especially in rural Savannah, poverty incidence increased in Accra, from 8.5% in 1985 to 23% in 1992. Similarly, data on Sudan given by Farah and Sampath (1995) between 1967-8 and 1978-80, suggest that poverty is much more severe in rural areas but that there was a much more rapid increase in urban than in rural poverty. In Nigeria between 1985 and 1992, the number of poor in rural areas fell from 26.3 to 222.8 million, while in urban areas, it rose from 9.7 to 11.9 million. For the extreme poor, there was a similar trend in urban areas with a huge increase from 1.5 million to 4 million people (rural extreme poverty rose from 9 to 10 million).

Sectoral Correlates of Poverty

Poverty is usually linked to economic activities or sectors, particularly agriculture. This is especially important for policies that target or affect particular sectors. In South Africa in 1993, the poorest were much more likely to depend on agriculture as a main source of income than the rich. Of the poorest households, 37% depended on agriculture as a main source of income, against less than 1% of households in the richest quintile. The richest households depended largely on regular wages (84%), against 19% for the poorest. In Ghana, while poverty declined for all socio-economic groups between 1988 and 1992, the incidence and intensity of poverty remained the highest among food crop and export crop farmers. In 1992, poor households derived 48% of their income from agricultural activities, and non-poor households 37%.

In Nigeria, employment status of the household head was closely related to poverty in both 1985 and 1992. In 1985 and 1992, both in rural and urban areas, the highest incidence of poverty was found among the self-employed. At the national level, in 1985, their poverty incidence was 53% against 46% for wage earners. In 1992, it was 35% against 28%. Agricultural workers formed the largest component of the extreme poor in 1992, albeit falling from 87% in 1985 to 67% in 1992. Detailed data from Côte d'Ivoire (Grootaert et al. 1997) show that in rural areas, households with diversified income sources managed the recession relatively well. So did public sector workers and export crop farmers.

Table 6   **Rural-urban poverty differences**

	Year	Poverty incidence			Poverty gap		
		National	Rural	Urban	National	Rural	Urban
Cameroon	1983-84		71	25			
	ibid.	40	41-47	1-34			
Côte d'Ivoire	1988	45.9	77.0	23.0			
Egypt	1997	26.5	29.1	23.1	6.7	7.5	5.7
The Gambia			66.0	33.0			
Ghana	1988	36.9	42.0				
	1992	31.4	34.0				
Guinea-Bissau			58.0	24.0			
Kenya	1992	46.4 (48.7)	46.4	29.3			
Lesotho			54.0	55.0			
Madagascar			37.0	44.0			
Malawi			63.0	10.0			
Mauritania	1990	57.0	62-75	18-54	0.50	0.53-0.57	0.29-0.40
Niger	1993	63.0	66.0	52.0	0.22	0.23	0.18
Nigeria	1985	43.0					
	1992	34.1	36.0	30.0	15.0	16.0	12 .0
South Africa	1993		73.7	40.5			
Tanzania	1991	50.5	59.0	61.0			
Tunisia	1985	11.2	19.1	4.6			
Uganda			57.0	38.0			
Yemen, Rep. Of	1992	19.1	19.2	18.6	5.7	5.9	5.1
Zaire			76.0	32.0			
Zambia			88.0	46.0			

N.B.   Poverty lines are not the same, and therefore poverty estimates are not comparable across countries.

Sources: World Bank Poverty Assessments: Ghana, Kenya, Mauritania, Niger, Nigeria, South Africa, Yemen, Tunisia and Cameroon 2nd row.   Cleaver and Donovan (1995): Cameroon (1st row), Côte d'Ivoire, Gambia, Ghana, Guinea-Bissau, Lesotho, Madagascar, Malawi, Nigeria, Tanzania, Uganda, Zaire and Zambia. Datt et al. (1998): Egypt

Female-Headed Households

Although ambiguities and variations are recognized in definitions of the term "female-headed households", it is commonly argued that they deserve special public attention because they face the triple burdens of poverty, gender discrimination and absence of support as heads of households (Buvinic and Gupta, 1997). Poverty within female-headed households may also be related to the perpetuation of poverty over generations because children in these households tend to be more vulnerable. Three reasons may cause the link between female headship and poverty: (a) higher child dependency unsupported by transfers from absent fathers; (b) gender-related gaps in economic opportunities; and (c) demands and disruptions of domestic chores and childbearing.

However, poverty data show that female-headed households are not always worse off. On the one hand, for example, the Participatory Poverty Assessment conducted in 35 Kenyan villages in 1994, indicates that there were twice as many female-headed households (44%) than male-headed households (21%) among the very poor. Similarly, in South Africa the poverty incidence in female-headed households was around 67%, while it was 44% for male-headed households. Extreme poverty incidence was 38% among female-headed households and 24% among male-headed households (Pillay 1996). In Ethiopia, while overall poverty declined by 15% during 1989-1994, female-headed households experienced no significant decline (Dercon and Krishnan 1998).

By contrast, in Nigeria, the incidence of poverty was greater among male-headed households than female-headed households (44% at the national level in 1985 and 36% in 1992 for male-headed households, against 37% and 21% respectively for female-headed households). In Ghana in 1992, male-headed households had a slightly higher incidence of poverty than female-headed households, i.e. 32% versus 29%. The same was true in Niger where divorced or widowed women traditionally live under the guardianship of a male relative. Poverty incidence among male-headed households was 64%, and among female-headed households 55%. Poverty depth and severity was also higher in male headed households. In Côte d'Ivoire, female-headed household was not a significant factor in explaining poverty.

Underlying some of these variations is the fact that the significance and meaning of female-headed households – or indeed the term "households" itself – vary across countries, e.g., in areas with a tradition of women living apart from partners in polygamous societies of West Africa, in areas with matrilineal descent where women have economic means, or where male remittances are regular and generous (Buvinic and Gupta, 1997). Relating poverty to household characteristics is one of the most difficult issues in poverty research, for at least four reasons. Firstly, it touches directly on intra-household inequalities, an area which household surveys do not deal with. Secondly, it emphasizes the importance of household size and composition for the very measurement of poverty. Thirdly, across the region, household forms differ so fundamentally that it is difficult to generalize about the status of men, women and children. Finally, even if female-headed households are not over-represented as compared to male-headed households, they may still be more vulnerable in other respects. The data that exist, moreover, present a varied picture about the vulnerability of various types of households. These suggest that policies should be sensitive to the specific forms in specific areas.

Age and Poverty

Different age groups experience different poverty risks. This is often related to life cycle effects, and to the earner-dependent ratios of households. However, this is not uniform. In Nigeria, poverty incidence was the lowest among households whose head was between 16 and 25 years old. The older the household head, the more likely the household was to be in poverty In 1985, 46% of the households with heads between 36 and 55 years were poor, and 52% of the households with heads over 66 years. In Ethiopia, households with younger heads experienced larger declines in poverty than those with older heads. In South Africa, children constitute a large part of the poor population. In 1993, 61% of children lived in poverty, against 47% of the 16-64 years old and 52% of the over 64 years old.

The World Bank's 1997 Status Report on Africa provides an overview of the probability of being poor by age group in 14 countries. In all countries, in both rural and urban areas, the probability of people in the age group 0-14 years is higher than in the age group 15-59 years. The difference is particularly high in rural Côte d'Ivoire, with a difference of 12 percentage points. But the probability of being poor is not usually higher among the elderly (60 and over).

Education

Lack of education is often linked with poverty. In 1987/88, among Ghana's heads of households without any education, 28% were in the poorest expenditure quintile. No households whose heads had secondary or university education were in this quintile. Only 12% of the households with heads without education, as against 60% of the households with heads with secondary education were in the richest quintile. In Kenya in 1992, the primary enrolment rate in rural areas was 63% for households in the poorest decile and 78% in the richest decile. In Ethiopia, human capital variables mattered in accounting for changes in poverty between 1989 and 1994.

But again, these correlates are not uniform. Using the 1987-8 panel from the Côte d'Ivoire dataset, Grootaert et al. (1997) relate household characteristics to changes in household per capita expenditure. Education, up to but not beyond basic diploma level, mattered most in explaining welfare over time in urban areas, while in rural areas, physical capital (land and farm equipment) mattered most.

Ethnicity

Relatively little is known about the contribution of ethnicity and race to differences in poverty. It is clear however, that this is a significant factor. South Africa shows extreme inequality between different racial/ethnic groups, but differences also exist in other countries. According to Whiteford and McGrath, while the incidence of poverty has decreased between 1975 and 1991 for Africans from 68 to 67.2%, coloreds from 52 to 38.6%, and Indians from 30 to 19.6%, it has increased for whites from 3% of households to 9.5%. In 1991, the bottom quintile included a significant proportion of whites, contrary to 1975. The top quintile comprised a greater proportion of blacks than in 1975. The distribution however, remains still extremely unequal, and South Africa's poverty map is still one dominated by racial divides. Sometimes regional variations in poverty indicate ethnic variations, and sometimes, they also correspond to divergences in poverty between nomadic groups and the rest of the population.

In summary, an important conclusion from the limited data presented here, is the diversity in profiles of the poor. In some cases, economic growth is accompanied by a worsening of income distribution among the poor, for example in Nigeria during 1986-1992. It may involve a redistribution of poverty between urban and rural areas even if rural poverty remains higher overall. Data on Ethiopia suggest that some of the poor, the better educated and younger, have profited more from economic growth than others. Poverty correlates show some generalities, but it is not always the case, e.g., that female-headed households are worse off. This diversity reinforces the earlier conclusion that good quality data, at a sufficiently disaggregated level, are essential for policy interventions related to poverty.

Is Poverty Information Sufficiently Available?

The poverty profiles presented are based on nationally representative household surveys. Without the conclusions about poverty at the national level and about trends, these become meaningless. They are essential to provide disaggregated information about the poor, and hence are essential for targeting. To obtain reliable information on poverty, expenditure surveys are usually preferred over income surveys. This is because they provide more reliable and stable information about welfare due to consumption smoothing. Such surveys are essential for anti-poverty policies, but they have disadvantages as well. In the first place, it takes time for the results to become available not only because of the time required to process the data, but also because of the need to collect data throughout the year to capture the effects of seasonality. Secondly, the data themselves do not explain poverty, they merely record it. To explain poverty, qualitative information is essential to shed light where survey data have not, such as regarding vulnerability, assets depletion, survival strategies, etc.

This section discusses whether sufficient poverty information, both of the quantitative and qualitative types, is available in the region. It is generally acknowledged that too little information is available about the socio-economic condition of Africa's population. A major difficulty is that, except for a few countries of the region (Ivory Coast, South Africa, Ethiopia and Zimbabwe), household panel data do not exist. This means that most poverty analyses provide a static picture of poverty. Discussions of poverty trends focus on some aggregate level, rather than on individual level. Thus, the mobility of households in and out of poverty – which tends to be more common than often assumed – and the processes determining poverty status and changes, remain unknown.

Data on consumption poverty based on household surveys, have become available for an increasing number of countries. Around 1993, about 66% of the people in SSA countries and 47% in the Middle East and North Africa, were covered by a recent, fairly reliable household survey (Ravallion and Chen, 1996). Appendix A is based on this information. This is an enormous improvement over 1990 when less than 10% of SSA's population had been covered by a household survey. The improvement has continued since Ravallion and Chen's count.

Appendix Table A lists the data collected from internationally available sources. This indicates that data more recent than 1980, exist for 30 countries in SSA, and 5 in North Africa and the Middle East. For 23 countries, international comparable data on poverty levels are available. For another 7 countries, nation-wide representative poverty data are available but are not internationally comparable. Data presented by Cleaver and Donovan (1995) add 2 countries, Malawi, Zaire, to the list. A publication by van Holst Pellekaan and Hartnett (1997) presenting data on relative poverty, adds another 3, i.e. Burkina Faso, CAR and Sierra Leone to the list of non-comparable data.[9] The recent *Status Report on Sub-Saharan Africa* of the World Bank's Africa Region indicates that since the mid 1980s, 72 national surveys of different types have been carried out in SSA in 35 countries. This suggests a near complete coverage of the region, even if not all data have been analyzed or published.

Many of these nationally representative surveys have been sponsored and technically supported by the World Bank. Its initiatives to generate data on levels of living date back to 1980, when the Living Standards Measurement Study surveys (LSMS) were established. These aimed to develop methods for monitoring progress in raising levels of living, identify the consequences for households of current and proposed government policies, and improve communications between survey statisticians, analysts and policy makers.[10] The surveys include many dimensions of household well-being, and use extensive quality control procedures. The Social Dimension of Adjustment Project assumed responsibility for the LSMS surveys in Côte d'Ivoire, Ghana, and Mauritania. It also sponsors Integrated Surveys (similar to LSMS surveys), for example in Uganda, Mauritania, Madagascar, Senegal and Guinea, and also Priority Surveys, and Community Surveys.[11] More recently, the *Core Welfare Indicators Questionnaire* (CWIQ) was developed in collaboration with UNICEF and UNDP. This rapid monitoring tool to measure key indicators for different population groups is seen as useful in monitoring outcomes of policies. Apart from these World Bank initiatives, organizations like the IFPRI, Cornell's University Food and Nutrition Policy Program, and Universite Laval (with UNDP and the University of Benin), have sponsored surveys.

Most countries in the region therefore, have some nationally representative household surveys. Obviously, in countries like Liberia and Somalia, these are not administered because of the conflicts. Only in a few politically stable countries, i.e. Equatorial Guinea and Togo, that no poverty monitoring takes place. According to the *Status Report of the World Bank,* in 20 countries, poverty monitoring has taken place in the past and is planned for the future. Most of those countries included have been referred to above. For example:

- Kenya has been the subject of intensive socio-economic analysis, and has a well developed statistical information system. The results of two Household Budget Surveys, for 1981/82 which had information only on rural poverty and for 1992, have become available. Another survey was carried out in 1994. Participatory assessment has also become common, with a second central one carried out in 1997.

- In Ghana since the second half of the 1980s, substantial research on poverty has been undertaken. The three Living Standards Household Surveys of 1988, 1989 and 1992 provide comparable data. The World Bank produced two Poverty Assessments synthesizing the results obtained in the surveys. The Participatory Poverty Assessment (Norton et al., 1995) broadly confirms the quantitative analysis.

- Nigeria is the largest country in SSA with nearly 20% of the region's population, but until recently, little information on poverty was available. The World Bank's *Poverty Assessment on Nigeria* provides a first good overview of poverty and its correlates over the 1980s, relying mainly on two national consumer surveys of 1985 and 1992. In 1993 a sample survey of agriculture was carried out, and in 1996, a national consumer survey.

- South Africa's Integrated Household Survey, conducted between 1993 and 1994 by the Southern African Labour and Development Research Unit (SALDRU), offers nationally representative data. However, it provides income but not expenditure data. The absence of earlier large-scale studies impedes conclusions on the evolution of poverty and related indicators over time. Before the 1980s, much poverty research focused on poverty among white South Africans. However, since 1970, several authors have attempted to estimate the incidence of poverty in South Africa, using mainly the Minimum Living Level (MLL) poverty line.

It is clear that there have been many initiatives to improve the data collection in Africa. However, they vary in scope and quality. Striking even in the World Bank's Poverty Assessments is the lack of uniformity. Some assessments have been considered deficient by the World Bank itself. Often, data are so outdated as to make them useless for policies. There is also a lack of information on the links between economic growth and poverty reduction, and it is difficult to estimate the effect on poverty of alternative policies.

One of the main problems which continues to hinder the analysis of poverty is the lack of trend data. Trends cannot be deduced from one-off surveys, and where surveys are available for two points in time, care is needed before trends can be ascertained because they may come from unusually good or bad years (e.g. Guinea-Bissau). Appendix Table 2 lists 10 countries in the region for which data are available about changes in poverty but these are mostly for two or three points in time only. According to the 1997 World Bank Status Report, 15 countries in SSA have implemented two surveys although some have carried out more. But in much fewer cases are the surveys comparable.

Tables 2, 3, 4 and 5 report available data on indicators related to consumption poverty. Like the poverty data, such data mask significant informational problems. Estimates on the prevalence of food intake inadequacy (Table 2) amount to little more than guesswork in many countries. For example, such prevalence estimates should rely on the distribution of dietary energy between individuals, but information is available on the distribution between households. And even then, data are available for only 18 countries. Dietary energy intake distributions for some other countries are determined from distributions of income or expenditure. Yet in some countries this approximation is not feasible and so "figures are imputed based on neighbouring countries with similar socio-economic situations" (FAO 1996: 41).

Trends in child anthropometry are shown in Table 3. Beyond the FAO source, this type of data is also becoming increasingly available through the World Bank-sponsored Integrated Surveys and Priority Surveys. According to the World Bank's 1997 *Status Report*, anthropometric data are available in 22 data sets for 14 countries.[12] But these data suffer from the common concerns about comparability, as surveys even within the same countries use different methodology, sample frames, and reference age-groups which are of crucial relevance for the outcome. Finally, data on child or infant mortality, life expectancy, literacy or enrolment rates, according to some sources are available for almost all countries in the region. However, these data can seldom be disaggregated in the desired way, and are reasonably reliable only for the census year.[13]

Qualitative or participatory approaches to monitoring poverty have now become common. They are included in the World Bank Poverty Assessments with differing degrees of effectiveness. They have been instrumental in rapidly tracing the effects of the crisis in East Asia (Robb 1998). In Ghana, for example, the Living Standards Household Surveys of 1988, 1989 and 1992 have been complemented by Participatory Poverty Assessments (PPA) which broadly confirmed the quantitative analysis (Norton et al. 1995). The PPA categorized levels of poverty in villages following a subjective wealth-ranking exercise, and a group discussion of the characteristics of the very poor, poor, average and rich people. Once consensus was reached, people were asked to categorize each household in the community in one group. Common methods are community maps which illustrate where people live, flow diagrams showing links and causes, seasonal calendars, matrix analysis and wealth ranking. They often involve traditional anthropological methods such as semi-structured interviews with key informants and contact persons, which aim to obtain information from individuals who are thought to have sufficient knowledge about issues or groups of people of interest. A key feature is the concern with obtaining only "enough information" rather than "as much information as possible". The primary strength is in assessing relative values, which can be useful in monitoring situations where policy impacts are assessed. While such assessment usually have been carried out in small locations by local NGOs, attempts have been made to scale it up. In Kenya and Tanzania, participatory rural assessment (PRA) was used in poverty assessment by sampling a large number of communities and using pre-designed scoring cards and categories to produce comparable results.

There are problems with PPAs as well. Firstly, scaling up is not simply a matter of duplicating the exercise in several localities; institutional mechanisms for coordination and analysis need to be in place. Secondly, while most PRA exercises focus on relative values, absolute values are crucial for comparative purposes which relates to the problem of scaling up. Thirdly, the explanatory power of subjective data has been questioned. Ravallion (1996) compares the predictive power of subjective and objective data and concludes that subjective welfare questions did predict consumption with some degree of accuracy, but not as much as objective indicators. Answers and discussions of subjective questions are also prone to being influenced by the presence of a facilitator and other community members. PPA is usually seen as a cheap alternative to more expensive household surveys. However, in the context of poverty monitoring, PPA is a relatively expensive method compared to the monitoring of a limited number of indicators, whether from existing data sources or through short surveys. Finally, it is unlikely that participatory monitoring could accurately track the full primary and secondary effects of macroeconomic and sectoral reforms.

Participatory techniques are particularly useful in adding depth of understanding to the quantitative data collected by large-scale household monitoring surveys. Some of the methods can be usefully implemented for rapid tracing of effects of crises. But none of these can substitute for nationally representative household data. The most important challenge is in combining the various methods, using the strength of quantitative techniques to provide generalizable data with the strength of qualitative approaches to provide deeper insight into the meanings of poverty, and the strength of rapid appraisals to provide insights more quickly than household surveys. Part of the issue between the two approaches depends on exactly what the information is required for. Obtaining context-specific information through participatory approaches may be, at times, the best way of evaluating certain questions about poverty.

The approaches are not substitutes for each other, and therefore it remains crucial to continue to stress the need for representative data. As noted above, in the context of the wide range of new initiatives, perhaps the most important problem is the lack of trend data. Beyond the problems that this poses for policy-relevant analyses, it may also indicate the relative lack of sustained effort to monitor poverty. The initiatives described of the LSMS type, have to a large extent, been donor-driven. In many cases, this has not been accompanied by efforts to build in-country capacity and contribute to a constituency that enables sustained efforts towards poverty monitoring over time. The World Bank's 1997 *Status Report* is rightly concerned that in a fairly large number of countries in SSA, there are no future plans for administering surveys, and that the number of planned surveys in the region is declining. There are doubts whether there is, both among donors and within the countries concerned, sufficient constituency to enforce such sustained efforts.

How Useful is the Existing Information for Policy?

What can policy makers do with the kind of information previously described? Particularly, how useful are the poverty profiles for targeting? There are three types of targeting: (a) Sectoral targeting; (b) Self targeting; and (c) Administered targeting (Van de Walle, 1998).

- Sectoral targeting: This targets types of spending which are relatively important to the poor without attempting to reach the poor directly as individuals.   Information is required about the types of spending most relevant to the poor.   Estimates of "incidences of benefits" across income deciles from different kinds of public spending are central for poverty-reducing sectoral targeting policies.
- Self targeting: By assuming that the poor will identify themselves, this saves on considerable information demands.   However, to design the program, reliable key information is required. Self-targeting subsidies on "inferior goods" require information on consumption preferences to ensure that most non-poor will not consume the subsidized good. Improving self-targeting programs requires beneficiary evaluation, but the existence of a recent nation-wide survey contributes to adequate poverty responses, particularly to identify the most vulnerable areas. For public works employment, often praised as an effective anti-poverty intervention (Lipton et al., 1998), wage data are essential for determining the correct programme wage (which should not be above the market rate, to keep the program self-targeting.   Data on local wage rates are fairly easy to obtain, and do perhaps not need household surveys. But to target the programs and to evaluate the outcome of the programs which should involve a comparison with situations where the project is not implemented, survey information can be of great help.[14]
- Administered targeting: Many anti-poverty policies rely on administered targeting which requires detailed information on the poor. Households income can be used directly as a means of targeting. However, this is administratively difficult, and it may induce households to claim to be poorer than they actually are. Therefore, other means of administrative targeting are often preferred, i.e.   using characteristics that are easily observed, not easily changed and highly correlated with poverty, such as region of residence, landholding, gender, and household size. Also a focus on such indicators, if they better reflect long-run living standards, may provide a better identification of the chronically poor.[15] The more a poverty profile is able to indicate long-term living standards, the better it will be for targeting the chronically poor. Education and land ownership may be considered as long-run welfare indicators.

Thus, poverty characteristics already discussed can be helpful, not only in the understanding of poverty, but also for policies targeting the poor. But it is important to stress that such correlates are by no means easy to identify, and can be very sensitive to definitions of poverty, and the setting of poverty lines. For example, Ravallion and Bidani (1994) show that the method used to derive the poverty line can have a large impact on the poverty profile. They show this for Indonesia and it is likely to hold in other places. According to the "cost of basic needs method" for determining the poverty line, rural poverty is substantially greater than urban poverty (as are poverty gap and poverty severity). However, using "the food energy intake method", this rural-urban ranking is reversed for all three poverty measures. A similar re-ranking is observed when the two methods are compared for poverty across provinces and regions. Thus, careful sensitivity analysis of poverty profiles is required to see whether they are robust as to the choice of methods, assumptions and poverty lines. Ravallion and Bidani (1994: 98) state that policymakers should be wary of how underlying poverty measures have been constructed before using the derived poverty profiles to formulate poverty-reduction policies. But the reality is that data are often unavailable for the relative luxury of sensitivity analysis. Moreover, sensitivity analysis only indicates the effect of choices for different groups but choices still have to be made for practical policymaking.

To further illustrate the point about how different methods and definitions can lead to different profiles of the poor, outcomes of recent research that compare quantitative and qualitative and participatory methods are referred to. Shaffer (1998) compares the groups identified as poor in Guinea through survey data and through a participatory assessment, and finds discrepancies between the two approaches in terms of the poverty status, particularly of women. Survey data clearly indicate that male-headed households in Guinea were poorer than female-headed households (for poverty incidence, depth and severity measures), and this was not affected by the choice of poverty line. Correspondingly, female-headed households are found to be under-represented among the poor, and even more so among the ultra-poor. Survey data also indicate that the incidence of both stunting and wasting was higher in boys than girls, and a higher percentage of men had body mass indices which put them in the ranges of "health risk" and "underweight". Figures for child mortality under-5 years indicate excess male mortality. The participatory study reveals that both men and women believed that in terms of work-load and decision-making authority, women were disadvantaged, these being elements of welfare not exposed by the survey information. In well-being ranking exercises, groups of both men and women separately ranked all but two married village women below males, and the materially poorest man in the village was ranked "better-off" than materially better-off women. This example cited illustrates that survey information may give a misleading or incomplete picture of deprivation. Basing policy entirely on survey data, may therefore be insufficient.

Comparisons of subjective poverty assessment and survey-based objective poverty assessment have been carried out for Jamaica and Nepal, based on qualitative questions on perceptions of consumption adequacy (Pradhan and Ravallion, 1997). Poverty measures and poverty rankings of regions, based on objective poverty lines have striking similarities to those based on subjective poverty lines. Both subjective and objective poverty lines address consumption adequacy only, and not other aspects of welfare. The results show that with good survey information, an objective method of estimating consumption poverty can be devised which accords quite well with what the poor consider inadequate.

The point here is not to debate which kind of poverty monitoring is better. In any case, qualitative and quantitative methods should reinforce each other. This discussion focuses on whether poverty profiles can be used for targeting anti-poverty policies. The examples illustrate that such profiles can be essential for targeting, but that they should be applied with careful recognition of how they are constructed, and their sensitivity to changes in the specification of poverty lines and/or poverty concept. Different definitions, methods and approaches can give radically different outcomes, even to the extent that rankings can be reversed, potentially leading to great targeting errors. Policies therefore, should be based on representative quantitative data, but these should be carefully analyzed, and should be supported by more contextual information and knowledge about the priorities, perceptions and needs expressed by the poor themselves.

Conclusion

Much has been written during the 1990s about poverty, the characteristics of the poor, its status in Africa and how it relates to economic growth. The main objective of this paper is to look at the underlying information that forms the basis of these debates. Poverty research (e.g. Lipton et al., 1998) provides clear suggestions regarding effective, cost-efficient responses to poverty. However, the successful application in a given context requires specific information on the poor in that particular country, at that particular point in time. The main argument is that too little is known about poverty, particularly in Africa, the very continent where human deprivation is worst.

There are less than 20 SSA countries for which internationally comparable data are available, usually for one point in time only. This makes it very difficult to draw reasonably reliable conclusions about, for example, the link between economic growth and poverty.

This paper also investigates what poverty data are available at the national level in Africa and the Middle East, about trends in countries and characteristics of the poor, and how useful these data can be for policy makers. In terms of coverage, data on poverty are becoming increasingly available. Whereas at the beginning of the 1990s, perhaps only 10% of the population was covered by nationally representative surveys which are essential for many policy purposes, now they are available in all but a few countries. Availability is not the whole story, however. Governments and donors may still be paying insufficient attention to sustained monitoring of poverty. In many cases, surveys have been implemented only once, and have not become a regular exercise nor integrated in policy-making processes. The lack of trend data is a major hindrance for poverty analysis which may also signify that there is inadequate commitment to provide regular data.

Nationally representative expenditure surveys can usefully describe the welfare of a population. These surveys also provide information about the characteristics of the poor, which are essential for understanding poverty, as well as targeting anti-poverty policy. This paper has attempted to demonstrate how much variety there is in this respect, and that results of research are very sensitive to definitions employed. But other forms of measurement can contribute to the monitoring of poverty and identifying the poor. Health and education are often correlated with poverty, but much of the data on these issues in the region are not of high quality. Proxies of poverty, such as land ownership or rural wage rates, may also be instrumental in the continuous and timely monitoring of poverty. Finally, participatory assessments not only provide in-depth knowledge essential to understand poverty, but can also be helpful in rapidly tracing effects of sudden shocks. None of these methods are substitutes for each other. The challenge in monitoring poverty lies in an eclectic combination of various approaches.

Poverty analysis is not cost-less. Approaches to poverty analysis are neither cheap nor easy. Adequate poverty monitoring will remain contingent upon many things, including continued commitment by donors, but especially within the countries to obtain regular data on the welfare of the population.   Neglecting the need for poverty information may lead to higher costs later and to policy mistakes and inefficiency.

Notes

1 These data are discussed in greater details. Regarding the growth-poverty link, Ravallion and Chen (1996) conclude that generally speaking, growth usually benefits the poor. Lipton (1998) shows that about one-third of variation in poverty across countries may be explained with variations in GNP. Roemer and Gugerty (quoted by Killick 1997: 13) find almost a one-to-one relationship between overall GNP/capita growth and the incomes of the poorest 20% and 40% of the population. Findings by Bruno *et al.* (1996) which suggest that growth does not automatically result in rising inequality, strengthens expectations that growth will reduce poverty. de Haan (1998) discusses these themes in more detail.

2 Cleaver and Donovan (1995) and Ravallion and Chen quoted in Demery and Walton (1998) have estimated that a per capita growth rate of 1.9% is required to halve $1/day poverty in SSA by 2015 (the International Development Target), when the actual growth rate between 1991 and 1995 was -1.35 though projected to be 1.1% for 1997-2000.

3 Purchasing power exchange rates at 1985 prices are used by the World Bank to establish an international PL. PPP exchange rates are defined as the nominal exchange rate multiplied by the ratio of an index of world prices over an index of domestic prices. There have been questions about this method, however, because of uncertainties over local prices. Moreover, the lack of data which would allow PPP rates to relate more closely to the bundles purchased by the poor, poses additional problems for the poverty estimates.

4 Part of the review of the literature, particularly for Nigeria, Kenya, Ghana and South Africa, was carried out earlier by Eliane Darbellay for the *1997 Human Development Report*. For these countries, information is based on *World Bank Poverty Assessments*, unless otherwise stated. The list of poverty correlates is by no means exhaustive. It does not include, for example, information about household size, or ownership of assets (e.g., in Ethiopia, ownership of land as well as oxen were found to be important factors in the decomposition of poverty changes between 1989 and 1994 (Dercon and Krishna, 1998: 27), or regional differences, which are usually substantial. The 1997 World Bank *Progress Report on Africa* lists household welfare indicators for urban and rural expenditure quintiles for 15 SSA countries.

5 Along with the reduction in all poverty measures, there has also been a slight decrease in income inequalities between 1988 and 1992. Deininger and Squire (1996) give values of Gini coefficients of 0.36 for 1988, 0.37 for 1989 and 0.30 for 1992.

6   Dercon and Krishnan (1998: 21). However, the same study also shows that changes in poverty differed across the villages. For example, distance to towns and roads mattered in accounting for the poverty changes over time.

7 The line for extreme poverty was set at 1/3 of mean per capita household expenditure. Along with the worsening condition of the poorest in terms of poverty incidence and intensity, income inequalities have increased over the 1980s.   The Gini coefficient

increased from 0.51 to 0.56 between 1981/82 and 1992 at the national level, and from 0.40 to 0.49 in rural areas (World Bank, Kenya, 1995).

8 Income inequalities among the whole population increased from Gini 0.387 in 1985 to 0.449 in 1992, and among the poor from 0.188 to 0.251.

9 Data in Deininger and Squire (1996a) show an additional 3 countries for which survey data are available, i.e. Gabon, Seychelles, Sudan, but all from the 1970s. For South Africa which does not have similar data, Whiteford and McGrath (1994) argue that the distribution of mean household income within the poorest deciles of households deteriorated between 1975 and 1991 which is a period with relatively low economic growth, while the income of the upper deciles remained relatively stable.

10 Grosh and Glewwe (1995) provide a catalogue of LSMS data sets; this is being updated. Grootaert and Marchant (1991) describe the initiatives with regard to data collection under the *Social Dimensions of Adjustment in Sub-Saharan Africa Programme*. They conclude that the SDA programme is fundamentally different from that of the LSMS. Aho *et al.* (1998: 28) describe earlier pioneering *African Consumer Expenditure Surveys*, and the *National Household Survey Capability Programme of the UN*.

11 *Priority Surveys* provides rapid information to policy makers that would be used to identify target groups, and to provide key socio-economic indicators for such groups. The survey is based on a relatively short questionnaire for a relatively large sample of households. *Integrated Surveys* provides detailed information to investigate responses of different households to adjustment. It uses lengthy and detailed questionnaires on a somewhat smaller sample. *Community Data Collection Programme* aims to provide a baseline, and monitor information on markets and infrastructure in the economy.

12 This allows testing of the correlation between anthropometric data and income poverty data. According to the Status Report, stunting is closely related to income levels, but wasting is highly variable.

13 Composite indicators, such as UNDP's Human Development Index, have been proposed and have rapidly obtained political significance. These give a rough indication of welfare, but provide little added value to the primary indicators on which they are based and are subject to the same data constraints.

14 Ravallion's *Appraising Workfare Programs* (1998) provides a relatively simple analytical tool for a rapid appraisal of workfare programs. Nevertheless, data requirements appear substantial.

15 Much of poverty is dynamic with people repeatedly slipping into and out of poverty. This does not imply that transitory poverty is not a problem. Temporary poverty can damage capabilities in the long run. An example is when households because of temporary crises or life cycle events, are forced to withdraw children from school, or cannot afford sufficient nutrition at early ages.

References

African Development Bank. 1997. African Development Report. *Africa in the Work Economy.* New York: Oxford University Press.

Aho, G., S. Larivière and F. Martin. 1998. *Poverty Analysis Manual. With Application in Benin.* Québec: Université Laval and UNDP.

Baker, J.L. and M.E. Grosh. 1994. 'Poverty reduction through geographical targeting: How well does it work?' *World Development* 22, No 7:983-995.

Barro, R.J. 1997. *'Determinants of economic growth. A cross-country empirical study.* Development Discussion Paper No. 579, Cambridge: Harvard Institute for International Development.

Bruno, M., M. Ravallion and L. Squire. 1996. *Equity and growth in developing countries: Old and new perspectives on the policy issues.* Policy Research working Paper 1563, World Bank, Washington, D.C.

Buvinic, M and G.R. Gupta. 1997. 'Female-headed households and female-maintained families: are they worth targeting to reduce poverty in developing countries?' *Economic Development and Cultural Change* 45, No 2:259- 280.

Cleaver, K.M. 1997. Rural development strategies for poverty reduction and environmental protection in Africa. In *Overcoming Rural Poverty in Africa.* Edited by Breth. Geneva.

_____ and W.G. Donovan. 1995. *Agriculture, poverty and policy reform in Sub-Saharan Africa.* World Bank Discussion Papers, Africa Technical Department Series, Washington D.C.

Datt, G., D. Jolliffe and M. Sharma. 1998. A profile of poverty in Egypt, 1997. IFPRI and Government of Egypt.

Deininger, K. and L. Squire. 1996. 'A new data set measuring income inequality'. *The World Bank Economic Review,* 10, No 3: 565-591.

Demery, L. and M. Walton. 1998. 'Are poverty and social goals for the 21st century attainable? Paper presented at the IDS Conference *What Can Be Done About Poverty,* Sussex, 29 June - 1 July 1998.

Dercon, S. and P. Krishnan. 1998. Changes in poverty in rural Ethiopia 1989-1995: Measurement, robustness tests and decomposition. Mimeo, Oxford Centre for Study of African Economies.

El-laithy H. 1998. Poverty measures in Egypt. Paper presented at the International Conference on *Poverty: Emerging Challenges,* Bangladesh Institute of Development Studies, Dhaka, February.

Farah, A.A.M. and R.K. Sampath. 1995. *'Poverty in Sudan'. Journal of Asian and African Studies* 30, No 3-4: 146-161.

Food and Agriculture Organization of the United Nations. 1996. *The Sixth World Food Survey.* Rome, Italy.

Grootaert, Christiaan and R. Kanbur. 1995. The lucky few amidst economic decline: Distributional change in Côte d'Ivoire as seen through panel data sets, 1985-88. *Journal of Development Studies* 31, No 4: 603-619.

_____, R. Kanbur and Gi-Taik Oh. 1997. 'The dynamics of welfare gains and losses: An African case study'. *Journal of Development Studies* 33, No 5: 635-658.

_____ and T. Marchant. 1991. *The social dimensions of adjustment priority survey. An instrument for the rapid identification and monitoring of policy target groups.* SDA Working Paper Series No.12, World Bank.

Grosh, M.E. and P. Glewwe. 1995. A guide to living standard measurement study surveys and their data sets. LSMS Working Paper No.120, World Bank, Washington.

de Haan. 1998. Economic growth, poverty, and policies: national experiences in Sub-Saharan Africa. Paper for the IDS Conference *What Can Be Done About Poverty,* June 1998.

Hassan, F.M. A. 1997. 'Economic reform: Is it hurting the poor? A country specific study'. *Journal of International Development* Vol 9, No 1: 21-38.

Jayarajah, C., W. Branson and B. Sen. 1996. *Social Dimensions of Adjustment. World Bank Experience.* World Bank, Washington, D.C.

Killick, T. 1997. *'Adjustment, Income Distribution and Poverty in Africa: A Research Guide.* Nairobi, AERC.

Lipton, Michael, S. Yaqub and E. Darbellay. 1998. *Success in Anti-poverty.* ILO, Geneva.

Lundberg, M.K.A. and P.K. Diskin. 1995. Targeting assistance to the poor and food insecure. A literature review. USAID, SD Publications Series, Technical Paper No.9 (available on Internet).

Morrison, C. 1991. Adjustment, incomes and poverty in Morocco. *World Development* 19, No 11: 1633-1651.

Norton, A., A. Bortei-Doku Aryeetey, D. Korboe and D.K. Tony Dogbe. 1995. *Poverty assessment in Ghana. using qualitative and participatory research methods.* PSP Discussion Papers, World Bank, Washington, D.C.

Pillay, P. 1996. An overview of poverty in South Africa. In *South Africa: Wealth, Poverty and Reconstruction.* Edited by L. Deng and E. Tjonneland. Chr. Michelsen Institute.

Pradhan, M. and M. Ravallion. 1997. Measuring poverty using qualitative perceptions of welfare. Mimeo, Free University, Amsterdam and World Bank, Washington, D.C.

Ravallion, M. 1996. 'How well can method substitute for data? Five experiments in poverty analysis'. *The World Bank Research Observer* 11, No 2.

_____. 1998. *Appraising workfare programs.* World Bank Policy Research Working Paper No. 1955, World Bank, Washington, D.C.

_____ and B. Bidani. 1994. 'How robust is a poverty profile?'   *World Bank Economic Review* 8, No1: 75-102.

_____ and S. Chen. 1996. What can new data tell us about recent changes in living standards in developing and transitional economy?   World Bank, Poverty and Human Resources Division. Mimeo.

Robb, C.   1998.   Social aspects of the east Asian financial crisis: Perceptions of poor communities.   Paper presented at the IDS Workshop *Crisis in East Asia* , 13-14 July.

SALDRU.   1994.   *South Africans Rich and Poor: Baseline Household Statistics, Project for Statistics on Living Standards and Development.* University of Cape Town.

Shaffer, P.   1998.   'Who's poor? Comparing household survey and participatory poverty assessment results from the Republic of Guinea'. *World Development* 26, No12 (Forthcoming).

UNDP Ukraine. 1996. *Ukraine Human Development Report.* Regional Bureau for Europe and CIS, UNDP.

van de Walle, D.   1998. 'Targeting revisited'.   *World Bank Research Observer* 13, No 2:231-248.

Van Holst Pellekaan, J.W., and Teresa Hartnett. 1997. "Poverty in sub-Saharan Africa: Causes and characteristics".   In: *Overcoming Rural Poverty in Africa.* Edited by S.A. Breth. Geneva: Centre for Applied Studies in International Negotiations.

Whiteford, A. and M. McGarth.   1994.   *The Distribution of Income in South Africa.* Human Sciences Research Council, Pretoria.

World Bank.   Various years.   *World Development Report.*   Oxford: Oxford University Press.

_____.   1995.   *Ghana: Poverty past, present and future.* Report No 14504-GH, World Bank, Washington, D.C.

_____.   1995.   *Kenya poverty assessment.*   Report No 13152-KE, World Bank, Washington, D.C.

_____.   1996.   Taking action for poverty reduction in Sub-Saharan Africa: Report of an Africa Region Task Force, World Bank, Washington, D.C.

_____.   1996. *Poverty Reduction and the World Bank. Progress and Challenges in the 1990s.* World Bank, Washington, D.C.

_____.   1996. Nigeria: *Poverty in the midst of plenty. The challenge of growth with inclusion, a World Bank poverty assessment.* Report no 14733-UNI, World Bank, Washington, D.C.

_____.   1997.   *Status report on poverty in Sub-Saharan Africa 1997: Tracking the incidence and characteristics of poverty.*   September, World Bank, Africa Region, Washington, D.C.

Appendix Table A Poverty in African and Middle Eastern countries

	GNP/cap PPP 1995	GNP/cap % gwth 85-95	$1/day poverty Year survey	HCI	PGI	GDP/cap PPP survey	HCI, national poverty line Year survey	National	Rural	Urban	Relative poverty Year Survey	National	Rural	Urban	Inequality Year survey	Avge Gini
Sub-Saharan Africa																
Burkina Faso	780	-0.2					1995	33.0			1995	56	65	13		
Benin	1760	-0.3													1986	54.2
Botswana	5580	6.1	85-86	34.7	13.3	2337										
Burundi	630	-1.3					1990	36.2								
Cameroon	2110	-6.6					1984	40.0	32.4	44.4					1983	49
CAR	1070	-2.4									1993	61	77	33	1992	55.0
Côte d'Ivoire	1580	-4.1	1988	17.7	4.3	1419	Early 90s		77	23	1995	40	49	31	85-88	39.2
Ethiopia	450	-0.3	81-2	33.8	8.0	322	(93-4)	(53)								
Eritrea																
Gabon		-8.2													75-77	61.2
The Gambia	930	-1.1					1992	64.0			1992	49	73	21		
Ghana	1990	1.4	1991	26.3	12.4		1992	31.4	34.3	26.7	1993	39	45	26	88-92	35.1
Guinea		1.4				763					94-95	52	52	51		
Guinea-Bissau	790	2.0	1991	87.0	57.8	593	1991	48.8	60.9	24.1	1991	54	65	29	1991	56.1
Kenya	1380	0.1	1992	50.2	22.2	914	1992	46.4	46.4	29.3	92-93	61	69	12	1992	54.4
Lesotho	1780	1.2	86-87	50.4	24.8	928	1993	49.2	53.9	27.8					1987	56.0
Madagascar	640	-2.2	1993	72.3	33.2	579	Early 90s		37	44	1993	51	59	21	1990	43.4

Appendix Table A Cont

	GNP/cap PPP 1995	GNP/cap % gwth 85-95	$1/day poverty Year survey	HCI	PGI	GDP/cap PPP survey	HCI, national poverty line Year survey	National	Rural	Urban	Relative poverty Year National Survey	Rural	Urban	Inequality Year survey	Avge Gini
Malawi	750	-0.7					Early 90s		63	10					
Mali	550	0.8					Early 90s			50					
Mauritania	1540	0.5	1988	31.4	15.2	788	1990	57.0						1988	42.5
Mauritius	13210	5.4					1992	10.6						80-91	40.7
Mozambique	810	3.6													
Niger	750		1992	61.5	22.2	420					1993	38	43	1992	36.1
Nigeria	1220	1.2	92-93	28.9	11.7	978	92-93	34.1	36.4	30.4	1992	44	52	86-92	38.6
Rwanda	540	-5.4	83-85	45.7	11.3	769	1993	51.2						1983	28.9
Senegal	1780	-0.7	91-92	54.0	25.5	1120					1991	55	78	1991	54.1
Seychelles														78-84	46.5
Sierra Leone	580	-3.6									89/90	56	74	1968	60.8
South Africa	5030	-1.6	1993	23.7	6.6	2954					1993	63	82	1992	62.3
Sudan							1991	51.1						1971	38.7
Tanzania	640	1.0	1993	16.4	3.7	518					1993	42	52	69-93	40.4
Togo	1130	-2.7					87-89	32.3							
Uganda	1470	2.7	89-90	50.0	14.7	548	1993	55.0			1993	42	46	89-92	36.9
Zaire							Early 90s		76	32					
Zambia	930	-0.8	1993	84.6	53.8	709	1993	86.0			1993	52	75	76-91	47.3
Zimbabwe	2030	-0.6	90-91	41.0	14.3	1182	90-91	25.5						1990	56.8

Appendix Table A Cont

	GNP/cap PPP 1995	GNP/cap % gwth 85-95	$1/day poverty				HCI, national poverty line				Relative poverty				Inequality	
			Year survey	HCI	PGI	GDP/cap PPP survey	Year Survey	National	Rural	Urban	Year Survey	National	Rural	Urban	Year survey	Avge Gini
Middle East and North Africa																
Algeria			1995	<2	-		1995	22.6	30.3	14.7					1988	38.7
Egypt			90-91	7.6	1.1			-							59-91	38.0
Iran				-	-			-							69-84	43.2
Jordan			1992	2.5	0.5		1991	15.0							80-91	39.2
Morocco			90-91	<2			90-91	13.1	18.0	7.6					84-91	39.2
Tunisia			1990	3.9	0.9		1990	14.1	21.0	8.9					65-90	42.5

Sources:

World Development Report (1997): GNP/capita and growth

Ravallion (1996): $/day poverty and GDP/capita at survey year (in PPP, 1985 prices) and National poverty line except Eritrea (World Bank Poverty Assessment)

Cleaver and Donovan (1995): data marked with 'early 90s' as the survey year

van Holst Pellekaan and Hartnett (1997): Relative poverty data from Deininger and Squire (1996)

Appendix Table B   Trends in poverty during the 1980s and 1990s (population below the poverty line)

	Year	National Poverty		Rural poverty	Urban poverty
		ModeratePO	Extreme PO	Moderate PO	Moderate PO
Sub-Saharan Africa					
Cote d'Ivoire	1985	30			
	1988	45.9			
Ethiopia	1989			61.3	
	1994			49.6 / 33.3	
	1995			45.3	
Ghana	1988	36.9	10.2	42	
	1992	31.4	6.0	34	
Kenya	81/82	(51.5)		47.9	
	1992	46.4		46.4	29.3
		(48.7)			
Nigeria	1985	43	12.0		
	1992	34.1	13.6	36	30
Tanzania	1983	64.6			
	1991	50.5			
Sudan	1978	38			
	1990	72			
North Africa/ Middle East					
Jordan	86/87				
	1992				
Morocco	1970	42	42		
	1985	30	30		
Tunisia	1985				
	1990				
Egypt	1981/2			26.8	33.5
	1995/6			50.2	45.0

Sources: Jayarajah *et al.* (1996): National data for: Cote d'Ivoire, Ghana, Jordan, Morocco, Tunisia, and rural data for: Ethiopia, Kenya, and Tanzania.

Cleaver and Donovan (1995): Cote d'Ivoire (rural & urban), Ghana (rural & urban), Kenya (rural & urban), Nigeria (rural & urban), Tanzania (rural & urban).

Demery and Squire (1996): Cote d'Ivoire (national), Ethiopia, Kenya (in brackets) and Tanzania. Dercon and Krishnan (1998): Ethiopia - the two figures are the results of two different rounds, the second one held at the beginning of the harvest when food was relatively plentiful; panel data for 351 households.

Hassan (1997): Sudan – however, questions exist regarding the quality of these data.

Morrison (1991): Morocco, but PL is not specified.

El-laithy (1998): Egypt – however, Datt et al. (1998) calculate poverty incidence in 1997 to be 26.5%.

5 Priorities of Social Policy Measures and the Interest of Low-Income People: The Egyptian Case

Karima Aly Korayem

Introduction

Social policy measures are important means to reduce poverty and raise the standard of living of low-income people in general. However, since there are budget constraints for the government, priorities have to be set in allocating government expenditure for different social measures. These priorities may be set by the government according to its own criteria or may be set according to the interest of low-income people as revealed by their expenditure patterns; i.e., giving higher priorities to those social services representing higher relative shares in the budget of low-income people. This paper espouses the second alternative which is to set a scale of priorities that serves the interest of low-income people, including the poor as a subgroup. Thus, the objective of this study is to assess social policy priorities set by the government with respect to the needs of low-income people in Egypt. The social policy measures examined in this context are government expenditures on food subsidy, education,and health. The two latest Household Expenditure Sample Surveys (HESS), which were carried out in 1990/91 and 1995/96, were used to analyze the expenditure pattern of the low-income people on food subsidy, education and health *vis-à-vis* the Egyptian government's expenditure pattern on these three items.

Low-Income Household Group in Egypt: Its Evolution by Size and Relative Expenditure Share for the Period 1990/91 - 1995/96

To identify the low-income households group in Egypt, a set of measurement criteria has to be developed since such kind of criteria is not available in the literature.   Thus, the first step in this study is to formulate such an indicator to differentiate between low-, middle- and upper-income household groups, and apply it to the Egyptian case.

Income-Inequality Index: A Measure for Income-Inequality and for the Identification of Low-Income Households Group

Income is equally distributed among the population if a given percentage of the population receives an equal percentage of national income, e.g., 5% of the population receives 5% of the national income, 10% of the population receives 10% of the national income, etc. Accordingly, income is unequally distributed if a   given percentage of the population receives a smaller percentage share of national income, while other equal percentage of the population receives a greater percentage share of national income. The former group is the population who falls in the lower-income intervals, while the latter group belongs to the upper-income intervals. The income inequality index (III) is based on this concept. The III is presented mathematically as follows:

$$III = \frac{\left[\sum_{i=1}^{N}|(X - RS_i)|\right]/2}{(100 - X)} \tag{1}$$

where   X = fixed population interval = equal income-distribution share (EIDS)

   RS_i = relative income share of the ith population interval
   N = number of the population intervals, i.e., N = 5 for the quintile distribution of the   population, N = 10 for the decile distribution, etc.

Meaning of the III

The numerator: $[\sum_{i=1}^{N} |(X - RS_i)|]/2$

represents the relative share of national income (or expenditure) that is unequally distributed. Since the sum of the absolute value of differences from EIDS is computed, it is necessary to divide by 2 in order to avoid double counting.

The denominator: $(100 - X)$

represents the extreme case of inequality in income distribution, when all the national income is received by one population interval (X), i.e., by one quintile, or one decile, etc.

In the extreme case of equality in income distribution, III = 0, since in this case RS_i = X for all i, and hence the numerator in Equation 1 is equal to zero. In the extreme case of income inequality, the general solution of Equation 1 is:

$$III = \frac{\left[\sum_{i=1}^{N-1} |(X-0)| + |(X-100)|\right]/2}{(100-X)} = 1 \qquad (2)$$

where N = 5 for the quintile distribution of the population; N = 10 for the decile distribution, etc.[1]

Thus, the value of the income inequality index falls between 0 and 1, i.e. $0 < III < 1$. The two extreme cases of quintile income distribution are shown in Figures 1 and 2. Figure 1 shows the case of extreme equality in income distribution. In this case, each of the households' quintile receives an income share equal to EIDS, which is equal to 20% of the national income; i.e., EIDS = X. Figure 2 shows the case of extreme inequality in income distribution where all the income quintiles, except one, receive zero income; while one quintile receives all the national income. As shown in Figure 2, 80% of the national income is unequally distributed. This is the share of national income above the EIDS (= the shaded area in Figure 2).

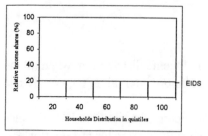

Figure 1: Extreme equality of income-distribution

Figure 2: Extreme inequality of income-distribution

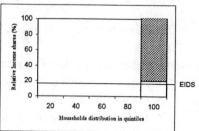

is the share of national income wich is unequally distributed

EIDS = equal income distribution share

Identification of Low-Income Households

In the decile income-distribution, one may differentiate three groups: (a) the household deciles whose shares of the national income are less than 10% for each decile; (b) those deciles whose shares of national income are around 10% of the national income for each decile; and (c) those household deciles whose relative shares are greater than 10% of the national income for each decile. Hence, in the decile income-distribution, 10% share of the national income is the EIDS, while in the quintile income-distribution pattern, the EIDS refers to 20% of the national income, etc. The EIDS is used in identifying the three household groups: (a) the lower-income households, (b) the middle-income households, and (c) the upper-income households. The first group includes the poor and the last group includes the rich.

Because of non-availability of income distribution data, the expenditure data in the HESS are used to identify the low-income households group in Egypt. Since household expenditure and income are closely related, the lower-expenditure and lower-income households are used interchangeably throughout the study. The same applies to middle-expenditure (middle-income) and upper-expenditure (upper-income) households. Using the expenditure data in the HESS, the equal expenditure-distribution share (EEDS) instead of the EIDS, is used to differentiate the three household groups: (a) the lower-expenditure households group which includes all deciles whose expenditure shares are below the EEDS; (b) the middle-expenditure households group consisting of all deciles whose expenditure shares are around the EEDS; and (c) the upper-expenditure households group encompassing all deciles whose expenditure shares in total expenditure are higher than the EEDS. The first group is expected to include the poor who live at the poverty line (PL) and below, and the non-poor who live at low-income level (above the PL). The second group is expected to include the lower middle-income and middle-income households. The third group is expected to include the upper middle-income and high-income households.

Table 1 presents the decile distribution of households expenditure in urban and rural sectors in Egypt, as computed from the HESS 1990/91 and 1995/96. The EEDS is at 10% of total households expenditure as explained above. An arbitrary equal expenditure-distribution range (EEDR) is assigned around the EEDS to identify the middle-expenditure households group. The EEDR is defined at 20% around the EEDS; i.e., the EEDR will be higher than 8%, and lower than 12% of total expenditure. Thus, 8% <EEDR <12% of total expenditure. The three household groups are: (a) the lower-expenditure (and lower-income) households with decile expenditure share equal to, or less than 8% of total expenditure; (b) the middle-expenditure (and middle-income) households with decile expenditure share higher than 8% and lower than 12% of total expenditure; and (c) the upper-expenditure (and upper-income) households with decile expenditure share equal to, or greater than 12% of total expenditure. The decile expenditure-distribution of urban and rural households in 1990/91 and 1995/96 are presented in Figures 3, 4, 5 and 6.

Table 1   Distribution of households total expenditure in urban and rural sectors in Egypt

Households Distribution in Deciles	Relative Expenditure Shares			
	1990/91		1995/96	
	Urban	Rural	Urban	Rural
I	3.3	3.4	2.9	3.2
II	5.0	5.2	4.6	5.2
III	6.2	6.0	5.7	6.3
IV	6.9	7.6	6.7	7.7
V	7.7	8.1	7.9	8.6
VI	9.0	9.3	8.8	9.5
VII	10.3	10.6	10.3	10.8
VIII	11.8	12.3	11.7	12.1
IX	14.7	14.4	14.9	14.4
X	25.2	23.2	26.4	22.1
III*	0.244	0.227	0.259	0.216
Gini coefficient	0.304	0.283	0.326	0.275

* Calculated by applying Equation 1 in the text.

Source : Calculated from Appendix Tables A1 and A2

According to the decile expenditure-distribution of households in 1990/91 and 1995/96 as presented in Table 1 and Figures 3 - 6, the lowest five household deciles in the urban sector and the lowest four deciles in the rural sector represent the lower-expenditure (and lower-income) households. The next three household deciles in the urban and rural sectors represent the middle-expenditure (and middle-income) households. The last two household deciles in the urban sector and the three last household deciles in the rural sector represent the upper-expenditure (and upper-income) households. In other words, in both periods 1990/91 and 1995/96, the lower-income households represent 50% of the urban households and 40% of the rural households. The middle-income group represents 30% of the households in both sectors. The upper-income households represent 20% of the urban households and 30% of the rural households.

The next step is to identify the expenditure intervals in the HESS 1990/91 and 1995/96 for the lower-expenditure, middle-expenditure and upper-expenditure households, guided by the relative size of each of the three household groups as identified above. In other words, one would need to locate the expenditure brackets in the HESS within which the lower-income households who represent 50% of the households in the urban sector and 40% of the households in the rural sector fall. According to the HESS data in 1990/9, the lower-expenditure households whose average expenditure falls below the EEDS are those who fall in the expenditure intervals below £E4800 in the urban sector and £E4000 in the rural sector, representing 46% in the former sector and 44% in the latter (Tables 2 and 3). In the HESS of 1995/96, the lower-expenditure households whose average expenditure falls below the EEDS are those who fall in the expenditure intervals below £E6800 in the urban sector and £E5600 in the rural sector, representing 46% of the households in both sectors (Tables 4 and 5). These are the closest figures to the estimated lower-income group size of 50% in the urban sector and 40% in the rural sector in both periods 1990/91 and 1995/96. The middle-expenditure (and middle-income) households whose expenditures are around the EEDS, are those who fall in the expenditure intervals £E4800 and 5600 in the urban sector, and £E4000 and 4800 in the rural sector in 1990/91, and in the expenditure intervals £E6800 and £E8000 in the urban sector and £E5600 and £E6800 in the rural sector in 1995/96. These represent 26% and 27% in the urban and rural sectors in 1990/91, and 29% and 32% of households in the two sectors respectively in 1995/96. These are the closest figures to the estimated size of the middle-income households group in both sectors in the two mentioned years. The estimated size is 30% of the households. Consequently, the upper-income households belong to the expenditure intervals of £E6800 and above in the urban sector and £E5600 and above in the rural sector in 1990/91, and in the expenditure intervals of £E10000 and above in the urban sector and £E8000 and above in the rural sector in 1995/96. These represent 27% and 29% of urban and rural households in 1990/91, and 25% and 23% of urban and rural households in 1995/96 (Tables 2, 3, 4 and 5).

It should be emphasized that the objective is to find out the expenditure intervals in which most of the households of the lower-expenditure group falls, and to examine their expenditure pattern with respect to food subsidy, education and health. The same applies to the households in the middle-expenditure and upper-expenditure groups. Thus, the identified size of each group derived from the household expenditure deciles is only used as a means to reach this objective.

Figure 3 The decile expenditure-distribution of the urban households in Egypt: 1990/91

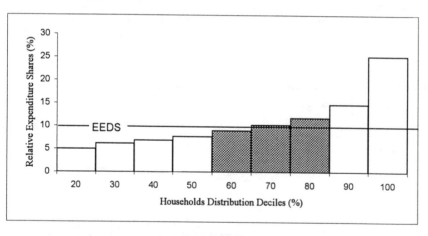

- Lower-expenditure household deciles : left of the shaded area
- Middle-expenditure household deciles : the shaded area
- Upper-expenditure household deciles : right of the shaded area
Source : Table 1

Figure 4   The decile expenditure-distribution of the rural households in Egypt; 1990/91

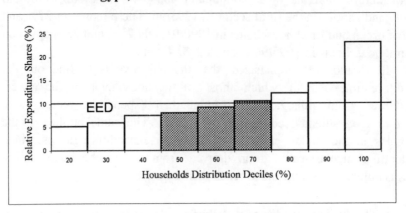

- Lower-expenditure household deciles : left of the shaded area
- Middle-expenditure household deciles : the shaded area
- Upper-expenditure household deciles : right of the shaded area
Source : Table 1

Figure 5   The decile expenditure-distribution of the urban households in Egypt; 1995/96

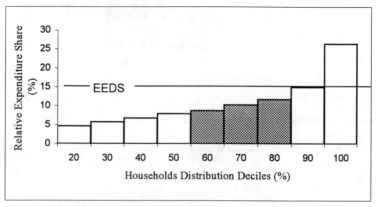

- Lower-expenditure household deciles : left of the shaded area
- Middle-expenditure household deciles : the shaded area
- Upper-expenditure household deciles : right of the shaded area
Source : Table 1

Figure 6   The decile expenditure-distribution of the urban households in Egypt; 1995/96

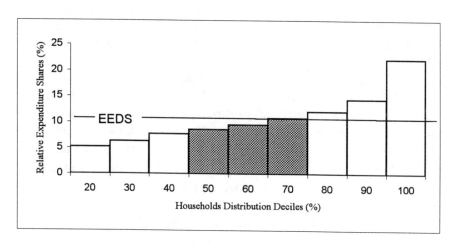

- Lower-expenditure household deciles : left of the shaded area
- Middle-expenditure household deciles : the shaded area
- Upper-expenditure household deciles : right of the shaded area
Source : Table 1

Evolution of the Low-, Middle-, and Upper-Expenditure Household Groups

The size of the lower-expenditure households group in both years 1990/91 and 1995/96 was larger in the urban sector as compared to rural sector. It was 50% in the urban sector and 40% in the rural sector. The size of the middle-expenditure households group in the two years was the same in the two sectors. It included 30% of the households in each sector. Finally, the size of the upper-expenditure households group in both years was smaller in the urban sector with 20% as compared to the rural sector with 30%. To summarize, the urban sector has a larger lower-expenditure households group and a smaller upper-expenditure households group as compared to the rural sector in Egypt. The middle-expenditure households group is at the same size in both sectors.

The relative shares of the three groups in total expenditure in 1990/91 and 1995/96 are derived from Table 1. The relative share of the lower-expenditure (and lower-income) households in total expenditure was 29.1% in the urban sector and 22.2% in the rural sector in 1990/91, and 27.8% in the former sector and 22.4% in the latter in 1995/96. The relative share of the middle-expenditure (and middle-income) households in total expenditure was 31.1% in the urban sector and 28.0% in the rural sector in 1990/91, and 30.8% and 28.9% in both sectors respectively in 1995/96. For the upper-expenditure (and upper-income) households, the relative share in total expenditure was 39.9% in the urban sector and 49.9% in the rural sector in 1990/91, and 41.3% and 48.6% in both sectors respectively in 1995/96.

Comparing the overall income-distribution picture in the urban and rural sectors in Egypt as shown in Table 1, it may be observed that in both years, income was more equally distributed in the rural sector as compared to the urban sector, as reflected in the values of the III and the gini coefficient. They had lower values in the rural sector as compared to the urban sector.[2] In 1990/91, the III was 0.244 in the urban sector as compared to 0.227 in the rural sector, and the gini coefficient was 0.304 and 0.283 in the two sectors respectively. In 1995/96, the III was 0.259 in the urban sector and 0.216 in the rural sector, and the gini coefficient was 0.326 and 0.275 in the two sectors respectively.

Looking at the evolution of the size and the relative expenditure share of the lower-income households group over the periods 1990/91 and 1995/96, one finds that in the urban sector , its size was the same in 1995/96 as it was in 1990/91, including 50 % of the households in the sector, while its relative share in total expenditure fell from 29.1% in 1990/91 to 27.8% in 1995/96. In the rural sector, the size of the lower-income households group was also constant over the period. It included 40% of the rural households, while its relative expenditure share increased slightly from 22.2% of total rural expenditure in 1990/91 to 22.4%.

In the urban and rural sectors, the size of the middle-income households group did not change over the periods 1990/91 and 1995/96, while its relative share in total expenditure fell from 31.1% to 30.8% in the urban sector, and increased from 28.0% to 28.9% in the rural sector. The size of the upper-income households group was also constant over the period at 20% of households in the urban sector and 30% in the rural sector. However, the group's share in total expenditure changed over the period in the two sectors. It increased from 39.9% in 1990/91 to 41.3% in 1995/96 in the urban sector, while it decreased from 49.9% to 48.6% in the rural sector.

To recapitulate, over the periods 1990/91 and 1995/96, there was a redistribution of total expenditure from the lower- and middle-income household groups to the upper-income households group in the urban sector in Egypt. The larger squeeze fell on the lower-income group as reflected by the relative drop in its expenditure share as compared to the middle-income group. In the rural sector, the redistribution was in the opposite direction.

There was a redistribution of total expenditure from the upper-income households group to the middle- and lower-income household groups during 1990/91 and 1995/96. The largest gain went to the middle-income households group as revealed by the relative increase in its expenditure share as compared to the lower-income group. Thus, from the changes that took place in the expenditure distribution in urban and rural sectors in Egypt, it may be concluded that income distribution worsened in the urban sector, and improved in the rural sector over the periods 1990/91 and 1995/96. This conclusion is supported also by the change in the values of the III and the gini coefficient over the period under consideration. In the urban sector, the III increased from 0.244 in 1990/91 to 0.259 in 1995/96, and the gini coefficient rose from 0.304 to 0.326. On the other hand, the III fell from 0.227 to 0.216 and the gini coefficient decreased from 0.283 to 0.275 in the rural sector over the period.

Low-Expenditure Households' Patterns on Food Subsidy, Education, and Health

Food subsidy in Egypt in 1995/96 was allocated totally to four commodities: *baladi* bread (a local type of bread), wheat flour (82% extraction), edible oil (cotton seeds oil), and sugar. In 1990/91, these four commodities represented 93% of the total food subsidy (Korayem, 1998, Table 1). In the HESS of 1990/91 and 1995/96, the data available are for households expenditure on the four food items (bread, wheat flour, edible oil, and sugar) with subsidized and non-subsidized components of those items combined. For example, bread sold in Egypt includes besides the subsidized *baladi* bread, other types of bread (*fino* and *shami*) which are sold at market prices. The same applies to the other three items.[3] Thus, to analyze the expenditure of the low-income households on food subsidy, the expenditures on the four food items with their subsidized and non-subsidized components were examined. Because of the difference in household size in the different expenditure brackets in 1995/96 as compared to 1990/91, the household's member as the unit of measurement was used, although the household was considered the decision unit.

Looking at the expenditure of the urban lower-expenditure household's member on food items with subsidized components, education and health in 1990/91 and 1995/96, one finds that the relative expenditure share spent on the first item was 10.6% in 1990/91 as compared to 9.0% in 1995/96. The relative share of expenditure allocated to health was 4.1% and

4.9%, and to education was 2.0% and 2.5% in the two years respectively. In the rural sector, the relative expenditure share of the low-expenditure households' member on food with subsidized components was 10.0% in 1990/91 and 9.3% in 1995/96, while the relative expenditure shares in the two mentioned years were 3.2% and 3.4% for health and 1.1% and 2.2% for education (Tables 2, 3, 4 and 5). Thus, in both urban and rural sectors and in both 1990/91 and 1995/96, the lower-expenditure households spent the highest budget share on t food items with subsidized components. Next in order came the expenditure share on health, and lastly, education. These expenditure shares on the three items reflect the relative importance of food subsidy, education and health in the budget of the lower-income households in Egypt.

This expenditure pattern of the lower-income households does not apply to the upper-income households, which indicates that expenditure priorities differed in the two groups. As shown in Tables 2, 3, 4, and 5, the relative importance of the food items with subsidized components, education and health differed in the household budget of the upper-expenditure households as compared to the lower-expenditure ones. These were reflected in the levels and the ranking order of the budget shares spent on the three items. In the upper-expenditure households group, the relative share of expenditure on the food items with subsidized components was quite close to the relative share spent on the three items. This differed in the upper-expenditure households as compared to the lower-expenditure group. The highest expenditure share of the urban households' member in the former group was on education with 7.0%. Next came the expenditure shares on food with subsidized components and health. Both budget shares were also close as in 1990/91, 4.5% and 4.4% respectively. This big jump in the expenditure share spent on education is probably due to the considerable increase in the cost of education in 1995/96 as compared to 1990/91, especially in the private sector. In the rural sector, the ranking order of the expenditure shares on the food items with subsidized components, on health and on education was the same for both the upper-expenditure and the lower-expenditure household groups in 1990/91. The difference was in the level of the expenditure shares allocated to the three items (Table 3). In 1995/96, the ranking order between education and health changed in the upper-expenditure households as compared to the lower-expenditure ones. The budget share spent on education was higher than that spent on health (Table 5).

Table 2 **Relative share of expenditure on food items with subsidized components, health and education in aggregate expenditure per urban household member, 1990/ 91 (%)**

Annual Household Expenditure Intervals (£E)	Relative Share of Individuals in the Population Sample	Food Items with Subsidized Components	Health	Education
Group 1: Lower-Expenditure Households:				
- 1000	0.3	12.3	4.4	1.0
1000-	0.2	11.4	6.1	0.3
1200-	0.7	11.6	5.6	0.3
1600-	4.4	11.9	4.8	1.2
2400-	10.2	13.1	3.9	1.7
3200-	14.4	10.1	4.1	2.2
4000-	15.9	9.1	3.9	2.4
Average* of Group 1	46.1	10.6	4.1	2.0
Group 2: Middle-Expenditure Households:				
4800-	12.8	8.1	4.1	2.7
5600-	13.6	7.0	4.4	2.8
Average* of Group 2	26.4	7.5	4.3	2.8
Group 3: Upper-Expenditure Households:				
6800-	9.3	6.2	4.6	3.2
8000-	8.6	5.2	4.4	3.2
10000-	4.0	4.5	4.5	9.6
12000-	2.0	3.7	4.0	3.4
14000-	3.5	2.3	4.7	3.5
Average* of Group 3	27.4	5.0	4.5	3.3

*Weighted average - weights used are the relative shares of individuals in the population sample.
Source: Calculated from Appendix Table A3

Table 3   **Relative share of expenditure on food items with subsidized components, health and education in aggregate expenditure per rural household member, 1990/ 91 (%)**

Annual Household Expenditure Intervals (£E)	Relative Share of Individuals in the Population Sample	Food Items with Subsidized Components	Health	Education
Group 1: Lower-Expenditure Households:				
-1000	1.1	14.8	3.3	0.1
1000-	0.7	14.6	4.2	0.1
1200-	2.2	13.5	3.3	0.4
1600-	8.6	9.0	3.5	0.8
2400-	14.3	10.3	3.0	1.1
3200-	16.7	9.2	3.1	1.4
Average* of Group 1	43.6	10.0	3.2	1.1
Group 2: Middle-Expenditure Households				
4000-	15.3	8.4	3.1	1.7
4800-	11.6	7.5	3.2	1.8
Average* of Group 2	26.9	8.0	3.1	1.7
Group 3: Upper-Expenditure Households				
5600	11.7	6.6	3.4	1.9
6800	7.6	6.5	3.7	1.9
8000-	5.0	6.1	3.7	1.9
10000-	2.3	6.0	3.6	1.8
12000-	1.0	3.8	2.9	1.7
14000-	1.8	3.3	3.3	1.4
Average*of Group 3	29.4	6.1	3.5	1.9

*Weighted average - weights used are the relative shares of individuals in the population sample.
Source: Calculated from Appendix Table A4

Table 4   Relative share of expenditure on food items with subsidized components; health and education in aggregate expenditure per urban household member, 1995/ 96 (%)

Annual Household Expenditure Intervals (£E)	Relative Share of Individuals in the Population Sample	Food Items with Subsidized Components	Health	Education
Group 1: Lower-Expenditure Households:				
-1000	0.04	17.1	3.4	-
1000-	0.1	12.6	4.7	-
1200-	0.2	11.3	6.1	0.2
1600-	1.6	9.4	6.7	0.5
2400-	3.6	9.5	5.3	1.1
3200-	5.9	8.9	4.4	1.7
4000-	9.0	8.6	4.9	2.1
4800-	10.2	11.5	5.7	3.5
5600	15.5	7.4	4.2	3.1
Average* of Group 1	46.1	9.0	4.9	2.5
Group 2: Middle-Expenditure Households				
6800-	12.9	7.1	4.1	4.3
8000-	16.0	6.4	3.9	5.0
Average* of Group 2	28.9	6.7	4.0	4.7
Group 3: Upper-Expenditure Households:				
10000-	8.7	5.5	3.9	5.4
12000-	5.1	4.9	4.0	5.4
14000-	11.1	3.5	4.9	9.1
Average*of Group 3	24.9	4.5	4.4	7.0

*Weighted average - weights used are the relative shares of individuals in the population sample.
Source: Calculated from Appendix Table A5

Table 5 Relative share of expenditure on the food items with subsidized components; health and education in aggregate expenditure per rural household member, 1995/ 96 (%)

Annual Household Expenditure Intervals (£E)	Relative Share of Individuals in the Population Sample	Food Items with Subsidized Components	Health	Education
Group 1: Lower-Expenditure Households				
- 1000	0.2	14.2	4.0	-
1000-	0.1	13.5	4.8	0.3
1200-	0.5	11.9	5.0	0.1
1600-	2.3	11.4	4.4	0.5
2400-	5.8	10.9	3.6	1.2
3200-	9.6	9.6	3.3	1.8
4000-	13.1	8.9	3.3	2.4
4800-	14.1	8.4	3.1	3.0
Average* of Group 1	45.7	9.3	3.4	2.2
Group 2: Middle-Expenditure Households				
5600-	18.7	7.8	3.2	3.3
6800-	13.0	7.3	3.1	3.9
Average* of Group 2	31.7	7.6	3.2	3.5
Group 3: Upper-Expenditure Households				
8000-	11.5	6.7	3.4	4.3
10000-	4.9	6.2	3.5	4.7
12000-	2.4	5.5	3.5	4.0
14000-	3.7	4.4	5.4	3.1
Average*of Group 3	22.5	6.1	3.8	4.2

*Weighted average - weights used are the relative shares of individuals in the population sample.
Source: Calculated from Appendix Table A6

To recapitulate, taking the relative expenditure shares on the three items as indicators of their relative importance for the lower-income households, it was found that the highest priority was given to the food items with subsidized components, next came health, and lastly education. This implicit order of priorities applies to urban and rural households in both 1990/91 and 1995/96. For the upper-expenditure households in the urban and rural sectors in 1990/91, the ranking of the budget shares spent on the three items was the same as that of the lower-expenditure households, with a comparable lower level allocated to food items with subsidized components and comparable higher expenditure levels on education and health. In 1995/96, the ranking of the relative expenditure shares of the upper-expenditure households on the three items diverged from the comparable ranking of the lower-expenditure ones. The budget share spent on education in the former group exceeded that spent on health; and in the urban sector, it exceeded even the budget share allocated to the food items with subsidized components.

Allocation of Government Expenditure to Food Subsidy, Education and Health

In 1990/91, the relative share of government expenditure spent on food subsidy was 5.3% of the total expenditure as compared to 1.1% allocated to education and 0.7% to health (Table 6). Over the periods 1990/91 and 1994/95, the relative share of government expenditure allocated to food subsidy declined steadily, reaching 4.3% of total expenditure in 1994/95. It started to rise again in 1995/96, and reached 5.5% of total expenditure in 1996/97. The budget shares spent on both education and health showed a rising trend over the period 1990/91 and 1996/97. The relative expenditure shares spent on education and health were raised to 3.6% and 2.2% respectively in 1996/97 (Table 6).

Looking at the absolute value of government expenditure on food subsidy, education and health in real terms, one finds that total government expenditure fell from £E25424.6 million in 1990/91 to £E17858.4 million in 1996/97; i.e., it fell by 29.8% over the period. But, inspite of the fall in real total expenditures, real government expenditure on education and health increased as shown in Table 7. Expenditure on education increased from £E286.6 million in 1990/91 to £E641.4 million in 1996/97, i.e., by 123.8%. Expenditure on health increased from £E184.4 million to £E400.9 million over the period, i.e., by 117.4%. On the other hand, real government expenditure on food subsidy fell from £E1340.8 million in 1990/91 to £E933.4 million in 1995/96, i.e., by 30.4% over the period, then increased to £E980.2 million in 1996/97 (Table 7).

Government expenditure on education and health are policy measures that affect income distribution, while expenditure on subsidy affects income redistribution. Expenditure on education and health increase the capabilities of the individuals thus raising their marginal productivity and increasing total output. Since labor earning is a function of labor productivity, these types of government policies have positive impacts on both the individuals and the economy as a whole. The situation differs with respect to government expenditure on food subsidy. Food subsidy has positive impact on the standard of living of the low-income people in general and the poor in particular, since they are those who spend a relatively large portion of their budget on food. Supplying basic food commodities at low affordable prices has positive impact on the health of the poor and the low-income people, which raises their productivity and consequently will have a positive impact on national output.

On the other hand, it may be argued that measures of redistribution may reduce output, since work effort may fall off, as work incentives are reduced by high marginal rates of tax. Redistribution may also retard economic growth, since high tax rates may reduce the level of savings of the upper-income people and/or curtail incentives to innovation and enterprise (Musgrave and Musgrave, 1973).

One may conclude that the high relative share of government expenditure on food subsidy as compared to education and health implies that the Egyptian government gives higher priority to food subsidy as compared to education and health. But, if one examines the evolution of these expenditure shares over the periods 1990/91 and 1996/97, one finds that the reverse is true, i.e., the government gives higher priorities to education and health as compared to food subsidy. However, in real terms, the absolute value of government expenditure on food subsidy is still larger than government expenditure on each of education and health. The gap between food subsidy and the two social services is declining over time. This becomes obvious if the sum of government expenditure on education and health together is compared with expenditure on food subsidy. One finds that in real terms, government expenditure in 1990/91 on education and health was £E471 million as compared to £E1340 million on food subsidy. In 1996/97, real government expenditure on education and health was £E1042.3 million as compared to £E980.2 million spent on food subsidy, i.e., over the 6-year period, government expenditure on education and health together exceeded that on food subsidy, while the reverse was true in 1990/91 (Table 7).

Table 6 **Government expenditure* on food subsidy, education and health, 1990/91-1996/97 (at current prices, £E million)**

Fiscal Year	Food Subsidy Value	% of the total	Education Value	% of the total	Health Value	% of the total	Total Government Expenditures
	(1)		(2)		(3)		(4)
1990/91	2400	5.3	513	1.1	330	0.7	45510
1991/92	2482	5.2	796	1.7	487	1.0	47563
1992/93	2450	4.7	1336	2.6	752	1.4	52223
1993/94	2486	4.4	1609	2.9	806	1.4	56264
1994/95	2492	4.3	1800	3.1	1000	1.7	58256
1995/96	3098	4.8	2000	3.1	1200	1.9	63889
1996/97	3668	5.5	2400	3.6	1500	2.2	66826

*Excluding wages
Source : Column 1: Ali and Adams Jr., 1996 and the last two years : Ali, Abdel Rahman and Ibrahim, 1998 . Columns 2 and 3 from 1990/91-1993/94: Official Gazette and from 1994/95: Preliminary figures taken from People's Assembly, minutes of debate of government budget proposals. Column 4: Central Bank of Egypt, Annual Report, 1992/93 (Table 6/1) and 1996/97 (Table 9/1)

Table 7 **Real government expenditure on food subsidy, education and health, 1990/91-1996/97 (£E million)**

Fiscal year	Urban Consumer Price Index (1986/87=100)	Food Subsidy	Education	Health	Total Government Expenditures
	(1)	(2)	(3)	(4)	(5)
1990/91	179.0	1340.8	286.6	184.4	25424.6
1991/92	214.3	1158.2	371.4	227.3	22194.6
1992/93	243.5	1006.2	548.7	308.8	21446.8
1993/94	280.3	886.9	574.0	287.5	20072.8
1994/95	313.8	794.1	573.6	318.7	18564.7
1995/96	331.9	933.4	602.6	361.6	19249.5
1996/97	374.2	980.2	641.4	400.9	17858.4

Source : Column 1: National Bank of Egypt, 1998, Economic Bulletin , Vol.51 (1), Table 2/8. Columns 2, 3, 4, and 5 are calculated from Table 6 using the Consumer Price Index as a deflator

How Appropriate are the Social Policy Priorities Set by the Government in Meeting the Needs of Low-Income People?

There is no single unanimous theory that explains the determinants of government expenditure. Different theories have been formulated to explain the objective of government expenditure and derive their determinants accordingly (e.g., see Premchand, 1983; and Sandford, 1984). One may differentiate between three approaches in this respect (Premchand, 1983). The first approach defines the objective of government expenditure to maximize social welfare. Theories of marginal utility and public goods are used to explain government expenditure composition according to this approach. The second approach compares government behavior with the firm behavior with respect to the allocation of resources. Public choice, represented by voting and other factors such as economic growth, externalities, etc. is used to explain the composition of government expenditure in this approach. The third approach is related to the empirical school that attempts to explain government expenditure by analyzing government behavior in different countries (rich and poor), and under different circumstances (wars and social disturbances).

The objective of this study is to assess the appropriateness of the social policy priorities set by the Egyptian government to the needs of low-income people, specifically with respect to expenditure on food subsidy, education and health. The "social welfare" approach seems to be the appropriate one to adopt in this respect. The assessment was made by comparing the relative budget shares of the low-income households spent on food subsidy, education and health in 1990/91 and 1995/96 with the corresponding present composition of government expenditure on these items and the evolution of this expenditure composition that took place over the periods 1990/91 and 1996/97. This would give the relative weights assigned to food subsidy, education and health in the budget of the low-income households as compared to government budget, and the divergence or convergence, that may take place in the near future between the sets of priorities of the government and the low-income households.

Looking at the budget shares spent on the food items with subsidized components, education and health by the low-expenditure household's member, it was found that the highest share was spent on the first item. Next came health, and then education. This expenditure pattern applies to both urban and rural household members in the two years 1990/91 and 1995/96 (Tables 2, 3, 4, and 5). In the government budget, the set of priorities as revealed by the expenditure shares allocated, had a different ranking order with respect to education and health. The highest share was allocated to food subsidy, next came education, and lastly came health. This budget shares' ranking applies over the years 1990/91 and 1995/96 (Table 6).

Comparing the ranking of priorities for food subsidy, education, and health of the low-expenditure households' member and the government as reflected in their budget shares allocated to the three items, two points are worth making. Firstly, the largest share of expenditure in both budgets is allocated to food subsidy.[4] However, the order of priorities of the government and the low-income households differed with respect to expenditure on education and health. The lower-income households' member spends a larger share of his budget on health as compared to education, while the government allocates a relatively larger share of its budget to education as compared to health. However, this government pattern of expenditure coincides with the pattern of the urban and rural households' members in the upper-expenditure households group in 1995/96, i.e. they spent a higher budget share on education as compared to health (Tables 4 and 5). Secondly, looking at the change in the pattern of government expenditure over the periods 1990/91 and 1996/97, one finds that the expenditure share allocated to food subsidy was on the decline, while the budget shares spent on education and health were on the rise. This indicates that the composition of government expenditure on social services may change in the near future in favor of education and health, and against food subsidy, if this trend continues. On the other hand, this may not happen, if the budget share spent on food subsidy continues its rising trend which started in 1995/96 (Table 6). It should be mentioned, however, that some changes in the composition of government expenditure have already taken place since 1994/95. Since then, the combined budget share of education and health exceeded the relative share spent on food subsidy (Table 6).

Given the existing divergence in the expenditure patterns of the government and low-expenditure households as shown in this study, does this mean that the order of priorities of government expenditure on social services does not meet the needs of the low-income people in Egypt? As mentioned the "social welfare" approach is adopted in assessing the appropriateness of government expenditure on social services with respect to the needs of low-income people. According to this approach, the objective of the government is to maximize social welfare. Since there is more than one definition of "social welfare", the answer to the question raised depends on the definition applied in this respect. One may point out two schools of thought, the origin of which goes back to the continental writers, and particularly to the Italian writers in the nineteenth century (Premchand, 1983). One school believes in the individualistic state, the welfare function of which is the additive sum of the individuals' welfare.. The other believes in the paternalistic state, the welfare function of which transcends the sum total of the individuals' welfare and may provide services that are different from individual wants.[5] If the first school of thought is adopted, the answer to the question raised is positive; i.e., indeed government expenditure on social services does not meet the needs of the low-income people in Egypt. But, if the second school of thought is adopted, the answer to the question is negative, if it is believed that the social benefit of education exceeds those of health.[6]

One may conclude that the divergence between government expenditure on food subsidy, education and health, and the relative budget shares spent on those items by the lower-income households does not necessarily mean that the Egyptian government fails to maximize the welfare of the society, including the lower-income people as a subgroup. Indeed, it all depends on how the society conceives its welfare function. Generally speaking, the welfare function of the society has to be specified first, preferably by voting, before it is feasible to assess the success or failure of government policy in maximizing social welfare.

Appendix

Table A1 Average and total household expenditure in urban and rural sectors, 1990/91 (£E)

Annual Household Expenditure Intervals	Urban Sector			Rural Sector		
	Number of Households	Total Household Expenditure	Average Household Expenditure (=2/1)	Number of Households	Total Household Expenditures	Average Household Expenditures (= 5/4)
	(1)	(2)	(3)	(4)	(5)	(6)
1000-	76	55541	780.8	85	61405	722.4
1000-	40	43929	1098.2	57	63103	1107.0
1200-	131	186625	1424.6	148	209486	1415.4
1600-	518	1061547	2049.3	556	1144089	2057.7
2400-	989	2794504	2825.6	910	2567935	2821.9
3200-	1243	4473448	3598.9	1001	3608472	3604.9
4000-	1275	5596268	4389.2	898	3940696	4388.3
4800-	1003	5201586	5186.0	661	3421488	5176.2
5600-	1016	6249656	6151.2	636	3915105	6155.8
6800-	679	4995734	7357.3	409	2992800	7317.4
8000-	647	5755983	8876.4	264	2337595	8854.3
10000-	297	3246528	10931.1	115	1261506	10969.6
12000-	59	2050974	12899.2	55	705527	12827.8
14000-	281	5777684	20561.2	86	1653531	19227.1
Total	8354	47490007	5684.7	5881	27882738	4741.2

Source: Central Agency for Public Mobilization and Statistics (CAPMAS), *Households Income and Expenditure Sample Survey, 1990/91 Cairo*, Vol. 2 (Part 1), Table 2-1 and Vol.3 (Part 1), Table 2-1

Table A2 **Average and total household expenditure in urban and rural sectors, 1995/96 (£E)**

Annual Household	Urban Sector			Rural Sector		
Expenditure Intervals	Number of Households	Total Households Expenditures	Average Household Expenditure (=2/1)	Number of Households	Total Households Expenditures	Average Household Expenditure (= 5/4)
	(1)	(2)	(3)	(4)	(5)	(6)
1000-	11	8631	784.6	77	58217	756.1
1000-	26	28545	1097.9	44	48318	1098.1
1200-	48	68608	1429.3	166	233851	1408.7
1600-	267	544970	2041.1	445	899188	2020.6
2400-	394	1115002	2830.0	738	2093731	2837.0
3200-	516	1857681	3600.2	987	3564249	3611.2
4000-	662	2922652	4414.9	1123	4957307	4414.3
4800-	678	3528933	5204.9	1123	5833178	5194.3
5600-	968	5985619	6183.5	1333	8220353	6166.8
6800-	755	3363364	7368.7	838	6157649	7348.0
8000-	889	7909311	8896.9	710	6278293	8842.7
10000-	498	5453714	10951.2	288	3110488	10800.3
12000-	280	3599982	12857.0	129	1653384	12816.9
14000-	630	13253534	21037.4	182	3631888	19955.4
Total	6622	51840546	7828.5	8183	46740094	5711.9

Source : Central Agency for Public Mobilization and Statistics (CAPMAS), *Households Expenditure Sample Survey, 1995/96 Cairo*, Vol.2, (Part 1), Table 2-1 and Vol.3, (Part 1), Table 2-1

Table A3 Annual average expenditure on food items with subsidized components, health and education per urban household member, 1990/91 (£E)

Annual Household Expenditure Intervals	1000-	1000-	1200-	1600-	2400-	3200-	4000-	4800-	5600-	6800-	8000-	10000-	12000-	14000-
Relative Share of Individuals in the Population Sample (%)	0.3	0.2	0.7	4.4	10.2	14.4	15.9	12.8	13.6	9.3	8.6	4.0	2.0	3.5
Food Item with Subsidized Components*	55.3	70.3	71.6	65.6	82.2	72.1	73.5	75.9	74.0	77.0	79.4	82.9	84.8	87.4
Health	19.5	37.7	34.2	26.5	24.5	29.1	31.3	37.9	46.1	57.0	67.4	83.2	91.5	175.3
Education	0.4	1.8	2.0	6.8	10.9	15.4	19.6	24.7	29.8	39.9	48.2	66.3	78.6	131.1
Annual Aggregate Expenditure	440.8	618.7	615.9	553.5	626.0	713.0	806.3	931.3	1052.0	1236.3	1526.4	1857.3	2314.9	3739.6

*Consist of all types of bread (*baladi, fino* and *shami*), wheat flour (regular and super), edible oil (cotton seeds oil), and sugar.

Source: Taken and calculated from CAPMAS, *Household Income and Expenditure Sample Survey, 1990/91, Cairo*, 1993, Vol. 2 (Part 1), Tables 2-1 and 18-1.

Table A4   Annual average expenditure on food items with subsidized components, health and education per rural household member, 1990/91 (£E)

Annual Household Expenditure Intervals	1000-	1000-	1200-	1600-	2400-	3200-	4000-	4800-	5600-	6800-	8000-	10000-	12000-	14000-
Relative Share of Individuals in the Population Sample (%)	1.1	0.7	2.2	8.6	14.3	16.7	15.3	11.6	11.7	7.6	5.0	2.3	1.0	1.8
Food Item with Subsidized Components*	20.6	35.9	34.0	30.8	47.7	51.6	56.4	57.2	57.3	67.1	74.5	84.7	72.1	76.5
Health	4.6	10.3	8.2	12.1	14.1	17.7	20.7	24.7	29.7	37.7	45.5	51.7	54.8	75.8
Education	0.2	0.2	1.1	2.8	5.1	8.1	11.6	13.5	16.5	19.1	23.6	26.0	32.0	32.9
Annual Aggregate Expenditure	139.6	246.5	251.8	341.7	465.3	562.7	667.5	764.4	867.5	1027.4	1225.2	1422.2	1876.4	2328.9

*Consist of all types of bread (*baladi*, *fino* and *shami*), wheat flour (regular and super), edible oil (cotton seeds oil), and sugar.

Source: Taken and calculated from CAPMAS, *Household Income and Expenditure Sample Survey, 1990/91, Cairo,* 1993, Vol. 2 (Part 1) , Tables 2-1 and 18-1.

Table A5   Annual average expenditure on food items subsidized components, health and education per urban household member, 1990/91 (£E)

Annual Household Expenditure Intervals	1000-	1000-	1200-	1600-	2400-	3200-	4000-	4800-	5600-	6800-	8000-	10000-	12000-	14000-
Relative Share of Individuals in the Population Sample (%)	0.04	0.1	0.2	1.6	3.6	5.9	9.0	10.2	15.5	12.9	16.0	8.7	5.1	11.1
Food Item with Subsidized Components*	123.2	133.4	129.4	111.2	100.6	96.9	96.7	98.7	98.9	105.3	109.0	116.3	120.2	143.3
Health	25.1	52.0	69.5	78.8	56.0	48.1	54.4	49.2	56.4	60.5	66.1	83.1	98.9	201.8
Education	-		2.3	5.4	11.6	18.0	23.5	30.5	41.1	63.4	84.9	114.3	131.9	376.4
Annual Aggregate Expenditure	719.3	1057.2	1143.5	1179.6	1059.9	1085.1	1121.5	861.1	1339.4	1488.7	1709.8	2115.1	2449.0	4125.0

*Consist of all types of bread (*balaadi, fino* and *shami*), wheat flour (regular and super), edible oil (cotton seeds oil), and sugar.

Source: Taken and calculated from CAPMAS, *Household Income and Expenditure Sample Survey 1990/91, Cairo,* 1993, Vol. 2 (Part 1) , Tables 2-1 and 8-1.

Table A6   Annual average expenditure on food items with subsidized components, health and education per rural household member, 1990/91 (£E)

Annual Household Expenditure Intervals	1000-	1000-	1200-	1600-	2400-	3200-	4000-	4800-	5600-	6800-	8000-	10000-	12000-	14000-
Relative Share of Individuals in the Population Sample (%)	0.2	0.1	0.5	2.3	5.8	9.6	13.1	14.1	18.7	13.0	11.5	4.9	2.4	3.7
Food Item with Subsidized Components*	103.2	120.7	119.7	97.5	87.4	79.5	74.6	76.9	76.0	77.1	81.6	86.4	83.1	95.3
Health	29.2	42.9	50.6	37.7	29.2	27.3	27.6	28.2	30.9	32.6	41.1	49.1	53.3	116.2
Education	-	3.0	1.2	4.2	10.0	15.0	20.3	27.3	32.5	41.2	52.5	65.2	61.2	66.9
Annual Aggregate Expenditure	727.7	894.8	1008.0	857.2	802.8	824.3	842.4	917.7	974.3	1052.9	1213.9	1400.5	1523.9	2165.7

*Consist of all types of bread (*baladi, fino* and *shami*), wheat flour (regular and super), edible oil (cotton seeds oil), and sugar.

Source: Taken and calculated from CAPMAS, *Household Income and Expenditure Sample Survey, 1990/91, Cairo,* 1993, Vol. 2 (Part 1) , Tables (2-1) & (18-1).

Notes

---

1 Applying the general solution (Equation 2) to the quintile and decile distribution of the population:
(a) For the quintile distribution: $X = 20$, $N = 5$

$$III = \frac{\left[\sum_{i=1}^{4} |(X-0)| + |(X-100)|\right]/2}{(100-X)} = [(4X+80)/2]/80 = 80/80 =$$

(b) For the decile distribution: $X = 10$, $N = 10$
$$III = [(9X + 90)/2]/90 = 90/90 = 1$$

2 Needless to say, the values of both indicators - the III and gini coefficient- must move in the same direction, since both measure the state of income distribution. The difference in their values is due to the difference in their construction. The III measures the inequality in income-distribution by the income shares above the EIDS, while the gini coefficient measures income inequality by the area between the Lorenz curve and the equal income-distribution line.

3 For more details on the food subsidy system in Egypt, see Korayem (1998).

4 This refers to "food items with subsidized components" in the households' member budget.

5 There is a third type of state according to the Italian writers in the nineteenth century, which is the monopolistic state in which the concern of the government is to maximize the welfare of its members (Premchand, 1983).

6 Some of the social benefits of education are: (a) the impact of education on raising the marginal productivity of labor and promoting economic growth; (b) a certain level of literacy should prevail if the market economy is to work properly (e.g., consumers must be able to read advertisements for new products and workers be able to read advertisements for jobs); (c) education is also important for an efficient and stable government, and is essential for effective democracy. Among the social benefits of health is the prevention of the spread of epidemic diseases across the country. The growth in population due to the reduction in mortality rate will stimulate demand for goods and services and, hence, promote economic growth (Sandford, 1984).

References

Ali, S., Abdel-Rahman, A. and Ibrahim, A. (1998), Overview and Assessment of Food Subsidy Expenditure in Egypt, A study prepared for: Egypt: *Human Development Report 1997*, Institute of National Planning, Cairo, Egypt.

Ali, S., and Adams, R.H. Jr. (1996), 'The Egyptian Food Subsidy System Operation and Effects on Income Distribution', *World Development*, Vol. 24 (1), pp. 1777-1791.

Central Agency for Public Mobilization and Statistics (1993), *Household Income and Expenditure Sample Survey 1990/91*, CAPMAS, Cairo, Egypt.

_____. (1997), *Household Expenditure Sample Survey 1995/96*, CAPMAS, Cairo, Egypt.

Central Bank of Egypt (1992/93 & 1996/97) *Annual Report*, Cairo, Egypt.

Korayem, K.   (1998), Impact of Food Subsidy Policy on Low-Income People and the Poor
         in Egypt, A study prepared for Egypt: *Human Development Report 1997,* Institute
         of National Planning, Cairo, Egypt.

Musgrave, R.A., and Musgrave, P.B. (1973),   *Public Finance in Theory and Practice,*
         McGraw Hill, Inc., USA.

National Bank of Egypt. (1998), *Economic Bulletin,* Vol. 51 (1).

Premchand, A.   1983), *Government Budgeting and Expenditure Controls; Theory and
         Practice,* International Monetary Fund, Washington, D.C.

Sandford, C. (1984), *Economics of Public Finance,* 3rd ed., Pergamon Press, Oxford.

6 Evaluating Psychological and Biological Deprivation in Low-Income Countries: Focus on the Angolan Experience

Mwangi S. Kimenyi[1]

Introduction

Despite being blessed with valuable resources including vast oil reserves and huge deposits of high- quality diamonds, Angola is one of the poorest countries in the world. A primary reason for this has been a civil war that ravaged the country between 1974 and 1994. In addition to claiming thousands of lives, the war adversely affected production and severely constrained the government's ability to invest in services such as health, education, and infrastructure. During the war years, virtually all earnings from oil and diamond exports were directed toward military activities. The quality of life in the country has been further undermined by widespread displacement of the population and the prevalence of landmines which have greatly handicapped food production. The result has been an extremely low quality of life: malnutrition, prevalence of disease, high infant and maternal mortality, and extremely unsanitary living conditions.

With the cessation of the civil war, an opportunity has opened for the government to adopt policies to alleviate poverty. Central to the design of appropriate policies is a clear understanding of the current state of poverty. Although there are visible indicators of extreme poverty in Angola, reliable data that may be used to evaluate the extent of deprivation and also the effectiveness of poverty alleviation policies were previously not available. To more accurately quantify the extent of poverty in Angola, the World Bank funded a household consumption survey in 1995. Data from this survey, though not perfect, are the best available for the country. The data set is comprehensive and may be used to evaluate poverty status in Angola.

The paper seeks to determine the extent of biological and psychological deprivation based on accepted international standards. A primary motivation of this paper is to analyze how well existing measures of poverty capture the extent of deprivation in very low-income countries like Angola.

Biological and Psychological Deprivation

Poverty may be defined in both relative and absolute terms. An absolute poverty definition is based on a specified minimum level of consumption. Individuals and families that do not have resources to consume this level of goods and services, are considered poor. Relative poverty not only considers the ability to consume a certain minimum, but also compares the welfare of those with the lowest amount of resources with others in society (Kimenyi, 1995). In poor countries where the most pressing problem has to do with a large proportion of the population unable to consume basic necessities, absolute poverty is of primary policy concern. Absolute poverty focuses on the idea of biological deprivation and is based on the biological necessities perspective that defines the poor as those that "do not consume or who do not receive income sufficient to purchase those commodities which are indispensably necessary for the support of biological life," (Randolph, 1982, p.6).

Statistics

Using the biological deprivation perspective, an absolute poverty line (PL) may then be established. The first step is to determine the income necessary to provide for adequate nutritional needs. This amount of income is the food component of the poverty line. The next step is to determine the amount of income necessary to meet other basic needs. This amount is the non-food component of the PL. The income necessary to meet both the food and non-food components is then defined as the z, monetary PL. Once the PL is determined, then several statistics may be computed showing the extent of deprivation in society. The simplest measure of poverty is what is referred to as the *headcount statistic* which is simply the total number of all individuals with resources less than z. If the total number of poor is q and n is the total population, then *incidence of poverty* is simply $[(q/n)*100]$. Identifying the size of the biologically deprived population as revealed by the headcount statistics is crucial to the design of anti-poverty policy. However, the headcount statistics have a major shortcoming in that these statistics do not reveal the intensity of poverty among the poor and rather consider all poor to be equivalent. Thus, an individual whose income falls by only $1 from the PL is considered equivalent to one with a much larger income shortfall. This clearly indicates that counting the number of poor is not sufficient to measure the degree of deprivation.

An alternative statistic that captures the intensity of poverty is based on the idea of a *poverty gap*. An individual's poverty gap is that individual's income shortfall from the PL. Simply, if a poor person's income is y_i and z is the PL, then that individual's poverty gap is $z-y_i$. Essentially, the poverty gap is the amount by which i's income must be augmented to permit the individual to achieve a level of consumption necessary to meet the biological needs. The greater the poverty gap, the greater the intensity of poverty. The sum of the poverty gaps of all the poor individuals gives the *aggregate poverty gap*. This statistic indicates the amount by which the income of the poor must be augmented to eliminate all poverty. Several other poverty gap statistics may be computed from the aggregate poverty gap. The most important of these are the *average poverty gap*, the *poverty gap ratio*, and the *poverty burden ratio*. The average poverty gap is obtained by dividing the aggregate poverty gap by the number of poor. The poverty gap ratio is the ratio of the poverty gap to the PL $[(z-y_i)/z]$. Again, the higher this ratio is, the more intense the poverty. The poverty burden ratio is arrived at by dividing the aggregate poverty gap by the total income of non-poor households in excess of their PL, also called the luxury income. The ratio shows the amount of non-poor's income which would need to be transferred to the poor to eliminate poverty. If the poverty burden ratio is greater than 1, then poverty cannot be eliminated by transferring luxury income from the non-poor.

The above poverty gap statistics are an improvement on the headcount statistics in that they capture the intensity of poverty. However, these measures are insensitive to the distribution of income among the poor. In essence, the measures assume a proportional relationship between income shortfall and biological deprivation (Randolph, 1982, p.56). Thus, a transfer made from an extremely poor individual to a less poor individual, leaves the measures unchanged for so long as the total number of poor remains unchanged. Thus, the measures equate the loss in welfare of the giver to be equivalent to the gain by the recipient. In reality, the relationship between income shortfall and biological deprivation is not proportional but rather, there is diminishing biological returns to income. Thus, the poorer an individual is, the greater the impact of biological deprivation from a further reduction in income. It is therefore crucial that measures of biological deprivation weigh income shortfalls from the PL with weights that increase with the size of the shortfall.

Another justification for weighing individual's income shortfalls from the PL, is to capture psychological or relative deprivation. Transfers from a poor person to a wealthier one increases psychological deprivation of the giver more than it decreases the psychological deprivation of the recipient.   Such a transfer increases poverty and thus the weight of income shortfall must increase with the size of the shortfall to capture the change in psychological deprivation. For so long as there is inequality in the distribution of income among the poor, a good measure of poverty should capture not only biological deprivation but also psychological deprivation. This requires that not only the measure consider the income shortfall from PL but also the measure should apply a weighting scheme that captures the idea that psychological deprivation increases with the size of income shortfall.   These type of measures are referred to as weighted poverty gap measures.

Sen (1976) was the first to propose a weighted poverty gap measure. His measure, the *Sen Index of Poverty* is the sum of all the poors' biological deprivation weighted by the psychological deprivation and is given by the following expression:

$$Poverty = \frac{2}{(q+1)n}\left[\sum_{i=1}^{q}\left(\frac{z-y_i}{z}\right)(q+1-i)\right]$$

Where: q = the number of poor individuals;
n = the number of poor individuals plus the number of the non-poor individuals;
z = the PL per adult equivalent;
y_i = the income of the ith person; and
i = rank in the income distribution where individuals are ranked from the poorest to the wealthiest.

The term *[(z-y)/z]*   is an individual's poverty gap ratio and measures the extent of biological deprivation. $(q+1-i)$ is the measure of psychological deprivation which is essentially the rank of the poor individuals where the poorest is assigned the highest number. For example, suppose there are 1000 poor people. Then the poorest is assigned *i=1000* while the least poor is assigned *i=1.* In other words, the poorer the individual, the higher the weight assigned. The term *[(2/q+1)n]* to the right of the summation sign is a normalizing factor to make the index equal to the product of incidence of poverty and poverty gap ratio when all poor receive the same income.

Several researchers have provided alternative weighted poverty gap measures. All the measures include a measure of biological deprivation weighted by psychological deprivation. The main difference between the various weighted poverty gap measures is the weighting scheme selected.

For example, Kakwani (1980) proposed a family of poverty indices whose members differ by the magnitude of psychological deprivation. *Kakwani Family of Poverty Indices* is computed as follows:

$$Poverty = \frac{q}{n\sum\limits_{q} i^k}\left[\sum\limits_{i=1}^{q}\left(\frac{z-y_i}{z}\right)(q+1-i)^k\right]$$

Where k is an exponent differentiating family members. Other variables are as defined in the computation of the Sen Index. The size of the exponent k differentiates between the class of members. A higher k implies strong perception of relativity. If $k-0$, individuals are viewed as totally unaffected by relative deprivation.

Thon (1983) proposed an alternative, the *Thon Index of Poverty*, expressed as follows:

$$Poverty = \frac{2}{n(n+1)}\left[\sum\limits_{i=1}^{q}\left(\frac{z-y_i}{z}\right)(n+1-i)\right]$$

The measure differs from that of Sen and Kakwani in a number of respects. Firstly, when the poor have same incomes, the measure is not identical to the product of incomes of the poor and the poverty gap ratio. Secondly, the psychological deprivation of the poor is not dependent on the number of the poor as is the case of the Sen's and Kakwani's measures of poverty but rather, depends on the total population (n).

Like Thon, Takayama (1979) considered psychological deprivation experienced by the poor to be dependent not just on the number of poor, but rather, on the total number of individuals that are wealthier. *Takayama Index of Poverty* is expressed as follows:

$$Poverty = 1 + \frac{1}{n} - \frac{2}{u*n^2}\left[\sum\limits_{i=1}^{n}(n+1-i)y_i^*\right]$$

Where Y_i^* is the income of the ith ranked individual in the censored income distribution. In the censored income distribution, $y_i^* = y_i$ *if* $y_i < z$, *and* $y_i^* = z$ *if* y_i. $U*$ is the mean of the censored income distribution.

Greer, Thorbecke and Foster (1984) proposed yet another class of weighted poverty gap measures. Like other measures, Greer, Thorbecke and Foster (GTF) defined poverty as a product of biological and psychological deprivation where biological deprivation is defined by the poverty gap ratio. GTF's measure of psychological deprivation depends on the rank of poverty gap ratios. They argued that psychological deprivation felt by a family is not dependent on the number of individual's between them and the PL but between its income and the income necessary to achieve a socially acceptable life style. The *GTF Family of Poverty Indices* is defined as:

$$
Poverty = \frac{1}{n}\left[\sum_{i=1}^{q}\left(\frac{z-y_i}{z}\right)\left(\frac{z-y_i}{z}\right)^{k-1}\right] = \frac{1}{n}\left[\sum_{i=1}^{q}\left(\frac{z-y_i}{z}\right)^{k}\right]
$$

In this expression, k differentiates between members of the family of indices. The larger the k, the more important is relative deprivation.

Each of these measures of poverty discussed, i.e. headcount, poverty gap, and weighted poverty gap measures, associate with some qualities but no measure is perfect. The choice of a particular measure primarily depends on the desired purpose, data availability, and one's concept of poverty. Nonetheless, a number of characteristics may be used to evaluate the various indices.

These properties include:
- Headcount sensitivity - increase in number of poor should increase the poverty measure, other things equal;
- Income shortfall sensitivity - a decrease in income received by a poor individual must increase poverty, other things equal;
- Deprivation sensitivity - if income of a poor person is increased by some unit, the poverty measure should decrease by a greater amount, the poorer the individual concerned;
- Non-poor's income insensitivity - a change in a non poor person's income should not affect poverty measure, other things equal; and
- Cardinality - the intensity aspect of poverty must be based on an interval or weighting scale.

The next step computes the various measures of poverty using Angolan data. The primary interest is on how well the various measures capture biological and psychological deprivation.

Analysis of Poverty in Angola

Data

The data used in this study are from a survey conducted in 1995 under the sponsorship of the Poverty Monitoring Group of the World Bank. Data collection was primarily undertaken by staff of the National Institute of Statistics in Luanda, Angola. The sample included slightly over 4000 households and nearly 26,000 individuals. As may be expected from surveys such as this, some data items were missing or inconsistent. For example, there were cases where income recorded was less than expenditures or missing. After discarding observations that were unusable, a total of 24,670 cases remained for analysis.

A cautionary remark to note is that the survey was conducted just one year after the cessation of the war. A large number of the population had moved into urban areas and others were in refugee camps. There were still parts of rural areas where there were frequent incidences of violence. Thus, most of the data from the survey is largely urban and not entirely representative of the population. The shortcomings notwithstanding, the data from the survey are quite rich and adequate for computing and evaluating the various measures of poverty.

Establishing the Poverty Line

As noted, it is typical to define a monetary PL in terms of food component and non-food component. The food component Y_f is the amount of income required to meet nutritional needs. The non-food component, Y_o is the income required to meet other basic needs. Estimating the PL then starts by determining the minimum necessary intake of calories per standard consumption unit, say an adult male. This is often based on some medical determination of what comprises adequate nutrition. Information is gathered on various diets available in a given area and their nutritional value recorded. The cheapest diet that can provide the necessary calories is selected and this then represents the food component of the PL for the standard consumer unit, i.e. the amount of money necessary to purchase food that provides the standard consumer unit with the required nutritional needs. Adjustments are then made to take into account differences in household composition because the caloric requirements vary across age and gender. Typically, individuals in the households are defined in terms of a standard unit such as adult male equivalents.

The non-food component Y_o is the amount of income that would permit a household unit to consume other necessary goods and services.

There are several methods of determining the non-food component of the PL but these approaches tend to be arbitrary. The most common approach is what is called the Engel's proportional (EP) method. This method utilizes statistical methods to estimate the functional relationship between total expenditures and food expenditures. The relationship is used to establish the average proportion of total expenditures on food (Engel's proportion) for households spending Y_f per adult equivalent on food. The idea is to obtain the amount spent on other goods and services by these households that are just on the food PL. The PL is then the ratio of Y_f to Engel's proportion (Y_f/EP), and $Y_o = Z - Y_f$.

Evaluating well-being of individuals in developed countries is primarily based on surveys of households' earnings. Because such earnings are mainly in monetary form, determining the households that fall below the PL, simply involves determining the threshold income necessary to achieve a certain level of consumption for a given household type (composition, age of members, rural, urban, etc). In developing countries, such data are difficult to obtain because most household earnings are not in monetary form. Obtaining the household income then, involves a complicated analysis of expenditures and production from which income is imputed. The 1995 survey of Angolan households is fairly detailed and contains information on both expenditures and earnings. The most important data in the survey that may be used to establish the PL are the annual monetized income, total expenditures, and expenditures on food. The data also record the household consumption of calories.

The food component of the PL in Angola is defined based on the assumption that the daily caloric intake requirements for an adult male is 2100. All units in the households are first defined in terms of adult male equivalents and the household daily caloric intake per adult male equivalent computed. Using expenditures data, the cost (Y_f) of purchasing food that provides the minimum required number of calories per an adult equivalent was determined. The EP method is then used to determine the PL. Based on the prices and dollar exchange rate prevailing in 1995, and assuming 2100 calories as the minimum nutritional requirements per adult equivalent, the PL per adult equivalent computed is just about $40 per month.

Profile of the Angolan Population

Tables 1a-c provide a summary of some key characteristics of Angolan households. The data provide information on the total sample and then split it into poor and non-poor households. The Tables provide information on age of head of households, house size, per capital annual income, household structure, and educational level of the head of household. The data reported in Table 1a reveal that the average age of households is relatively low (about 40 years), and the average size of households is about 6 members. The data also reveal a wide disparity between incomes of the poor and non-poor. Table 1b shows that the primary household structure is one headed by a monogamous male (69.7%). However, households headed by females are also quite prevalent (20% *de jure* female). Tables 1c reports levels of education of heads of households. The data show that the largest proportion of heads of households have no secondary education. Except for per capita income, there does not appear to be any systematic differences between the characteristics of poor and non-poor households.

Table 1a   Household characteristics

Variable	N	Mean	Standard deviation
Age of Household Head			
All	4109	39.44	11.38
Poor	3066	39.60	11.06
Non-poor	812	38.03	11.03
Household Size			
All	4109	6.30	2.91
Poor	3066	6.52	2.88
Non-poor	812		2.90
Per Capita Annual Income ($)			
All	4109	680.55	2696.99
Poor	3066	111.56	122.45
Non-poor	812	2829.67	5373

Source: Author's calculation using the Angolan Consumption Survey (1995).

Table 1b   Household structure

	N	Percent
Monogamous Male		
All	2865	69.7
Poor	2191	71.4
Non-poor	537	68.6
Polygamous Male		
All	14	03
Poor	11	04
Non-poor	2	02
Single Male		
All	342	8.3
Poor	247	8.1
Non-poor	64	7.9
De Facto Female		
All	64	1.6
Poor	48	1.6
Non-poor	13	1.6
De Jure Female		
All	825	20.1
Poor	570	18.6
Non-poor	176	21.7

Table 1c   Education level

	N	Percent
No Level		
All	568	13.8
Poor	378	12.3
Non-poor	119	14.7
Primary Not Completed		
All	464	11.3
Poor	361	11.8
Non-poor	79	9.7
Primary Completed		
All	669	16.3
Poor	511	16.7
Non-poor	125	15.4
No Secondary		
All	2048	49.8
Poor	1511	49.3
Non-poor	446	54.9
Secondary Not Completed		
All	361	8.0
Poor	306	10.0
Non-poor	43	5.3

Extent of Poverty in Angola

This section reports various poverty measures using data on individuals in the survey. To evaluate the suitability of the various measures to changes in both biological and psychological deprivation, three different PLs are defined: (a) Actual PL - $40; (b) Lower PL - $20; and (c) Upper PL - $60. Different PLs should associate with changes in headcount, poverty gap, and weighted poverty gap statistics. Defining different PLs allows for comparisons on how sensitive the measures are to changes in the number of poor. The various measures of poverty are computed as follows:

Headcount Measures

Headcount = q (population below the PL);

Incidence of poverty $= \dfrac{q}{n} * 100$; (n= total population);

Poverty Gap Measures

Aggregate poverty gap$= \sum (z - y_i)$ where y_i is the income per adult male equivalent;

Average poverty gap $= \sum \left(\dfrac{z - y_i}{q} \right)$;

Poverty Gap ratio $= \sum \left(\dfrac{z - y_i}{q} \right) / z$; (Average poverty gap divided by the PL);

Weighted Poverty Gap Measures

The weighted poverty gap indices are computed as follows:

$$\text{Sen Index} = \dfrac{2}{(q+1)n} \left[\sum_{i=1}^{q} (\dfrac{z - y_i}{z})(q + 1 - i) \right]$$

Kakwani Family of Indices:

a. Kakwani 0 $= \dfrac{q}{n \sum_{q} i^0} \left[\sum_{i=1}^{q} \left(\dfrac{z - y_i}{z} \right)(q + 1 - i)^0 \right]$

b. Kakwani 1 $= \dfrac{q}{n \sum\limits^{q} i^{1}} \left[\sum\limits_{i=1}^{q} \left(\dfrac{z - y_i}{z} \right) (q + 1 - i)^{1} \right]$

c. Kakwani 2 $= \dfrac{q}{n \sum\limits^{q} i^{2}} \left[\sum\limits_{i=1}^{q} \left(\dfrac{z - y_i}{z} \right) (q + 1 - i)^{2} \right]$

Thon Index $= \dfrac{2}{n(n+1)} \left[\sum\limits_{i=1}^{q} \left(\dfrac{z - y_i}{z} \right) (n + 1 - i) \right]$

Takayama Index $= 1 + \dfrac{1}{n} - \dfrac{2}{u^{*} n^{2}} \left[\sum\limits_{i=1}^{n} (n + 1 - i) y_i^{*} \right]$

Greer, Thorbecke, and Foster Family of Indices:

a. GTF 0 $= \dfrac{1}{n} \left[\sum\limits_{i=1}^{q} \left(\dfrac{z - y_i}{z} \right)^{0} \right]$

b. GTF 1 $= \dfrac{1}{n} \left[\sum\limits_{i=1}^{q} \left(\dfrac{z - y_i}{z} \right)^{1} \right]$

c. GTF 2 $= \dfrac{1}{n} \left[\sum\limits_{i=1}^{q} \left(\dfrac{z - y_i}{z} \right)^{2} \right]$

Table 2a reports the various poverty measures based on three PLs. As expected, the number of poor increases with increases in the threshold income. Based on the actual PL ($40), the 1995 poverty rate in Angola was 69.40%. The average income shortfall from the PL is $29.40, or 73.51% of the PL. The lower and upper PLs yield poverty rates of 55.33% and 77.41%, respectively. From the sample population of 24,670, the number of poor ranges from 13,650 for the lower PL, 17,126 for the actual PL, and 19,098 for the upper PL. Although the poverty rate increases with increases in the poverty threshold, the extent of deprivation is better revealed by changes in the aggregate poverty gap. For the lower PL, the aggregate poverty gap is $193,563. This figure increases to $503,594 for the actual PL, and to $867,316 for the upper PL. All the weighted poverty gap measures increase as expected, indicating increases in biological and psychological deprivation as the threshold income increases.

While it is in fact the case that all the weighted poverty gap measures show increases in the poverty as the threshold income is increased, it is not clear that these measures are necessarily much more useful than the headcount and poverty gap measures. To evaluate the responsiveness of the measures to changes in threshold income, relative changes of the measures are computed by dividing the values obtained from one PL by those obtained from another PL. Specifically, ratios of the measures are computed for the following PLs: $40 to $20; $60 to $20; and $60 to $40. The results of the relative changes of the measures are reported in Table 2b.

For discussion purposes, focus is on the relative values for the $40 PL to those of the $20 PL. The results show that the headcount statistics increase by 1.25 times when PL increases from $20 to $40. However, the aggregate poverty gap increases by a factor of 2.60. Clearly, the aggregate poverty gap is a much better indicator of the extent of deprivation than the headcount statistics. The results also reveal that the relative changes of the weighted poverty gap measures are not much different from the relative change in the headcount statistics. However, the relative changes recorded by the weighted poverty gap measures, are much smaller than the relative change in the aggregate poverty gap. By and large, the results are consistent when other PLs are considered.

The relative low responsiveness of the weighted poverty gap measures may be primarily due to the fact that different PLs do not necessarily result in large changes in the distribution of incomes among the poor. Nevertheless, given the much larger changes in the aggregate poverty gap, it does suggest that the weighted poverty gap measures do not necessarily capture the change in biological deprivation adequately.

Merely changing the PL is not sufficient to evaluate how well the measures capture biological and psychological deprivation. As noted previously, the weighted poverty gap measures take into account the income distribution among the poor. To evaluate the sensitivity of the various measures to changes in the income distribution among the poor and also changes in biological deprivation, the incomes of the poorest individuals are first increased. The subsidy does not alter the relative rankings of the poor nor is it sufficient to bring the incomes of the poor above the PL. Essentially, the subsidy just makes the poorest better off without reducing the number of the poor. Of course, such a subsidy reduces both the aggregate poverty gap and inequality among the poor.

Table 2c reports the poverty measures when the incomes of the poorest individuals are subsidized keeping the number below the PLs the same. Again, as expected, the weighted poverty gap measures increase as the income threshold is increased. It should be noted that the more informative comparison, is on the values of the measures for each PL with those reported in Table 2a. In all cases, the weighted poverty gap measures record a decrease when a subsidy is provided to the poor. But again, it is not clear whether the weighted poverty gap measures capture this change any better than the aggregate poverty gap measure.

To evaluate the relative responsiveness of the measures to the subsidy, ratios of the measures before and after the subsidy are computed for each PL. The results are reported in Table 2d. The results again reveal that the relative change of the weighted poverty gap measures with respect to the subsidy are very close to the relative change in the aggregate poverty gap. However, GTF 2 appears to outperform other measures and in one of the cases ($20 PL), this index is quite responsive.

The responsiveness of the poverty measures is then evaluated when the incomes of the less poor are reduced holding the number of poor constant and also keeping the original rankings of the poor. Such a change increases biological deprivation, but reduces income inequality among the poor. The results of the measures are shown in Table 2e. All measures show increase in poverty compared to the original poverty rate.

Table 2f reports the relative responsiveness of the measures to the income reduction of the poor. For the three PLs, the ratio of the aggregate poverty gap before and after income reduction, ranges between 0.81 and 0.95. The results show that the relative change of the weighted poverty gap measures are very close to the relative change in the aggregate poverty gap. Based on these results, the weighted poverty gap measures do not appear to be superior to the simple aggregate poverty gap measure in capturing the type of change discussed here.

Table 2a   Measures of poverty

Poverty line	$20	$40	$60
N	24670	24670	24670
Headcount	13650	17140	17638
Incidence	55.33	69.40	77.41
Aggregate Poverty Gap	193,563.99	503,594.47	867,316.85
Average Poverty Gap	14.18	29.40	45.41
Poverty Gap Ratio	70.90	73.51	75.68
Sen Index	0.452	0.609	0.691
Kakwani 0	0.392	0.510	0.585
Kakwani 1	0.452	0.609	0.691
Kakwani 2	0.469	0.642	0.726
Thon Index	0.610	0.735	0.800
Takayama Index	0.267	0.353	0.389
GTF 0	0.553	0.694	0.774
GTF 1	0.392	0.510	0.585
GTF 2	0.315	0.426	0.496

Table 2b   Relative changes of the poverty measures

Ratios of Poverty line	$40/20	$60/20	$60/40
Headcount	1.25	1.39	1.11
Incidence	1.25	1.39	1.11
Aggregate Poverty Gap	2.60	4.48	1.72
Average Poverty Gap	2.07	3.20	1.00
Poverty Gap Ratio	1.03	1.06	1.02
Sen Index	1.34	1.52	1.13
Kakwani 0	1.30	1.49	1.14
Kakwani 1	1.34	1.52	1.13
Kakwani 2	1.36	1.54	1.13
Thon Index	1.20	1.31	1.08
Takayama Index	1.32	1.45	1.10
GTF 0	1.25	1.39	1.11
GTF 1	1.30	1.40	1.14
GTF 2	1.35	1.57	1.16

Table 2c   Effect of subsidy to the poorest on measures of poverty

Poverty line	$20	$40	$60
N	24670	24670	24670
Headcount	13650	17126	19098
Incidence	55.33	69.42	77.40
Aggregate Poverty Gap	123,785.96	433,816.44	797,538.82
Average Poverty Gap	9.06	25.30	46.52
Poverty Gap Ratio	45.60	63.25	77.53
Sen Index	0.273	0.502	0.618
Kakwani 0	0.250	0.439	0.538
Kakwani 1	0.273	0.502	0.618
Kakwani 2	0.276	0.516	0.637
Thon Index	0.375	0.617	0.705
Takayama index	0.652	0.533	0.705
GTF 0	0.553	0.694	0.774
GTF 1	0.250	0.439	0.538
GTF 2	0.120	0.306	0.412

Table 2d   Relative measures of poverty before and after subsidy

Poverty line	$20	$40`	$60
N	1.00	1.00	1.00
Headcount	1.00	1.00	1.00
Incidence	1.00	1.00	1.00
Aggregate Poverty Gap	1.56	1.16	1.08
Average Poverty Gap	1.56	1.16	0.97
Poverty Gap Ratio	1.55	1.16	0.97
Sen Index	1.65	1.21	1.11
Kakwani 0	1.56	1.16	1.08
Kakwani 1	1.65	1.21	1.18
Kakwani 2	1.69	1.24	1.13
Thon Index	1.62	1.19	1.10
Takayama Index	1.19	1.65	1.53
GTF 0	1.00	1.00	1.00
GTF 1	1.56	1.34	1.08
GTF 2	2.62	1.39	1.20

Table 2e   **Effect of income reduction of the poor on the measure of poverty**

Poverty line	$20	$40	$60
N	24670	24670	24670
Headcount	13650	7140	19098
Incidence	55.33	69.42	77.40
Aggregate Poverty Gap	238,259.01	548,289.49	912,011.87
Average Poverty Gap	17.45	31.98	47.75
Poverty Gap Ratio	87.25	79.95	79.58
Sen Index	0.502	0.641	0.716
Kakwani 0	0.482	0.555	0.616
Kakwani 1	0.502	0.641	0.716
Kakwani 2	0.470	0.660	0.740
Thon Index	0.647	0. 784	0.883
Takayama Index	0.283	0.391	0.434
GTF 0	0.553	0.694	0.774
GTF 1	0.482	0.555	0.616
GTF 2	0.430	0.500	0.549

Table 2f   **Relative change in poverty before and after reduction of income of the poor**

Poverty line	$20	$40	$60
N	1.00	1.00	1.00
Headcount	1.00	1.00	1.00
Incidence	1.00	1.00	1.00
Aggregate Poverty Gap	0.81	0.91	0.95
Average Poverty Gap	0.81	0.91	0.95
Poverty Gap Ratio	0.81	0.91	0.95
Sen Index	0.90	0.95	0.96
Kakwani 0	0.90	0.91	0.94
Kakwani 1	0.90	0.95	0.96
Kakwani 2	0.99	0.97	0.98
Thon Index	0.94	0.93	0.90
Takayama Index	0.94	0.90	0.89
GTF 0	1.00	1.00	1.00
GTF 1	0.81	0.91	0.94
GTF 2	0.73	0.85	0.90

Alternative Weighted Poverty Gap Measure of Poverty

A primary shortcoming of the weighted poverty gap measures seems to be on the choice of the weighting scheme. The measures discussed above generally use the reverse order of rankings in the income distribution where individuals are ranked from the poorest to the richest. In this type of ranking, it is assumed that an individual who is poorer, suffers more psychological deprivation than an individual with slightly higher income. When individuals have the same incomes, they are necessarily assigned different rankings.   As it turns out, many individuals have the same incomes and there is no reason why they should be assigned different ranks.

But even if individuals with similar adult equivalent incomes are assigned similar ranks, it is questionable how realistic such a ranking approach is. The truth is that most people have incomes that differ by very small magnitudes, and for all practical purposes, actually enjoy similar living standards.   Is it realistic then to assume that a person whose income is 50 cents lower than that of another   person feels much more psychologically deprived? Is the 50 cents difference in income actually significant as to create perception   of differences in the well-being? It seems unlikely that such a difference would really matter nor would they be noticeable. Yet such a small difference could actually result in a huge difference in rankings.   The Angolan data reveal that such small differences in incomes sometimes result in rank differences of as much as 1000.   For example, in the Angolan case, income difference between individual ranked number 1701 and one ranked number 2,875 is only 50 cents!

It seems unrealistic to use the rankings based on income as the basis for the weights used to capture psychological deprivation. Instead, it seems more realistic that individuals compare themselves as a group with members of other groups who are better or worse off. In essence, a weighting scheme that uses groupings of individuals appears much more realistic than one that uses individual rankings in the income distribution.

A Proposed Weighting Scheme

A weighting scheme based on rankings by groups is proposed. Specifically, the population is ranked from the poorest to the richest and then divided into five groups (G=5), each with the same number of people. The poorest group is assigned $r=1$ and the richest group is assigned a value of $r=5$. The measure of poverty is then expressed as:

$$Poverty = \frac{q}{n\sum_q G_r^k} \left[\sum_{i=1}^q \left(\frac{z - y_i}{z} \right)^k (G + 1 - r)^k \right]$$

Essentially, this index uses a reverse order of the group rankings. k distinguishes the   family of class members. Table 2g.i reports the results of this index.   The focus is on only one class where $k=2$.

Table 2g.i   reports the value of the index based on a group weighting scheme.   It shows the results for the three PLs and also for the original data set and when a subsidy and tax are in place. Firstly, the index increases with increase in poverty threshold. Furthermore, as shown in Table 2g.ii   the index is more responsive to changes in the threshold income than the measures discussed previously (compare Table 2g.ii with Table 2b).

Table 2g.iii   shows that the proposed index is much more responsive to both the subsidy and tax than are the measures discussed previously. The new measure actually outperforms even GTF 2.

Table 2g.i   Measure of poverty using rankings of poor by quintiles

Poverty line	$20	$40	$60
Original Data	0.337	0.506	0.619
Subsidy	0.105	0.311	0.487
Tax	0.533	0.686	0.778

Table 2g.ii   Relative changes of poverty measures with respect to different PLs

Ratios of Poverty line	$40/20	$60/20	$60/40
Original Data	1.50	1.836	1.22

Table 2g.iii   Relative changes before and after subsidy and tax

Poverty line	$20	$40	$60
Original/Subsidy	3.20	1.62	1.27
Original/Tax	0.63	0.73	0.79

Conclusion

The primary purpose of this paper is to evaluate various measures of poverty using data for a low-income country. It has been demonstrated that the headcount measures that are so commonly in use in poor countries are not adequate to evaluate extent of deprivation. It may be in fact, misleading to policy makers. Poverty gap measures and weighted poverty gap measures are on the other hand, much more useful for evaluating extent of deprivation. This paper has evaluated the most popular measures by conducting sensitivity analysis. While the weighted poverty gap measures appear sensitive to changes in the incomes of the poor, their responsiveness to those changes is weak, particularly when rankings in the income distribution do not change.

An alternative weighted poverty gap measure that uses rankings by income groups as the basis for the weights to capture psychological deprivation is proposed. The results presented here show that such a weighting scheme is promising and may be superior to the other measures in capturing deprivation. However, it is noted that this measure has not been subjected to other sensitivity tests and therefore, the results should be considered tentative. Nevertheless, it is clear that there is an urgent need to focus on alternative measures of deprivation that are sensitive to even small changes in the well-being of the poor in low-income countries.

Note

1 The author is grateful to Mario Alberto Aduata de Sousa, Director of the National Institute of Statistics, Angola, for permission to use the data and to John Ngwafon of the World Bank for making the data available. Part of this study was conducted while the author was a consultant to the World Bank at the National Institute of Statistics and the final draft was prepared while with the Kenya Institute of Public Policy Research and Analysis (KIPPRA). The views expressed in this paper are those of the author and should not be attributed to the World Bank, the National Institute of Statistics nor KIPPRA.

References

Fisher, F.M. (1987). 'Household Equivalence Scales and Interpersonal Comparisons', *Review of Economic Studies*, Vol. 54 pp. 519-524. Not cited

Foster, J., Greer, J. and Thorbecke, E. (1984), 'A Class of Decomposable Poverty Measures,' *Econometrica*, Vol. 52, pp. 761-766.

Kakwani, N. (1980), 'On a Class of Poverty Measures', *Econometrica*, Vol 48 (2), pp. 437-446.

Kakwani, N.   (1993), 'Statistical Inference in the Measurement of Poverty', *Review of Economics and Statistics*, Vol No. 75(4) pp. 632-639.

Kimenyi, M. S.   (1995), *Economics of Poverty, Discrimination and Public Policy*, South-Western Publishers, Cincinnati, OH.

Randolph, S. (1982), Measures of Absolute Poverty, Monograph, Cornell University.

Sen, A.   (1976), 'Poverty: An ordinal Approach to Measurement', *Econometrica*, Vol 44, pp. 219-231.

Takayama, N. (1979). 'Poverty, Income Inequality and Their Measures: Professor Sen's Axiomatix Approach Reconsidered', *Econometrica,* Vol 47, pp. 774-759.

Thon, D. (1983).   'A Note on a Troublesome Axiom of Poverty Indexes', *The Economic Journal*, 93, pp. 199-200.

PART III:
SOCIAL REFORMS AND
SOCIAL SECURITY

7 A Welfare Analysis of the Price System Reforms' Effects on Poverty in Tunisia

Sami Bibi[1]

Introduction

Throughout the 1980s, the Tunisian economy has faced a deterioration of its external and internal deficits. The reason behind such deterioration may be partly attributed to the rapid consumption growth and to the subsidization of consumer prices which has been the main cause of the budgetary deficit. This situation led the government to adopt the structural adjustment plan proposed by the International Monetary Fund in 1986. This plan involved reforms aimed at the restructuring of the economy so as to enhance the traded goods sector, the rehabilitation of market mechanisms and the encouragement of private initiatives. These objectives were to be accomplished partly through the liberalization of the price system and through a fiscal reform with mainly the institution of the value added tax in July 1988. The goal of these reforms was to promote a sustainable economic growth without internal and external deficit deterioration. Nevertheless, macro-economic adjustment programs have often raised anxiety concerning their effects on poor population. The welfare reforms' effects on poor population have then to be evaluated. It is necessary to analyze the microeconomic implications of these macroeconomic reforms to be able to target correctly those social categories that need protection and identify the social measures that would have to accompany such reforms.

The aim of this paper is to propose a methodology, consistent with the consumer theory, that allows the evaluation of the implications of the price system reforms on the poor population's welfare. This issue poses an identification and a measure problem. It also delves on the poverty line estimation, using a utilitarian approach and the definition of the poor population welfare measures, that allow the assessment of social loss subsequent to the presence of poor people having an income level inferior to the poverty line. Welfare measures advocated in this paper are based on King's approach (1983). This approach presents the advantage of considering the households' reaction to price system reforms. It is based on the estimation of a demand system that has to respect economic consumer axioms. A methodology is presented allowing to estimate parameters of a flexible demand system, as the QAIDS system of Banks *et al.* (1993). The parameters estimation of this model have been made possible using the National Statistic Institute households' budget and consumption survey of 1990. The simulation of a price system reform's effects on the poor population and the identification of target groups is addressed. Within the framework of this section, a hypothetical reform is considered consisting of eliminating the budget devoted to food subsidies. The impact of this reform on the poor population welfare is examined and the possibility of reallocating a part of this budget to better tackle the poverty issue in Tunisia. Socio-demographic indicators are defined which are likely to lead to a better targeting of the poor populations. Such targeting would make it possible to reduce public expenditures and also to improve the well-being of these target groups.

Poor Population Welfare

The economic literature dealing with poor population welfare measures has considerably increased since the work done by Sen (1976). According to Sen, poverty analysis requires the solving of two problems, namely that of identification and that of aggregation. The identification problem consists in being able to spot the poor out of the total population with the definition of a poverty line (PL). It is also necessary to identify the sensitivity of the PL to price system reforms to establish a relationship between structural adjustment reforms and their microeconomic effects. The aggregation problem consists in finding a means through which the distribution of the individual well-being is moved to an aggregated poverty measure. This measure could be interpreted as being the social loss due to the presence of individuals having an income level lower than the PL. It would be preferable to see that this measure is consistent with certain axioms developed in the literature studying this subject.

The Identification Problem

The identification of the poor population, with the estimation of the PL, is a necessary step in analyzing the adjustment reforms on the well-being of the poor population. One of the methods commonly used consists in estimating this PL on the basis of needs in food energy (Greer and Thorbecke, 1986 ; Charmes, 1990). The shortcoming of this approach is that it does not account for all the needs created by society. A better alternative would be to derive the PL from the consumer theory (Ravallion, 1996).

The determination of the PL is rarely formulated in utilitarian terms. In theory, a utilitarian approach should enable the estimation of the PL corresponding to a minimum utility level, or again to an indifference curve that delimits the welfare level of a poor individual from the welfare level of a non-poor individual. The compensated expenditure function would allow therefore to determine for any given price system, the minimum expenditure level required to reach this indifference curve. As an example, the individual welfare may be represented by the Stone-Geary utility function $U(x) = \prod_i (x_i - \overline{x_i})^{\sigma_i}$, where x_i is the quantity consumed of good i, σ_i is a

positive parameter and $\overline{x_i}$ may be interpreted as some minimum consumption of good i; the maximization of this utility function subject to budgetary constraint $\sum_i p_i x_i = Y$, where p_i is the price of good i and Y is the

income level, gives the following non-compensated expenditures functions : [2]

$$d_i^h = z_i + \sigma_i \ (Y^h - z) \quad \text{with} \quad \sum_i \sigma_i = 1 \qquad (1)$$

where d_i^h is the per equivalent adult expenditure of good i by household h having a per equivalent adult income level, Y^h, and z_i is the constant of the model that indicates the minimum per equivalent adult expenditure of good i[3] Bourguignon and Field (1997) have underlined that when using this model to study the consumption behavior, it has to be assumed that all individuals having an income level below the minimum, $z = \sum_i p_i \overline{x_i}$, required to buy

the minimum bundle ($\overline{x}$), may be considered as being poor. Nevertheless, the definition of the poverty as compared to a reference bundle ($\overline{x}$) is too restrictive especially if a utilitarian approach is adopted for the estimation of the PL.[4]

A better approach is to choose another demand system that is more flexible. If $e(p,U)$ denotes the expenditure function which defines the minimum expenditure necessary to attain a specific utility level U at given price system p, a first order approximation to any demand system that satisfies axioms of the consumer theory, can be given by the PIGLOG class definite:

$$\ln(e(p,U)) = (1-U)\ln(z(p)) + U\ln(g(p)) \qquad (2)$$

Save a few exceptions, the utility level U lies between 0 (the subsistence level) and 1 (the bliss level).[5] So the functions $z(p)$ and $g(p)$ can be regarded as the costs of subsistence (or the PL) and bliss, respectively. For the AIDS demand system of Deaton and Muellbauer (1980a) or QAIDS of Banks *at al.* (1993), the z(p) function takes the following form:

$$\ln z(p) = \ln(\omega_0) + \sum_{i=1} \omega_i \ln(p_i) + \frac{1}{2} \sum_{i=1} \sum_{k=1} \theta_{ik} \ln(p_i) \ln(p_k) \quad (3)$$

The AIDS or QAIDS demand system estimation does not allow to deduce a PL if a value of ω_0^{6} is not first estimated. Since ω_0 can be interpreted as the PL if all prices are equal to 1, an arbitrary specification of this value can lead only to an arbitrary estimation of the PL . Thus, the recommendation made by Banks *et al.* (1993) is followed which suggests specifying a plausible interval for this parameter. This allows the avoidance of controversies concerning the estimation of the PL since the analysis of the price system reforms on the poor population will be made using a large interval of PLs. To do this, Atkinson's stochastic dominance conditions (1987) is used to evaluate the reforms impact on the welfare distribution of poor population with the use of a large interval of PLs.

The Aggregation Problem

To solve the aggregation problem, a mapping from the individual welfare distribution into a scalar poverty measure is required. The poverty measure which meets analysis needs must satisfy axioms of monotonicity, transfer, transfer-sensibility and decomposability.[7]

- The Monotonicity Axiom - A reduction of the poor's income must increase the poverty measure, all things being equal.
- The Transfer Axiom - An income transfer from a poor individual to a less one must increase the poverty measure, all things being equal.
- The Transfer-Sensibility Axiom - For any positive integer ρ and any pair of poor individuals h and j, if $j > h$, then $\Delta P^{h, h+\rho} > \Delta P^{j, j+\rho}$ where $\Delta P^{h, h+\rho}$ is the increase in poverty measure due to an income transfer from the hth poor to the $(h+\rho)$th poor.
- The Decomposability Axiom - Let Y^f be a vector of incomes obtained from Y by changing the incomes in subgroup c from Y_c to Y_c^f, where the total number of households in subgroup c (H_c) is unchanged. If Y_c^f has more poverty than Y_c, then Y^f must also have a higher level of

poverty than Y. The class of poverty measures proposed by Foster et al. (1984) and retained for this work satisfy all these axioms. It takes the next form:

$$P_\alpha(z,Y) = \frac{1}{H} \sum_{h=1}^{H_p} n^h \left(\frac{z - Y^h}{z} \right)^\alpha \tag{4}$$

where z and Y are as defined above, H (H_p) is the total number of households (poor households), n^h is the size of household h and α may be considered as a measure of poverty aversion: a larger α gives greater emphasis to the poorest poor. As α becomes very large, P_α approaches a Rawlsian measure which considers only the poorest households' welfare. The measure P_0 is known as the headcount ratio, while P_1 is a normalized average gap measure which is a good poverty measure only if all the poor have the same income.[8] The poverty measure P_α satisfies the monotonicity axiom for $\alpha > 0$, the transfer axiom for $\alpha > 1$, the transfer sensitivity axiom for $\alpha > 2$ and always the decomposability axiom.[9]

The decomposition of poverty measure is very useful since economic policies may have different impact on subgroups that compose the poor population. Also, a precise knowledge of the reforms' impact envisaged on the different subgroups will allow to identify better the most vulnerable social groups necessary to protect and social measures required that have to be inherent to these reforms. Thus, if C is considered to be mutually exclusive subgroups, if $P_{c,\alpha}$ is the poverty measure in the subgroup c and if f_c represents the weight of the subgroup c in the total population, then the measure P_α may be decomposed as follows:

$$P_\alpha(z,Y) = \sum_{c=1}^{C} f_c P_{c,\alpha}(z,Y_c) \tag{5}$$

To compare the levels of a household's welfare when it faces different price systems, it is equally necessary to define a welfare measure to each poor household. This measure may be presented in terms of values of the equivalent income function as defined by King (1983). For a given budget constraint (p, Y), equivalent income is defined as the income level which allows, at the reference price system p^r, the same utility level as can be reached under the given budget constraint:

$$V(p^r, Y_e) = V(p, Y) \tag{6}$$

where V is the indirect utility function and p is the price system. Notice that since p^r is fixed across all households, Y_e is an exact monetary metric of actual utility $V(p,Y)$ because Y_e is an increasing monotonic transformation of $V(.)$. Indeed, inverting the indirect utility function, equivalent income is obtained in terms of the expenditure function:

$$Y_e = e\left(p^r; V(p,Y)\right)$$
$$= y_e(p^r, p, Y) \tag{7}$$

where $e(.)$ is the expenditure function and $y_e(.)$ is the equivalent income function. The properties of the equivalent income function are derived from the properties of indirect utility and expenditure functions. Also, $y_e(.)$ is increasing in p^r and Y, decreasing in p, homogeneous of degree 1 in p^r and , homogeneous of degree 0 in (p, Y).

Suppose that the reference price system p^r is equal to the actual price system p^a , the distribution of equivalent income per equivalent adult in the actual situation (Y_e^a) is equal to the actual distribution of the income Y:

$$Y_e^a = y_e(p^a, p^a, Y) = Y \tag{8}$$

Suppose that the reform consists in substituting the price post-reform system p^p to the current price system p^a, the post-reform equivalent income Y_e^p would be given by:

$$Y_e^p = y_e(p^a, p^p, Y) \tag{9}$$

The post-reform equivalent income Y_e^p is a monetary assessment of utility level $V(p^p, Y)$ subsequent to the substitution of the price system p^p to the price system p^a. A natural per equivalent adult welfare measure variation of each household may be given by the change in equivalent income:

$$\Gamma = y_e(p^a, p^p, Y) - y_e(p^a, p^a, Y)$$
$$= Y_e^p - Y \tag{10}$$

Also, according to Equation 8, the PL z evaluated under the price system p^a corresponding to the equivalent PL z_e that allows reaching the utility level V_z in the current situation, characterized by the couple (p^a, z), and in the post-reform situation, characterized by the couple (p^p, Y_z):

$$V_z(p^a, z_e) = V_z(p^p, Y_z)$$
$$z_e = y_e(p^a, p^p, Y_z) \tag{11}$$

where V_z corresponds to the minimum utility level required to be non-poor and Y_z is the per equivalent adult PL correponding to the price system p^p. If the reform increases the price of some goods, households whose per equivalent adult income is between z and Y_z in the current situation will become poor people in the post-reform situation, given that the reform implies for them an equivalent gain (negative) per equivalent adult equal to:

$$\Gamma = y_e(P^a, P^p, Y_z) - y_e(P^a, P^a, Y_z)$$
$$= z_e - Y_z \tag{12}$$

The impact of macroeconomic reforms on the welfare of poor population may be evaluated by substituting in the retained poverty measure FGT Y_e and z_e to Y and z.[10] The poverty measure FGT in the actual situation and in the post-reform situation will then be given by the following equation:[11]

$$P_\alpha^o(z_e, Y_e) = \frac{1}{H} \sum_{h=1}^{H_p^o} n^h \left(\frac{z_e - y_e(p^a, p^o, Y^h)}{z_e} \right)^\alpha \qquad \text{with} \quad o = a, p. \tag{13}$$

where H_p^o is the number of poor households in the situation o.

Thus, the analysis of the price system reforms' effects on the welfare of poor population requires the specification of an equivalent income function. This function is closely linked to the estimation of a demand system that is coherent with the consumer theory.

Specification of a Demand System

The specification and estimation of a demand system as much as possible in harmony with the economic theory, is an essential element of a welfare analysis of the price system reforms' effects. The problem is that this choice can largely predetermine the selection of a fiscal reform (Deaton, 1988).[12]   With the absence of sufficiently long chronological series data on consumption at different prices of households in less developed countries (LDC), it is hard to estimate a demand system which is not additively separable, and the linear expenditure system (LES) hence becomes a natural choice.   Nevertheless, for the LES and for all additively separable demand systems, income elasticities are approximately proportional to price elasticities. Consequently, goods that have a weak price elasticity and which are desirable to tax on efficiency grounds, have equally a weak income elasticity and are undesirable to tax on equity grounds (Deaton and Muellbauer, 1980b).   Conversely, income elastic goods consumed by the non-poor which are natural targets for redistributive taxation, have high price elasticities and as a result, high deadweight or efficiency losses. The trade-off between equity and efficiency considerations is then given by a uniform tax structure independently of the LES parameters' estimations. The need to use the estimation results to deduce socially optimal reform directions has therefore motivated the authors to adopt a more flexible functional form, namely the QAIDS model of Banks *et al.* (1993) defined by:

$$w_i = \omega_i + \sum_k^K \theta_{ik} \ln(p_k) + \beta_i \ln(\frac{Y}{z(p)}) + \frac{\delta_i}{b(p)} [\ln(\frac{Y}{z(p)})]^2 + \vartheta_i \tag{14}$$

with $\sum_i \omega_i = 1$, $\sum_i \theta_{ik} = \sum_k \theta_{ik} = \sum_i \beta_i = \sum_i \delta_i = 0$ and $\theta_{ik} = \theta_{ki}$

where w_j, p_k, p, $z(p)$ and Y are as defined above, ϑ_j is a residual term and the $b(p)$ function is obtained according to the Cobb-Douglas form:

$$b(p) = \prod p_i^{\beta_i} \tag{15}$$

The QAIDS system, contrary to the AIDS system of Deaton and Muellbauer (1980a), allows not only income elasticities to vary with the income level, but also a good to be a luxury to some income levels and a first necessity good to others. This will be the case if coefficients β and δ are of opposite signs.

To a certain extent, the Deaton (1988) and Deaton and Grimard methodology (1992) is followed in estimating parameters of the QAIDS system. Statistical information contained under a double dimension to be able to develop a panel estimation data is used. The sample is then subdivided into different clusters. Each cluster contains about 20 households, characterized by a geographical proximity and surveyed during the same period. Also, as is assumed by Deaton (1988) and Deaton and Grimard (1992), households that belong to the same cluster are supposed to face the same price system. The variability between cluster prices is justified by a spatial and often a temporal effect.[13] Also, to linearize the problem of estimating the parameters of the QAIDS system, it is supposed that the PL $z(p)$ and the function $b(p)$ are exogenous.[14] Under these conditions, the budgetary equations to be estimated take the following form:

$$w_i^{ch} = \omega_i + \sum_{k}^{K} \theta_{ik} \ln(p_k^c) + \beta_i \ln(\frac{Y^{ch}}{z}) + \delta_i [\ln(\frac{Y^{ch}}{z})]^2 + \mu_i D^{ch} + f_i^c + \vartheta_i^{ch} \quad (16)$$

$$k = 1,...K, \quad c = 1,...C \quad et \quad h = 1,...H_c$$

where H_c is the number of households in the cluster c; D is a vector of regional and demographic variables, whose introduction seems very relevant given that these variables can influence the consumption levels with the classic variables like the price and the income, f is a specific fixed effect to the cluster[15] and p_k^c is the price of good k that is constant within the cluster c and variable between clusters. The equivalent income function relative to the QAIDS system is given by this equation:

$$\ln(Y_e^{ch}) = b(p^r) \left[\left(\frac{\ln(Y^{ch}) - \ln(z(p))}{b(p)} \right)^{-1} + \delta(p^r) - \delta(p) \right]^{-1} + \ln(z(p^r)) \quad (17)$$

where p^r is as defined above (King, 1983) and the function $\delta(p)$ is obtained according to the Cobb-Douglas form:

$$\delta(p) = \prod p_i^{\delta_i} \quad (18)$$

However, these prices are not observable. To bypass this problem, the unit value for each good as being expenditure relative to quantity is used as a price indicator. For each household having consumed good k, it is possible to calculate a unit value.[16]

Deaton (1988) has underlined that the unit values variability through the sample does not reflect only the spatial and temporal variability prices. It also reflects the quality choice that is itself a function of the price system and the income. Moreover, Deaton has developed a methodology which consists in cleaning unit values from qualities' effects and attributing their residual variability to a spatial price.[17] Furthermore, these unit values contain measurement errors coming from expenditures or quantities. Also, the use of average unit values as indicator of the price in each cluster is found to be reinforced because it allows the reduction of these measurement errors' misdeeds on estimation results.[18]

The first step consists in estimating the income, demographic and regional variables' effects by exploiting the variability within cluster of the budgetary equations. This will be done by applying the ordinary least square (OLS) on model 16 transformed by the transformation matrix Q defined as follows:[19]

$$Q = I - \frac{1}{H_c} SS'$$ (19)

where I is the identity matrix of order H_c and S is a sum vector also of order H_c; this consists in using deviated variables to their respective average in the cluster.[20] It follows that:[21]

$$w_i^{ch} - w_i^{c\cdot} = \beta_i \left[\ln(y^{ch}) - \ln(y^{c\cdot}) \right] + \delta_i \left[[\ln(y^{ch})]^2 - [\ln(y^{c\cdot})]^2 \right]$$
$$+ \mu_i [D^{ch} - D^{c\cdot}] + [\vartheta_i^{ch} - \vartheta_i^{c\cdot}]$$ (20)

This gives the estimate $\hat{\beta}_j$, $\hat{\delta}_j$ and $\hat{\mu}_j$. The second step consists in using the variability between clusters in order to identify prices' effects. To account for measurement errors that may appear in the unit values, the instrumental variable method is also applied to the next equation:[22]

$$w_i^{c\cdot} - \hat{\beta}_i \ln(y^{c\cdot}) - \hat{\delta}_i [\ln(y^{c\cdot})]^2 - \hat{\mu}_i D^{c\cdot} = \omega_i + \sum_{k=1}^{K} \theta_{ik} \ln(p_k^c) + f_i^c + \upsilon_i^c$$ (21)

The Hausman's specification test (1978) for the presence of measurement errors is implemented for each equation. The statistics of the test are as follows:

$$K = (\hat{\theta} - \hat{\theta}_{VI})'[\hat{V}(\hat{\theta}_{VI}) - V(\hat{\theta})]^{-1}(\hat{\theta} - \hat{\theta}_{VI}) \tag{22}$$

where $\hat{\theta}$, $\hat{\theta}_{VI}$, $V(\hat{\theta})$ and $V(\hat{\theta}_{VI})$ represent respectively the estimations of parameters' prices and their variances-covariances matrix according to OLS and instrumental variables methods.[23] Given that estimation results are used for fiscal reform analysis, it is necessary to use a demand system verifying the restrictions of the consumer theory. So, it is essential finally to impose homogeneity and symmetry constraints to the parameters of price effects.[24]

The application field of this method can only be based on food goods given that the survey conducted by the National Institute of Statistics reports expenditures only for non-food goods. Also, to insure the system's closure, the non-food budgetary equation has been omitted. Their respective parameters are deduced from constraints of additivity. The estimation of the QAIDS demand system has focused on the whole sample to improve the accuracy of the estimations.[25] Nevertheless, the urban - rural spatial dualism in the household consumption behavior has been taken into account by the specification of own price effects as follows:[26]

$$\theta_{ii} = \theta_{ii}^0 + \theta_{ii}^1 M^c \tag{23}$$

where M^c is a dummy variable that indicates if the region of household residence belonging to the cluster c, is urban or rural.[27]

Table 1 presents results of the Hausman's specification tests (1978). This Table shows that at the traditional threshold of 5% for all groups of goods, the presence of measurement errors hypothesis and correlation between unit values and the cluster specific effect may be rejected.

Table 1   Specification test of Hausman (1978)

Commodities	K
Hard Wheat	5.16
Tender Wheat	2.50
Other Wheat	6.64
Vegetables	9.08
Fruit	4.18
Meat	6.41
Poultry and Eggs	6.37
Milk	5.54
Sugar	8.20
Other Sugar Products	7.16
Mix Oils	9.65
Olive Oils	4.03
Fish	7.96
Canned Foods	11.75
Other Foods	2.19

N.B. The theoretical value of Chi-square is 28.9 when the freedom degree is equal to 18. The presence of measurement errors hypothesis in unit values in the budgetary equations can be rejected.

Finally, matrix of prices elasticities provided from these estimation results are presented in Tables 2 and 3. These Tables show that all own-elasticities prices in urban and rural area are, in accordance with the economic theory, negative and statistically significant. The performance of the estimation results must be equally considered according to the concordance of cross-elasticity signs with the goods nature. It is observed that the estimation results substantiate the substitutability between the various groups of goods such as cereals groups, olive and mix oils groups, and finally between the different proteins products such as meats, fish and poultry and eggs groups. Nevertheless, some inconsistency appears in the estimation results. For example, the negative sign of the cross-elasticity between poultry and eggs and fish groups or between meat and milk groups.[28]

Table 2 Own-price and cross-price elasticities in the urban area

	E_{i1}	E_{i2}	E_{i3}	E_{i4}	E_{i5}	E_{i6}	E_{i7}	E_{i8}	E_{i9}	E_{i10}	E_{i11}	E_{i12}	E_{i13}	E_{i14}	E_{i15}
Hard Wheat	-2.252 (-5.9)	1.553 (8.2)						0.311 (2.5)	-0.095 (-1.8)						-0.442 (-3.8)
Tender Wheat	1.377 (8.2)	-1.768 (-6.6)						-0.193 (-2.5)							0.273 (4.1)
Other Wheat			-0.528 (-3.8)	0.442 (2.9)			0.322 (2.7)							0.121 (3.3)	
Vegetables			0.069 (2.9)	-0.733 (-7.5)		0.221 (2.5)		0.240 (4.1)	0.067 (4)	0.082 (3.5)	0.194 (4.1)	-0.429 (-3.5)			
Fruit					-1.556 (-17)	-0.618 (-4.7)	0.204 (3.6)	-0.128 (-2.6)	-0.036 (-2.2)						-0.158 (-2.8)
Meat	0.439 (5.3)			0.187 (2.5)		0.600 (3.6)			-0.038 (-2.2)		0.043 (1.8)		0.210 (6.8)	0.106 (2.8)	
Poultry			0.125 (2.8)				-0.516 (-3)						-0.216 (-4.1)		
Eggs	0.211 (2.5)	-0.147 (-2.5)			0.156 (4.1)	-0.255 (-2.6)		-1.400 (-9.2)	-0.029 (-1.8)						
Milk	-0.234 (-1.8)			0.416 (4)	-0.087 (-2.2)	-0.280 (-2.2)		-0.106 (-1.8)	-0.011 (-2.6)	0.025 (2.3)	-0.172 (-2.9)	0.200 (3.3)		-0.070 (-2)	
Sugar										-1.000 (-1.9)			0.086 (2.3)	0.736 (2.7)	
Other Sugar Products			0.338 (3.5)					0.396 (2.3)				0.415 (3.6)			
Mix Oils			0.183 (4.1)			0.310 (1.8)	-0.416 (-2.9)				-0.627 (-3)	-1.920 (-8)	-0.122 (-2.4)		0.441 (3.4)
Olive Oils			-0.263 (-3.5)					0.463 (3.2)	0.074 (2.3)		0.270 (3.6)				0.235 (2.4)
Fish						1.306 (6.8)	-0.457 (-4.1)				-0.106 (-2.4)		-0.336 (-2.6)		
Canned Foods				0.292 (3.3)		0.305 (2.8)		-0.100 (-2)		0.068 (2.7)		0.156 (3.4)		-0.299 (-1.9)	0.144 (3.2)
Other Foods	-0.245 (-3.8)	0.171 (4.1)			-0.084 (-2.8)								0.062 (2.4)	0.082 (3.2)	-1 (-1.4)

Values between parentheses indicate the t-ratio. For clarities' sake, elasticities prices that are significant to the traditional threshold of 5% are presented.

Table 3   Own-price and cross-price elasticities in the rural area

	E_1	E_2	E_3	E_4	E_5	E_6	E_7	E_8	E_9	E_{10}	E_{11}	E_{12}	E_{13}	E_{14}	E_{15}
Hard Wheat	-1.863 (-6.2)	0.467 (8.2)				0.389 (5.2)		0.093 (2.5)	-0.028 (-1.8)						-0.133 (-3.8)
Tender Wheat	2.104 (8.2)	-2.173 (-5.3)						-0.295 (-2.5)							0.416 (4.1)
Other Wheat			-1.077 (-5.2)	0.306 (2.9)							0.135 (4.1)	-0.297 (-3.5)			
Vegetables			0.056 (2.9)	-0.783 (-9.9)		0.180 (2.5)	0.223 (2.7)			0.057 (3.5)				0.098 (3.3)	
Fruit					-2.028 (-8.7)			0.245 (4.1)	0.055 (4)						-0.161 (-2.8)
Meat	0.406 (5.3)		0.118 (2.8)	0.173 (2.5)		-0.647 (-5.3)	0.189 (3.6)	-0.118 (-2.6)	-0.037 (-2.2)		0.040 (1.8)		0.194 (6.8)	0.089 (2.8)	
Poultry Eggs						0.556 (3.6)	-0.543 (-3.3)						-0.204 (-4.1)		
Milk	0.274 (2.5)	-0.191 (-2.5)			0.203 (4.1)	-0.332 (-2.6)		-1.902 (-4.5)	-0.035 (-2.2)		-0.162 (-2.9)			-0.091 (-2)	
Sugar	-0.136 (-1.8)			0.241 (4)	-0.050 (-2.2)	-0.162 (-2.2)		-0.061 (-1.8)	-0.038 (-1.8)	0.033 (2.3)		0.259 (3.3)	0.050 (2.3)		
Other Sugar Products			0.385 (3.5)					0.451 (2.3)							
Mix Oils			0.102 (4.1)			0.173 (1.8)			-0.425 (-2.6)	-1.000 (-1.9)	-0.792 (-6.9)	0.231 (3.6)	-0.068 (-2.4)	0.839 (2.7)	
Olive Oils			-0.201 (-3.5)				-0.232 (-2.9)	0.354 (3.2)			0.206 (3.6)	-1.703 (-9.4)			0.337 (3.4)
Fish						3.283 (6.8)	-1.149 (-4.1)		0.187 (2.3)		-0.268 (-2.4)		-0.953 (-8.3)		0.591 (2.4)
Canned Foods				0.210 (3.3)		0.218 (2.8)		-0.072 (-2)		0.049 (2.7)				-0.764 (-5.8)	0.103 (3.2)
Other Foods	-0.254 (-3.8)	0.177 (4.1)			-0.087 (-2.8)							0.161 (3.4)	0.064 (2.4)	0.085 (3.2)	-0.728 (-1.4)

Reform of the Price System and Identification of Target Groups

The impact on poverty of a possible food subsidy suppression through a plausible interval of poverty line and a wide range of poverty measures is analyzed. This hypothetical reform is equivalent for each poor to an income loss equal to:

$$-\Gamma^h = y_e(p^a, p^p, Y^h) - y_e(p^a, p^a, Y^h)$$
$$= Y_e^h - Y^h \tag{24}$$

where Γ^h measures henceforth the per equivalent adult income loss of household h subsequent to the passage from the price system p^a to the price system p^p. The FGT class of poverty measures in the current situation and in the post-reform situation will be given respectively by equations 25 and 26:

$$P_\alpha^a(z_e, Y_e^a) = \frac{1}{H} \sum_{h=1}^{H_p^a} n^h \left(\frac{z_e - y_e(p^a, p^a, Y^h)}{z_e} \right)^\alpha$$
$$= \frac{1}{H} \sum_{h=1}^{H_p^a} n^h \left(\frac{z_e - Y^h}{z_e} \right)^\alpha \tag{25}$$

$$P_\alpha^p(z_e, Y_e^p) = \frac{1}{H} \sum_{h=1}^{H_p^p} n^h \left(\frac{z_e - y_e(p^a, p^p, Y^h)}{z_e} \right)^\alpha$$
$$= \frac{1}{H} \sum_{h=1}^{H_p^p} n^h \left(\frac{z_e - (Y^h - \Gamma^h)}{z_e} \right)^\alpha \tag{26}$$

where H_p^a and H_p^p represent respectively the number of poor households in the current and in the post-reform situation. Thus, the poverty measure variation resulting from the substitution of the price system p^p to p^a is given by the following equation:

$$\Delta P_\alpha = \frac{1}{H z_e} \left[\sum_{h=1}^{H_p^a} n^h \left[(z_e - (Y^h - \Gamma^h))^\alpha - (z_e - Y^h)^\alpha \right] + \sum_{h=H_p^a+1}^{H_p^p} n^h (z_e - (Y^h - \Gamma^h))^\alpha \right] \tag{27}$$

The left part of the equation 27 reflects the increase in the poverty measures explained by the well-being deterioration of the population part that was and remained poor following this reform. The right part expresses the poverty deterioration due to the increase in the number of poor households.

The food subsidies suppression entails essentially an increase of 58% of the hard wheat price, 54% of the tender wheat price, 10% of the other cereals price, 16% of the poultry and eggs price, 22% of the milk price, 32% of the sugar price and 49% of mix oils price. The reform effects on the poor population welfare, for different values of aversion to the poverty, are summarized in Table 4.

Table 4 Welfare impact of the reform on poor population

α	z_e	$P_\alpha(z_e, Y_e^a)$	$P_\alpha(z_e, Y_e^P)$	ΔP_α (%)
0	250	0.1087	0.1402	28.89
1	250	0.0271	0.0366	34.89
2	250	0.0102	0.0144	41.32
3	250	0.0047	0.0069	47.05
0	290	0.1563	0.1904	21.80
1	290	0.0418	0.0543	29.75
2	290	0.0164	0.0224	36.31
3	290	0.0078	0.0110	41.75
0	330	0.2095	0.2502	19.47
1	330	0.0589	0.0743	26.19
2	330	0.0242	0.0319	32.24
3	330	0.0118	0.0163	37.45

This hypothetical reform entails, if no compensation measure is taken, an important deterioration of all poverty measures. A monetary evaluation of the welfare deterioration indicates that the per equivalent loss (Γ) per equivalent adult would be equal to 22.2 dinars. This loss corresponds on the average to 9.34% of the poor population equivalent income. In addition, the greatest losers from this reform are found among the poorest people as is indicated the growing decline of the FGT measure when the aversion to poverty increases (Table 4).

The price system liberalization constitutes for the state a necessary option to reduce its budgetary deficit since most studies have shown that in nominal terms, food subsidies profit more to the richer people. In addition, these subsidies are a source of economic distortions given the relative prices alteration they engender. This reform has to be accompanied by compensation measures to minimize its harmful consequences on the poor population. This compensation, evaluated at the current price system (p^a), has to be at least equal to the equivalent loss per equivalent adult (Γ). If in addition, the state's objective is to eliminate the poverty problem in the post-reform situation, the budget required may be given by $HP_1(z_e, Y_e)z_e$. Table 5 gives the budget share relative to the food subsidies budget, according to different choice of PLs required to eliminate all poverty in the current (B^a) and in the post-reform situation (B^p), if a perfect procedure of targeting at no cost can be used to identify the poor from the non-poor population.

Table 5   Budget share relative to subsidies budget required to eliminate poverty

Actual Situation		Post-reform Situation	
z^a	B^a (%)	$z^p = Y_z$ [29]	B^p (%)
250	117.47	273	23.57
290	131.25	316	40..54
330	150.00	358	63.20

Thus, the state expenditures are considered to correspond exclusively to the budget devoted to food subsidies, its expenditures have to increase from 17.50 to 50% in the current situation to eliminate totally the poverty problem if the targeting cost of poor population is null. This course of action is not foreseeable given the tight budgetary policy which has been pursued by the Tunisian government since the adoption of the structural adjustment plan in 1986. On the other hand, the food prices liberalization would not only allow the state to have the required resources to eliminate poverty, but also help to save 36.8 to 76.43% of the budget devoted to food subsidies. Nevertheless, the success of this economic policy depends on the state's capacity to target perfectly the poor population and on the inherent costs of targeting.[30]

It is supposed that government decides to devote a part of the rise in its budgetary revenue which has resulted from the food subsidies suppression, to a program of poverty alleviation. Thus, in order to identify target groups, the state may proceed to the minimization of the FGT poverty measure subject to a budgetary constraint:

$$Min\, P_\alpha(z_e, Y_e) = \sum_{j=1}^{J} f_j P_{j,\alpha}\left(z_e, y_e(p^a, p^p, Y_j + T_j)\right) \text{ subject to } \sum_{j=1}^{J} n_j T_j = B \quad (28)$$

where P_α, $P_{j,\alpha}$, f_j, z_e, Y_e, y_e are as defined above, n_j is the individual number of subgroups j, T_j is the universal transfer in subgroup j and B is the budget devoted to the poverty alleviation program. Also, the decomposability of the FGT poverty measure would allow the identification of the priority target groups that must benefit from the budget devoted to the poverty alleviation program. Indeed, if the state desires to increase marginally the transfer granted to an individual of the subgroup *j*, the impact of this decision would be given by:

$$\frac{\partial P_{\alpha}}{\partial T_j} = -\frac{\alpha}{z_e} f_j \, P_{j, \alpha-1} \tag{29}$$

Equation 29 shows that if the objective is to minimize P_{α} at national level, groups having a strong contribution to the measure $P_{\alpha-1}$ have to be marginally favored.[31] Table 6 presents the subgroup contribution to the poverty according to various regional criteria (rural or urban zone, north or south regions...) or socio-demographic criteria (number of child by household, the occupation nature of the household head, his/her education level...).

A study of Table 6 shows that poverty is essentially a rural phenomenon in Tunisia. This problem is widespread in the northern regions and in West Central Tunisia. The targeting must also be considered according to other criteria such as the main occupation of the household head and his/her education level.

If the occupation of the household head is taken into consideration, poverty is pervasive among workers in agricultural and non-agricultural sectors. Targeting according to the main occupation of the household head may not altogether be reliable. Indeed, the poor who have activities in the informal sector may not have been included in this survey.

Finally, if targeting is to be made according to the education level of household head, illiterates have to be focused upon. As this population group is the largest for all the retained FGT measures, it may be concluded that any intervention which succeeds in better targeting, this group may entail a sensitive reduction of poverty.

Nevertheless, the targeting of poor population based on regional characteristics or socio-demographic criteria, is not without costs. Indeed, it is not excluded that an important part of the non-poor population is, for example, illiterate or residing in the rural zones. The analysis of the costs which result from such risks of errors should precede any proposal aiming at the use of these targeting procedures.

Table 6 Subgroup contribution to poverty

Contribution of subgroups (in %)		P_0	P_1	P_2	P_3
Zone	Urban	27.86	24.11	21.73	19.76
	Rural	72.14	75.89	78.27	80.24
Regions	Tunis	6.26	5.28	4.57	4.12
	North East	11.21	10.09	9.56	9.15
	North West	28.15	31.68	34.08	36.15
	East Central	6.11	5.99	5.96	6.04
	West Central	20.66	22.69	24.45	25.64
	Sfax	5.93	5.80	5.44	5.03
	South East	10.53	7.28	5.51	4.28
	South West	11.15	11.17	10.42	9.58
Profession	Inactive	11.06	11.59	12.53	13.54
	Agricultural Worker	22.67	24.61	25.77	26.72
	Agricultural	18.84	17.20	15.75	14.53
	Non-Agricultural Worker	31.60	32.15	32.50	32.63
	Non-Agricultural Independent	9.66	8.64	8.12	7.73
	Others	6.17	5.80	5.33	4.85
Education	Illiterate	70.62	73.10	74.70	75.81
	Primary	25.14	23.17	21.93	21.13
	Secondary 1st cycle	3.01	2.85	2.72	2.58
	Secondary 2nd cycle	0.92	063	0.43	0.30
	Academic	0.30	0.25	0.21	0.18

Estimation of a Plausible Interval of Poverty Lines

It has been shown that the estimation of QAIDS demand system does not allow to deduce a PL if an assessment is not identified beforehand, of the parameter ω_0 where this parameter indicates the cost of subsistence if all prices are equal to 1. Banks *et al.* (1993) propose that this parameter has to belong to a plausible interval chosen appropriatly. The Ravallion method (1994) is proposed to be used to estimate this interval.

It is both natural and convenient to decompose PL in two components: (a) food PL (z_f) and (b) non-food PL (z_{nf}). Nutritional requirements for good health are the most common approach in defining a food PL (Greer and Thorbecke, 1986; Charmes, 1990). To deduce a food PL consistent with the consumer theory, a better method would be to use a utilitarian approach. It is proposed to estimate this component of PL using a linear demand system LES.[32] To do this, it is supposed that food goods make up a group of goods separable from others.[33] This enables keeping the usage of the LES model solely for the estimation of the food PL. Thus, the following non-compensated expenditures functions are obtained:

$$d_i^h = z_i + \sigma_i \ (Y_a^h - z_f) + \vartheta_i^h \quad \text{with} \quad \sum_i \sigma_i = 1 \tag{30}$$

where d_i^h, z_i, z_f and σ_i are as defined above Y_f is the per equivalent adult food expenditure of household h and ϑ_i^h is a residual term. The estimation results of the model (Equation 30) using the ordinary least square (OLS) are given in the following Table 7:[34]

Table 7 Results of first stage estimation poverty line

Food Goods	Z_I	σ_i	R^2
Hard, Tender and Other Wheat	40.871	0.072	0.27
	(120)	(55)	
Vegetables	30.480	0.117	0.51
	(86)	(86)	
Fruit	7.369	0.094	0.40
	(19)	(65)	
Poultry and Eggs; Meat and Fish	40.355	0.334	0.76
	(72)	(154)	
Milk	13.536	0.095	0.41
	(39)	(71)	
Sugar and Other Sugar Products	6.423	0.027	0.14
	(31)	(33)	
Mix and Olive Oils	13.138	0.063	0.27
	(43)	(54)	
Canned foods	14.164	0.037	0.32
	(88)	(60)	
Other Foods	13.879	0.161	0.36
	(22)	(68)	

The non-food PL (z_{nf}) is estimated using the Ravallion method (1994). It consists of observing households' behavior whose income is just equal to the food PL ($Y^h = z_f$) where $z_f = \Sigma\, z_i$. These households are in a position to afford basic foodstuffs but prefer to devote part of their income to buy non-food goods. This income part may be considered as the lower non-food PL z_{nf}^l :

$$z_{nf}^l = Y - Y_f = z_f - Y_f \tag{31}$$

To estimate the non-food component of PL, the QAIDS model is used representing the food share (w_f) as a quadratic function of the total spending value per equivalent adult (Y^h) relative to the food PL (z_f):

$$w_f^h = \omega_f + \beta \ln\left(\frac{Y^h}{z_f}\right) + \delta \left[\ln\left(\frac{Y^h}{z_f}\right)\right]^2 + u_f^h \qquad (32)$$

The OLS estimation of model (Equation 32) gives the following results:

Table 8 Results estimation of the food share

ω_f	β	δ	R^2
0.5948	-0.0626	-0.02	0.328
(168)	(-12)	(-11)	

The coefficient ω_f is an estimated average food share of households having an income level equal to the food PL (z_f). The lower non-food PL (z_{nf}^l) is then given by the following equation:

$$z_{na}^l = (1 - \omega_f) z_f \qquad (33)$$

Equation 33 allows to have a relation between the food PL (z_f) and the lower PL (z^l) where $z^l = 253.2$ dinars per equivalent adult.

$$z^l = z_a + z_{nf}^l = (2 - \omega_f) z_f \qquad (34)$$

An upper PL (z^u) maybe deduced which is the minimum income level required at which a household will be able to devote a budget equal to the food PL (z_f) for food items. The upper PL that can be obtained only numerically, allows the estimation of an upper non-food PL corresponding to the maximum reasonable expenditure for basic non-food items.[35]

Conclusion

The purpose of this paper is to propose a methodology, inspired from the consumer theory, which would allow the assessment of the impact of price system reforms on the poor's welfare. These reforms may come as a result of the price system liberalization, fiscal reforms or a suppression of food subsidies.

The analysis of the price system reforms' impact on the poor population addresses an identification and a measure problem. To overcome these problems, an assessment of the effects of price system reforms on poverty using a wide range of PLs and measures was done. The estimation of PL was based on a utilitarian approach. On the measure problem, the class of FGT poverty measures was used, given that they meet minimum requirements of monotonicity, transfer, transfers - sensitivity and decomposability. In addition, poverty measures of King's (1983) equivalent income which is a monetary evaluation of the consumers welfare was used. Thus, the retained poverty measures reflect henceforth the social welfare loss resulting from the presence of some people living with an income level per equivalent adult under the PL.

The estimation of a demand system which would be, as much as possible, in harmony with the consumer theory has therefore been an essential stage in being able to deduce an equivalent income function. Also, the QAIDS demand system of Banks *et al.* (1993) was chosen because, compared to the AIDS demand system of Deaton and Muellbauer (1980a), it allows for a good to be a luxury to some income levels and a first necessity to other levels. The estimation results of the QAIDS model carried out on the Tunisian survey, are globally acceptable and in line with the economic intuition.

The estimation results have been used to simulate the welfare impact of price system reforms on the poor population. Dominance tests have then been used to evaluate the reforms' effects on a wide range of PLs and measures, encompassing different views on both the selection of the poverty measure, and the choice of the PL. Thus, some ideas from the recent literature on welfare modeling on the one hand, and the choice of the PLs and measures on the other, were considered.

This approach has been applied to simulate the impact of a hypothetical reform affecting subsidized food prices in Tunisia. The focus on subsidies problem is largely explained by their importance on the state's budget and also, by the limited available data that limit the study the households' reaction following prices' variation of non-food goods. The main result of this simulation is that this reform would entail an important deterioration of the poor households' welfare. This reform therefore, has to be accompanied by necessary compensation measures to avoid grave deterioration of the poor population's welfare than the one prevailing currently. It has been verified that the revenue saved by the state as a result of this reform, would it make it possible to eliminate all poverty and even save from 36.8 to 76.4% of the budget devoted to food subsidies, i.e., if a perfect targeting procedure likely to identify the needy groups at no cost, is applied. Targeting using criteria such as the residence area and the education level of the household head appear to be the most adequate that the state could think of to target its social transfers. However, it should be pointed out that this targeting method is characterized by two error types, the costs of which need to be assessed before suggesting an alleviation poverty program based on regional or demographic indicators of the poor population.[36] The first error type is due to the presence of a non-poor group, sharing the same indicator adopted for targeting. This group will take advantage therefore of this program while ideally, it should not be doing so. The second error type is explained by the presence of poor households which do not show the socio-economic or regional features adopted by the targeting procedure. This group will be deprived from benefiting from the alleviation poverty program measures whereas ideally it should be. The assessment of the costs engendered by such errors made up the extended investigations of this study.

Notes

1 This study is part of the author's thesis entitled Public Spending and the Targeting Problem of Poor Population. The author wishes to thank Professor Jean-Yves Duclos of Laval University, Professor Mohamed Goaied of Faculte des Sciences Economiques et de Gestion de Tunis, and his colleague Bechir Bouaicha for their valuable comments.

2 It is the linear system of expenditure known under the abbreviation LES.

3 Bibi(1998) estimates equivalence scales using the Engle method followed by Deaton and Muellbauer (1986).

4 Note here that Kanbur et al. (1995) have defended on the basis of a non-utilitarian approach, the idea of basing PL on a basket of reference consumption. The deprivation would be in this case proportional to the distance between the current basket consumption of each poor and the basket of reference consumption. Ravallion and Van de Walle (1991) find it difficult to base PL on a basket of reference consumption. They argue that even poor people make choice of consumption and it is necessary to be prudent before advancing judgement on what poor people have to consume.

5 See appendix of Deaton and Muellbauer (1980a).

6 Deaton and Muellbauer (1980a) consider that since $\omega 0$ can be interpreted as the outlay required for a minimal living standard (the PL) when all prices are equal to 1, choosing a plausible value is not difficult. Banks et al. (1993) propose that this parameter lies between

an appropriate interval. The Ravallion method (1994) is used to estimate this interval. The description of this method figures in the Appendix.

7 The two first axioms have been developed by Sen (1976), the third by Kakwani (1980) and the fourth by Foster et al. (1984).

8 See the Axiom N of Sen (1976).

9 The characteristic of any subgroup of poor population may be of regional nature (rural or urban zone, northern region or the south...) or socio-demographic (number of child by household, the occupation nature of the household head, his/her level of education...). Note that decomposability characteristic of the FGT poverty measure is not always respected in all poverty measures suggested in the literature dealing with this subject. As an example, this characteristic is not respected by Sen (1976) or Kakwani (1980) measures. See Foster et al. (1984).

10 This approach is equally followed by Ravallion and Van de Walle (1991).

11 The substitution of the equivalent income to the income in the class of poverty measures FGT was also done by Besley and Kanbur (1988) to study the impact of infra-marginal subsidies' reforms.

12 The subsidies reform analysis belongs to the same area of the optimal taxation theory given that subsidies are simply negative indirect taxes.

13 It is useful to point out that several clusters were not investigated during the same period.

14 To bypass the non-linearity version of the QAIDS model, it is supposed in the first iteration that $b(p)=1$. Also, it is supposed that $z(p)=z$ where z is estimated following Ravallion's method (1994). Since this approach gives a range of PL, the robustness of coefficients estimated relative to the choice of z is tested. It is noted that, apart from the constants of the model, all coefficients statistically significant are insensitive to the the PL choice.

15 The specific effect to the cluster not measurable in the consumption model, may be justified by the regional differences in the consumption custom.

16 To respect the constant prices hypothesis within the cluster, the average unit value of the cluster for each good i is taken.

17 This step has not been adopted in this application since the quality effect that unit values can contain, is neglected. This may not change results of elasticity estimation prices since a recent application, developing the procedure of Deaton (1988) on these same data, has shown the quasi - absence of the quality effect. For this subject, see the study of Ayadi et al. (1995a).

18 This affirmation is more legitimate when the number of households in the cluster is high. ($Hc \rightarrow \infty$).

19 It is easy to verify that $\varrho \, s = 0$.

20 It is clear that the constants variables contribution within cluster, the prices effects, are not identifiable in this first step.

21 $[\ln(y^{c})]^2 = \dfrac{1}{H_c} \sum_h [\ln(y^{hc})]^2$ the other averages are calculated using the same way.

22 If these two essential components are neglected, elasticity estimations obtained may be biased. Instrument vector is chosen for unit values: $t = \{\ln(Y)$, demographic, regional and temporal indicators variables$\}$.

23 This statistics is distributed according to a Chi - square to k freedom degrees, with k as the number of instrument variables. In the absence of quality effect and measurement errors, this statistics is close to zero.

24 If Hausman's (1978) specification tests are significant for most goods, it is useful to use the triple least square under restrictions of homogeneity and the symmetry. In fact, the application of OLS under these restrictions, is sufficient because the test is not significant for most of the goods items considered in this study.

25 This empirical step is more justified in the second step when the estimation of price effects is carried out on averages of clusters. Elsewhere, empirical results confirm it since the estimation of Equation 21 on the totality of clusters has improved the accuracy of elasticities in comparison to an estimation separated in the urban and rural zone. In addition, the estimation of price effects on the totality of clusters justifies more the thesis of the spatial price variation.

26 This is fundamental to improve food subsidies targeting for poverty alleviation in Tunisia. Indeed, 75% of the 20% of the poorest households live in the rural areas.

27 During the first step, it was not useful to apply the same procedure for parameters of income variables given that income elasticities of the QAIDS system depend on the income level of households.

28 These anomalies appear in the estimation results of Ayadi et al. (1995a) who used the same survey.

29 According to Equation 11, Yz corresponds to the PL in the post-reform situation evaluated under the price system Pp.

30 See Besley and Kanbur (1993).

31 See Besley and Kanbur (1988).

32 The linear demand system allows to estimate a poverty line by reference to a fixed consumption bundle that is too restrictive. To reduce disadvantages of the LES choice, the poverty line has been decomposed in two components and to use this system only for the estimation of food PL.

33 Ayadi and Matoussi (1995) have followed the nutritional approach to estimate this component. Also, they do not consider equivalence scales when estimatig their range of poverty lines.

34 Note that the estimation of the model (30) requires to use a non-linear estimation algorithm. To avoid the complexity of non-linear estimation, an iterative method is suggested to estimate this model.

35 The equation allowing to assess the upper poverty line is :

$$z_f = w_f z^u = \omega_f \, z^u + \beta \ln\left(\frac{z^u}{z_f}\right)(z^u) + \delta\left[\ln\left(\frac{z^u}{z_f}\right)\right]^2 (z^u)$$

what gives an upper poverty line equal to 327.5 dinars per equivalent adult. Note finally that these results are close to those found by Ayadi et al. (1995b).

36 See for example Baker and Grosh (1994) and Cornia and Stewart (1995).

References

Atkinson, A. B. (1987), 'On the Measurement of Poverty', *Econometrica*, Vol.55, No. 4, pp. 749-764.

Ayadi, M., Baccouche, R., Goaied, M. and Matoussi, M. S. (1995a), *Variation Spatiale des Prix et Analyse de la Demande en Tunisie*, Faculté des Sciences conomiques e de Gestion de Tunis.

Ayadi, M. and Matoussi M. S. (1995b), *Analyse de certains Aspects de la Pauvreté en Tunisie*, Faculté des Sciences Economiques et de Gestion de Tunis.

Baker, J. and Grosh, M. (1994), *Measuring the Effects of Geographic Targeting on Poverty Reduction*, LSMS Working Paper No. 99, World Bank, Washington, D.C.

Banks, J., Blundell, R. and Lewbel, A. (1993), *Quadratic Engel Curves, Welfare Measurement and Consumer Demand*, Institute for Fiscal Studies and University College, London.

Besley, T. and Kanbur, S. M. R. (1988), 'Food Subsidies and Poverty Alleviation', *The Economic Journal*, Vol. 98, pp. 701-719.

Besley, T. and Kanbur, S. M. R. (1993), 'Principles of Targeting', in M. Lipton and J. Van Der Gaag (eds), *Including the Poor*, World Bank, Washington, D.C., pp. 67-90.

Bourguignon, F. and Fields, G.S. (1997), 'Discontinuous Losses from Poverty, General $P\alpha$ Measures, and Optimal Transfers to the Poor', *Journal of Public Economics*, Vol. 63, No. 2, pp. 155-175.

Charmes, J. (1990), *Mesurer la Pauvreté, Identifier les Groupes Vulnérables: Enquête et Méthodes Utilisées En Tunisie*, Stateco No. 63, INSEE, pp. 57-83.

Cornia, G. A. and Stewart, F. (1995), 'Two Errors of Targeting', in D. Van de Walle and K. Nead (eds), *Public Spending and the Poor*, The Johns Hopkins University Press, Baltimore and London, pp. 350-386.

Deaton, A and Muellbauer, J. (1980a), 'An Almost Ideal Demand System', *The American Economic Review*, Vol. 70, No. 3, pp. 312-326.

Deaton, A and Muellbauer, J. (1980b), *Economics and Consumer Behavior*, Cambridge University Press, New York.

Deaton, A and Muellbauer,J.(1986), '*On Measuring Child Costs : with Application to Poor Countries'*,*Journal of Political Economy*, Vol. 97, No.1, pp. 179-201.

Deaton, A. (1988), 'Quality, Quantity and Spatial Variation of Prices', *The American Economic Review*, Vol. 78, No. 3, pp. 418-430.

Deaton A. (1990), 'Price Elasticities From Survey Data: Extension and Indonesian Results', *Journal of Econometrics*, Vol. 44, pp. 281-309.

Deaton, A. and Grimard, F. (1992), *Demand Analysis and Tax Reform in Pakistan*, LSMS Working Paper, 85, World Bank, Washington, D.C.

Foster, J., Greer, J. and Thorbecke, E. (1984), 'A Class of Decomposable Poverty Measures', *Econometrica*, Vol. 52, No. 3, pp. 761-765.

Greer, J. and Thorbecke, E. (1986), 'A Methodology for Measuring Food Poverty Applied to Kenya', *Journal of Development Economics*, Vol. 24, pp. 59-74.

Hausman (1978), 'Specification Tests in Econometrics' *Econometrica*, vol. 46, # 6,pp. 1251-1271.

Kakwani, N. (1980), 'On a Class of Poverty Measures', *Econometrica*, Vol. 48, pp. 437-446.

Kanbur, R., Keen, M. and Tuomala, M. (1995), 'Labor Supply and Targeting in Poverty Allviation Programs', in D. Van de Walle and K. Nead (eds), *Public Spending and the Poor*, Johns Hopkins University Press, Baltimore and London, pp. 91-113.

King, M. A. (1983), 'Welfare Analysis of Tax Réforms Using Household Data', *Journal of Public Economics*, Vol. 21, pp. 183-214.

Ravallion, M. and Van de Walle, D. (1991), 'The Impact on Poverty of Food Pricing Reforms: A Welfare Analysis for Indonesia', *Journal of Policy Modeling*, Vol. 13, No. 2, pp. 281-299.

Ravallion, M. (1994), 'Poverty Comparisons', *Fundamentals of Pure and Applied Economics Series,* Vol. 56, Chur, Switzerland, Harwood Academic Press, New York.
Ravallion, M. (1996), 'Issues in Measuring and Modelling Poverty', *The Economic Journal,* Vol. 106, pp. 1328-1343.
Sen, A. K. (1976), 'Poverty: An Ordinal Approach to Measurement', *Econometrica,* Vol. 44, No. 2, pp. 219-231.

8 Design Principles for an Efficient and Sustainable Social Security System

Peter Sturm

The Origin of Social Security

The concept of social security refers to a set of government programs providing transfer (i.e. unearned) income to individuals and families subject to pre-specified conditions.[1] The introduction of social security programs has been governments' response to the socio-economic changes accompanying the Industrial Revolution. The transformation of predominantly rural and agrarian societies into urban and industrial societies was in many cases, accompanied by the loosening of family ties. This increased the vulnerability of large parts of the population to economic changes outside their control. These changes manifested themselves in the transformation of the labor force from mainly self-employed farmers and crafts people (and in some more backward countries of feudal systems and serfs) into an industrial labor force of predominantly contractual workers and employees.

The perceived diminished control by individuals over their material fate in the industrializing society gave rise to demand for collective responsibility for citizens' welfare, most forcefully put forward by the moderate currents of socialism developing in Europe in the 19th century.[2] Nevertheless, the first great breakthrough in the implementation of state-sponsored social security occurred under the conservative government of Otto von Bismarck in 1883 in the newly founded German Empire. Bismarck's motivation for introducing a social security system was predominantly political. By providing workers with income guarantees in times of sickness and old age, he hoped to weaken the support for the socialist party and foster the loyalty of the work force to the German state as opposed to the internationalist orientation of the socialist movement.

The subsequent introduction of a variety of social security schemes in many countries was often linked to crisis situations in the countries concerned, and in contrast to the German precedent - introduced by left-leaning parties in government (Table 1). Since its modest beginnings in Germany in the last century, social security has gained increasing importance, making it the single most important government expenditure category in most countries (Table 2). While the coverage and extent of social security programs differ widely among different countries, the need for some government involvement providing insurance against sudden income loss or minimum income levels, is now universally recognized. Nevertheless, the rapid extension of these programs in the post-war period has lead to some disillusionment as to their efficacy. More recently, social security systems have come under scrutiny with respect to their effect on government finances, economic incentives and more generally, their ability to achieve declared objectives.

Table 1 Introduction of social security programs (selected nations)

Year	Country	Initial Coverage	Subsequent Major Extensions
1883/ 1884	German Empire	Sickness; Work injury	Old age pension (1889); Unemployment insurance (1927); Family allowance (1954)
1897	United Kingdom	Work injury	Old age pension (1908); Sickness, unemployment insurance (1911); Major reform and introduction of a comprehensive welfare state including family allowances, 1945)
1898	France	Work injury	Unemployment insurance (1905); Old age pension (1910); Sickness (1928); Family allowance (1932)
1898	New Zealand	Old age pension	Work injury (1908); Family allowance (1926); Unemployment(1930); Sickness(1938); Universal old age income (1972); Systematic review of the system since 1984.
1903	Russia/Soviet Union	Work injury	Sickness (1912); Unemployment insurance (1921); Old age pension (1922); Family allowance(1944)
1908	United States	Work injury	Old age pension, Unemployment insurance (1935); Health insurance for the elderly (MEDICARE) and for the poor (MEDICAID) (1965).
1936	Egypt	Work injury	Old age pension(1950); Sickness, Unemployment insurance(1959)
1942	Nigeria	Work injury	Old age pension, Sickness (1961)
1947	Saudi Arabia	Work injury	Old age pension (1962); Sickness(1969)

Source: US Social Security Administration (1997)

Table 2   Relative importance of social expenditures (selected OECD countries, 1993)

Country	GDP	Social Expenditure as Percent of Government Expenditure of which (Total = 100)				
		Total	Health	Unemployment (a)	Old Age	Others (b)
United States	16.3	48.2	37.9	8.3	34.1	19.7
Japan(b)	12.2	36.2	40.8	3.0	41.9	14.3
Germany	26.4	53.3	20.1	13.1	29.3	37.5
France	31.0	56.4	23.5	10.7	39.6	26.2
Italy	26.6	46.3	24.2	13.3	24.1	38.4
United Kingdom	24.8	56.9	23.2	8.6	27.2	41.0
Canada	20.2	40.6	35.6	14.1	23.2	27.1
Sweden	38.6	54.4	16.2	15.2	35.2	33.4
Denmark	31.6	53.9	17.7	24.0	27.4	30.9
Netherlands	31.0	56.3	21.8	11.2	26.8	40.2
Portugal	16.9	36.7	24.5	10.4	33.8	31.3
Turkey	7.1	...	19.1	0.2	41.2	39.5
Mexico(b)	3.8	...	75.5	0.3	5.2	19.0

a. Including active labor market policies, 1992.
b. Others: Family, child and housing benefits; survivor and disability pensions.
Source: OECD, Social Expenditure Data Base

Economic Rationale for Establishing Social Security Systems

There are basically two economic reasons for introducing social security programs. The first concerns various market imperfections which prevent private agents from achieving optimal outcomes by contracting and trading in competitive private markets. This creates second best situations, in which government intervention in the form of social security programs can improve in principle, on the economic outcomes that would otherwise result. Whether such intervention takes the form of government regulation or government direct involvement on financing and delivery of services, needs to be addressed separately.

The other rationale concerns income distribution issues. Even if private markets would function perfectly, the results may not constitute an optimal outcome or welfare maximizing. This is because the resulting distribution of real income may not correspond to the collectively preferred income or welfare distribution. If initial endowments, both material, e.g.

wealth and productive resources; or immaterial, e.g. education and health, are distributed unevenly among the population, the distribution of income resulting from private market processes may be uneven, including the possibility of failing to provide existence minima to a subset of the population.

It follows that one can distinguish between two broad objectives of government social security programs: (a) those aiming at modifying the *ex-ante* distribution of income; and (b) those aiming at raising economic efficiency resulting from market failures.[3] The difficulty facing policy makers is that these two objectives normally compete with each other. Achieving greater efficiency will lead to less equity and vice versa. A society's social welfare function will determine the optimal mix of equity and efficiency. This trade-off may be illustrated by a simple diagram (Figure 1). While the traditional view is that there is a trade-off between equity and efficiency over the whole range of possible outcomes, it has been argued more recently by the World Bank that there is a threshold of equity below which reducing income inequality does actually increase efficiency and facilitate economic development and growth. Equity and efficiency may, of course, be simultaneously improved for any outcome inside the transformation curve.

Figure 1   The Equity – Efficiency Trade-off

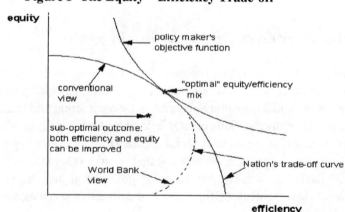

An additional reason underlying some social security programs is government "paternalism", based on the belief that individuals are not always the best judge of how to spend their incomes. Goods which the government feels tend to be under-consumed by individuals are called "merit goods". Subsidized provision of merit goods is often part of public welfare programs because the government feels that in households with tight budget constraints, the under-valuation of merit goods leads to their under-consumption. While easily distinguishable conceptually, the redistribution function, the insurance function and to a lesser degree, the merit goods rationale underlying social security programs is frequently intermingled and difficult to disentangle in practice.

Private contracting and trading will achieve pareto-optimal[4] outcomes only under fairly stringent conditions, which in the real world are seldom met. Violations of these conditions are called market failures.[5] The following section enumerates various market failures, providing a rationale for government-sponsored social security programs. Four components of social security are analyzed in detail, as the underlying rationale tends to differ somewhat between them: public health insurance, public old age (retirement) pension schemes, unemployment insurance and public welfare programs.

Health Insurance

The major market failures leading to sub-optimal outcomes in private markets for health care are externalities as well as imperfect and asymmetric information. Eradicating infectious diseases clearly implies major health and welfare benefits for the population at large. This is why most countries provide universal immunization and vaccination programs free of charge and often make them compulsory. In fact, this aspect of health care is usually not considered part of social security but of public health.

Positive external effects are less obvious in the area of personal health care, which in many countries, but not all, is considered part of social security. Government involvement in this area may take many different forms, ranging from publicly provided and administered universal health care as in the United Kingdom, government-run compulsory health insurance schemes with private provision of services as in Germany and France, or government financing of health care services for the elderly and the poor only, as in the United States.

As individual health care is in most respects a private service, one may indeed ask why the government needs to intervene in this market at all.

A common argument is based on a paternalistic attitude, i.e. that adequate health care is good for all citizens (a "merit good"), and that not all people are apt to realize this, thus requiring the government to make sure that adequate health care is indeed provided. In particular, it is possible that low-income people neglect personal health care with its long-term benefits, by giving priority to more urgent needs for food, clothing and housing, attending to medical needs only in emergency. This may lead to inefficiency whenever prevention is cheaper than cure. Another argument is "selective egalitarianism", i.e. the conviction that health care is a basic right that should be available to all citizens, just like the right to vote. The redistributive component of public health insurance is mainly introduced through a progressive contribution scheme (payroll taxes), while services provided are on an *ex ante* basis more or less equal for all persons covered.[6]

An additional obstacle facing private, voluntary provision of health insurance is the problem of adverse selection. If individuals have better information on their health status than the insurer, persons with higher health risk are more likely to opt for health insurance, driving up the average cost. If insurers respond with an increase in insurance premia, the insurance may become unattractive for another cohort of low-risk clients, who may then drop out of the scheme. In the extreme, this can lead to the disappearance of the market for the type of insurance services offered, depriving the population of sensible risk-sharing possibilities. This problem may be overcome by the introduction of compulsory and universal health insurance.

Old-Age Pension Schemes

Public pension schemes provide regular periodic income payments to retired persons in return for their compulsory contributions to the scheme during their professional life. In principle, private saving and well-functioning capital markets could fulfill an identical function, giving rise to the question whether and why government intervention is appropriate in this area. Petrie and Sturm (1991) argued that many individuals are unable to correctly assess their material needs in old age and tend to under-save thereby ending up in poverty in old age. If the government were to provide income transfers to poor people, such myopia may lead to transfers to individuals whose life-time income would have been adequate to provide for old age, but who chose not to save. In the extreme, this may entail perverse income redistribution from people with low life time income who pay taxes and provide for their own old age to old persons with higher life time incomes who receive welfare in old age because they decided to consume all earnings as and when received. [7]

Given the long-term character of a pension plan commitment, difficulties of individuals to properly evaluate and monitor private pension funds and their behavior, and the inability to correct past mistakes, it has also been argued that only the government can provide the desired degree of long-term security and stability, protecting individuals from bankruptcy of their pension insurance fund and from fraud.

Experience shows that transaction costs in compulsory public pension schemes are low relative to those in private pension plans. Under the latter, individual insurers spend considerable amounts of money competing for customers. It is, however, not clear whether this difference in cost represents a pure efficiency advantage of public pension schemes or whether it is the price to pay for greater diversity and choice which competitive private pension schemes offer. On the other hand, only public schemes are capable of insuring individuals against social upheavals like hyper-inflation and wars, by spreading of risk among generations.

Unemployment Insurance

Unemployment insurance provides individuals who lose their employment with income for a limited period of time. A commonly quoted rationale for unemployment insurance is that it improves the job matching process. Maintaining some income flow allows the unemployed individual to search for a job which best meets his preferences and abilities. Presumably, this facilitates a better overall allocation of labor resources in the economy, rather than forcing him to take the first best job which becomes available. Clearly, this argument holds for both public and private unemployment insurance, including self-insurance in the form of precautionary saving.

The efficiency rationale for public universal and compulsory unemployment insurance is that the private market will not provide such services, due to problems of moral hazard and adverse selection. The existence of unemployment insurance will make individuals more casual concerning job loss, increasing the incidence of unemployment (moral hazard) and driving up the average cost of insurance. This in turn, will induce people with a low probability or inclination to lose their job to drop out of the scheme unless it is compulsory. Thus, this raises the average cost per person covered even further (adverse selection). If insurers respond by increasing the insurance premia, this will induce another cohort of individuals with below average risk to opt out, and so forth, until the market for this particular type of insurance is eliminated.

In addition, it may be argued that individuals' job losses are not independent events. The incidence of unemployment rises during recessions, and since the frequency, duration and depth of recessions are difficult to predict, private providers of unemployment insurance risk bankruptcy. This risk does not exist, in practice, for the government, which has recourse to tax increases or deficit financing in case its unemployment insurance scheme becomes insolvent.[8] More generally, the government's ability to exert direct controls and to use compulsion, i.e. enforcing certain behavior through legislation, provides the means to deal with the moral hazard and adverse selection problems not normally available to private insurers.

Welfare Programs

Unlike public pension schemes, unemployment and health insurance where earmarked payroll taxes are collected in return for the benefits provided, social welfare is not based on any earmarked contributions.[9] It consists of need-based income transfers in either cash or kind. Thus, the principal motivation underlying social welfare programs is income redistribution. However, it may be argued that other motives are likewise present. Most people consider it unpleasant to be exposed to poverty in their entourage, implying that by reducing poverty, welfare schemes also have positive externalities. This argument is greatly strengthened to the extent that poverty reduction also reduces the incidence of crime and contagious diseases, as is often claimed.

Motivated by religious or other beliefs, many people consider it their moral duty to assist persons in need. This is the underlying reason why private charities, whose activities overlap considerably with public welfare, have a long tradition in most countries and long predate public welfare. But since the poverty relief resulting from private charity benefits all in the sense of reducing poverty levels, there is a tendency to "free ride", i.e. to rely on the action of others to relieve poverty. Thus, the private provision of poverty relief tends to be sub-optimal from a social welfare perspective. This is the rationale for the government to step in and to provide minimum thresholds of income, financed from compulsory tax revenues, obliging all citizens to share in the cost of poverty relief.[10]

Finally, to the extent that welfare transfers are delivered in kind, (e.g. in the form of foodstamps, housing subsidies or free health care), the redistribution rationale appears to coincide with some sort of merit good rationale, i.e. that the needy are unable to decide for themselves what constitutes the best way of spending their unearned income. The rationale for public welfare payments is most compelling in the case of recipients who are clearly unable to provide income for themselves, either because of chronic physical or mental sickness, or because of lack of maturity in combination with insufficient parental care.

Creating a Model Social Security System: Obstacles and Solutions

In the preceding section, various arguments were presented why government intervention may improve economic performance, both with respect to efficiency and equity outcomes. This point is illustrated in Figure 2. At point I, various market imperfections prevent the economy from operating on the utility possibility frontier, i.e. at a pareto-optimal point of production, where nobody can be made better of without making at least one other person worse off. Eliminating the pertinent production inefficiencies can move the economy to the utility frontier (point II),[11] but further government intervention may be required to achieve the social optimum (point III). The second fundamental theorem of welfare economics states that point III or any other point on the transformation curve, can be attained by the appropriate (re)-allocation of initial endowments if individuals' behavior is not affected by this redistribution.[12]

Figure 2 Government Intervention (the Pursuit of Efficiency and Equity)

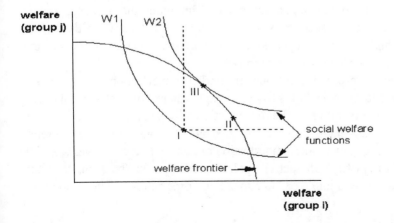

There is little that economic theory can tell about what the "best" distribution of income is, i.e. where point III is located on the utility frontier. This is a purely political or value judgement embodied in the social welfare function. It is properly addressed by political decision processes based on universal voting rights. Where economic theory may make a contribution, is by analyzing the effects which different methods of redistribution of either pre-tax income or initial endowments can have on individuals' incentives, and thus, the effect on efficiency.

Social Objectives and Government Failure

Given that income distribution objectives are an important motive behind the introduction and design of social security programs, a relevant question is what these distribution objectives are. Among OECD countries, there seem to be two different approaches to distribution objectives. One group of countries is concerned with the overall dispersion of individual incomes, considering that excessive income differences are detrimental to social cohesion. These countries' efforts to narrow income differentials rely heavily on a progressive tax system for revenue, and on various public expenditure programs including social security transfers to enhance the purchasing power of low income persons. The majority of North European countries, in particular the Scandinavian, have been favoring this approach. This has led to high shares of both government revenues and expenditures to GDP.

Another approach is favored mainly by the Anglo-Saxon countries. Policy makers are not so much concerned with income distribution *per se*, but primarily with people whose income is below a somehow defined poverty threshold, the lower tail of the income distribution.[13] The question may be posed as to which of the two alternative attitudes to the government's role in income distribution dominates may have an important influence on the design of the social security system, in particular the scale of the welfare programs and on the revenue side, the progressiveness of income and payroll taxes collected by the government.

The widespread incidence of market imperfections and failures in the real world in principle provides ample room for welfare enhancing government intervention. The introduction of comprehensive welfare state structures in many industrialized countries has been based on the assumption that identifying any market imperfection or distribution objective, would be sufficient to justify an active policy response in the form of either government regulation or tax/spending programs. The underlying assumption   has been that the government was run by benevolent civil servants, whose sole interest was the public good and who in general, had better access to information and pertinent analysis than private individuals, and thus were able to make better decisions on behalf of private persons and the public in general.

Actual experience with the performance of many social security programs and the comprehensive welfare state in general, has been disappointing in many instances. Consequently, policy makers have become more cautious in their assessment concerning the extent to which market failures may be effectively offset by government intervention. One of the reasons for the increased skepticism is the recognition that government officials do not necessarily, and indeed do not normally pursue exclusively the public good, but often have their own personal agenda and/or represent special interest groups. Fraud and corruption by civil servants are an extreme manifestation of this phenomenon.[14] In combination with limits imposed by the political process, this may prevent policy makers from achieving optimal results.

It is important to take these limitations to the effectiveness of government intervention into account when designing and implementing a national social security system. Several factors influence the government's capacity to operate such a system, including the technical competence of the country's civil servants, the material means at their disposal and the historical and cultural heritage of a nation. Thus, little can be said in general about the degree of optimal government involvement, and indeed it appears that opinions about this issue do not move uniformly in one direction, but seem to fluctuate over time.[15]

Nevertheless, a number of principles have gained acceptance in advanced countries aimed at limiting government failure and protecting government activity from inefficiency and/or abuse:

- The subsidiarity principle: No task which the private sector can assume properly should be taken over by the government;
- Any authority delegated to the government to execute a specific task or program should be subject to effective independent control;
- Effective control requires transparency of all government action. Therefore all activities need to be properly documented, and relevant information be made available to outside observers;
- Civil servants entrusted with the execution of government programs must be fully accountable to the general public or their legitimate representatives.

These principles which are applicable to most government activities in general, clearly will play an important role and provide relevant guidance in the design of public social security programs as well. To make them operative, they have to be translated into practical guidelines. For example, transparency requires the separation between the income redistribution function and the social insurance function of government intervention, a rule which is violated in most public insurance schemes as currently structured. Running clearly defined social insurance programs as independent funds financed from earmarked contributions will not only enhance transparency but will also facilitate financial control and monitoring the sustainability of the program.

The application of these principles may also have repercussions on the incentive structure of individuals covered by, and contributing to social insurance schemes. In fact, an additional reason for which social security programs have often fallen short of their aspired results, is that policy makers have failed to take into account individuals' reaction to the introduction of these programs, i.e. how government intervention affects individual incentive structures.

Negative Incentive Effects: Problems and Remedies

The introduction of social security programs may lead to the modification of individuals' behavior in various ways, depending on the nature of the program and how it is implemented. Much of the discussion about social security reform in OECD countries centers on the objectives of minimizing negative incentive effects of social security. Policy makers are most concerned about the reduction of incentives to work or to save, or more generally, any modification that tends to increase the probability that an individual will claim program -related services.[16]

When assessing the policy ramifications of these problems, it is important to note that they occur not only in the operation of social security programs, but that similar incentive problems affect private sector insurance programs and work incentives. Indeed, the private sector has developed various mechanisms to deal with the problem of moral hazard, which can be usefully applied to reduce incentive distortions of social insurance programs.

Public health insurance A major problem complicating efficient health care provision is caused by the consumers' imperfect knowledge of what constitutes an optimal medical treatment and their resulting reliance on experts, who in many cases are identical with the providers of the service, i.e. the treating physician.[17] In combination with universal public health insurance, this has led to an explosion of health care costs in many countries, which have shown much faster trend growth than national incomes, causing severe budgetary strains in those countries where health care is publicly financed.[18]

Interestingly, the same problem plagues countries where health insurance is predominantly privately run, e.g. the United States. The reason in both cases is that once a person is covered by health insurance, his marginal cost of service provision is well below the social marginal cost, i.e. the cost of producing the service. Patients, not knowing exactly what they need, want to play it safe and request any service they consider potentially helpful. As health care providers derive their income from supplying the service, they tend to pose little resistance to clients' demands and may even encourage them to increase the demand for their services.

There are various ways to deal with this excess demand problem. One is to permit corresponding oversupply, i.e. consumption of health services in excess of the social optimum. This is costly, and avoiding it requires the introduction of some sort of rationing system. This may be done by various types of co-financing, by direct controls on expenditures, or by introducing gate keepers.[19] Governments in OECD countries have experimented with these alternatives to curtail burgeoning health care expenditures. However, there is little agreement in what constitutes the most effective and *a fortiori* most efficient approach. As a consequence, public health care systems differ widely among countries. Nevertheless, based on past experience and experimentation, several principles have been elaborated providing useful guidelines for improving the effectiveness of public health care:[20]

- Rather than paying health care providers on the basis of sicknesses treated (fees for service), the insurer, i.e. the government, may offer contracts paying a fixed fee per person cared for (capitation fees), corresponding to the average health care cost for a large group of participants. Under this scheme, the provider maximizes his income by keeping his clients healthy, shifting the emphasis of medical care from cure to prevention.[21] This system may also be used to activate the efficiency enhancing forces of market competition by auctioning off contracts among competing groups of service providers.[22]

- Another way of substituting for the lack of market-driven efficiency improvements in public health care is for the government to collect detailed data on the cost of treatment for specific standardized sickness cases and medical procedures (Diagnostic Related Groups), and use this information to establish best practice or normal cost standards on the basis of which payments to providers are fixed. This should lead to specialization among providers and permit benefiting from economies of scale.

- Finally, the moral hazard problem in health insurance may be mitigated by experience rating, although if selective egalitarianism is the major motivation behind public health insurance, political resistance to such an approach may be strong. Similarly, making clients pay part of the cost incurred in treatment (co-payments) may help to discourage overuse of medical services and is used in most countries to some extent.

A serious incentive problem related to public health insurance is generated by the replacement of lost income in case of sickness, either from the public health insurance fund or through government regulation forcing the employer to continue payment of wages in case of sickness-related absence from work. This is a feature of social security in many OECD countries. There is substantial empirical evidence that the moral hazard created by these arrangements, increases the incidence of absenteeism attributed to sickness. It has turned out to be politically difficult and unpopular to prevent the abuse of such arrangements through direct administrative controls. Once such a system has been introduced, it is very difficult to scale it back or abolish it.

A radical solution to the limited information problem in health care would be to provide compulsory public health insurance only for very high cost (catastrophic) events, avoiding individuals to be ruined by medical emergencies. This would leave minor day-to-day medical expenditure to be covered by individuals out of their own pocket.[23] To avoid the problem of insufficient health care for children under this system due to parents' lack of income or concern, medical care could be provided free of charge for children up to a given age. In economic terms, this could be interpreted as a sort of public investment, just like compulsory free basic education.

Public pension schemes   In most countries, equity and efficiency motives are mixed up in the operation of the public pension schemes, either by design or by accident. As a result, the total value of lifetime contributions and benefits have little systematic relation. In addition, the system tends to lack transparency and is often subject to arbitrary changes by legislators, making it difficult for the individual to establish the relationship between contributions and benefits. In turn, this implies that contributions are largely considered equivalent to a general tax, while benefits are considered as unrelated government transfers. As a result, work incentives are distorted, both on account of the taxes collected and on account of the later pension transfers.

Another distortion feared by critics of public pension schemes as currently designed, is that they reduce private saving for retirement with no offsetting increase in public saving, since most public pension schemes are on a PAYG (Pay As You Go) basis, i.e. they are not funded. If this is so, the nation's physical capital stock is lower than it would be otherwise, implying a permanently lower level of income.[24] However, neither the theoretical argument nor the empirical evidence for the depressing effect of PAYG public pension schemes on national saving is conclusive.

A more tangible problem of PAYG pension schemes is that they are sensitive to unanticipated (at the time the schemes were introduced) changes in demographic trends, which may lead to large and arbitrary inter-generational income redistributions. Thus, the implicit public debt in many OECD countries from future pension obligations, is a multiple of the official public debt. Only drastic cuts in future pension benefits or corresponding increases in future pension contributions will prevent the system from running up public debt levels which are a multiple of these countries' GDP. This is basically a consequence of the lack of actuarial fairness of benefit-defined public pension schemes, in combination with the absence of funding.

The considerable experience gathered by countries who have recently undergone drastic reforms of their public pensions schemes, especially in Latin America, provides valuable lessons for other countries on how best to design an efficient and sustainable old-age pension system. The emerging consensus is that the optimal solution is a two-pillar system whose first pillar is a guaranteed universal minimum old-age income, which is means tested and financed from general revenue. The second pillar is a compulsory, funded, privately managed subject to strict prudential supervision and actuarially fair, i.e. contribution defined, old-age saving scheme. To accommodate different preferences among the population, e.g. degree of risk aversion, a third pillar consisting of voluntary contributions to the second pillar which raise pension entitlements, may be added to the scheme.

In such an ideal system, the first pillar looks after income re-distribution and old-age poverty relief where needed. The clear separation of this pillar from the insurance component of the scheme maximizes transparency of the system and thus reduces incentive distortions. The second pillar minimizes negative effects on work incentives by being actuarially fair, while the funding requirement reduces the risks of negative effects on national saving. Together with private management, the second pillar also offers the opportunity to promote the development of efficient domestic capital markets, a necessary condition for sound economic development in general. Finally, by making the second pillar compulsory, the system addresses the problem of individual myopia and moral hazard. Furthermore, a funded actuarially fair pension scheme adjusts automatically to large demographic changes, without imposing involuntary inter-generation income redistribution.[25]

Following recent reforms, the Australian old-age pension system comes close to the ideal scheme outlined above. The Swiss scheme has always displayed the essential characteristics of this model. While it is clear that developing countries cannot adopt such a sophisticated system overnight, it is important for them to keep the characteristics of such a desirable model in mind to avoid introducing elements which are incompatible with the ultimate aim of an efficient and sustainable scheme.

Unemployment insurance The major problem generated by unemployment insurance is moral hazard resulting from reduced employment incentives or unemployment traps. Many, though not all, OECD countries have witnessed a relentless increase in structural unemployment over the last quarter century. The combination of generous benefits relative to average earnings, and high effective marginal tax rates due to rapid withdrawal of other welfare benefit payments as the individual re-enters employment, are widely considered important contributors to this development.

There exist two alternative approaches to mitigate the detrimental incentive effects of unemployment insurance. The first is to keep both the level and duration of benefits low, which puts economic pressure on the individual to rapidly search for employment and to be less discriminating in the type of job he/she will accept. This is how the system is designed in the United States. Where such a system is considered to violate collectively agreed equity norms, benefit levels and duration may be kept high and entitlement duration long. However, this requires that the voluntary job search induced by economic necessity is replaced by administrative pressure and encouragement. This is the way the system is operated in Switzerland and a number of Scandinavian countries. Failure to encourage active job search by either of these methods, i.e. paying generous benefits, both with respect to level and duration, with little administrative pressure to look for employment, is bound to raise structural unemployment, as witnessed in many countries in the European Union.

The incentive problems created by unemployment insurance are often aggravated by the existence of a "black" labor market, providing employment opportunities outside the formal economy. This allows the unemployed to receive transfers from the unemployment insurance while engaging in gainful "black" employment at the same time. The tort inflicted to the public purse is twofold: (a) illegitimate receipt of unemployment benefits, and (b) avoiding income tax payments. Another potential misuse of unemployment insurance is for individuals to claim benefits, even though they have no intention to take active employment. Both these problems may be addressed by shifting from unemployment insurance to in-work- benefits, i.e. to make benefit receipt conditional on holding a job in the official economy.[26] To avoid this approach to entail the exclusion of workers not able to find any job, it is necessary to back in work benefits up with a residual unemployment benefit scheme or an employer of last resort, usually the public sector.[27] The overarching principle of this approach is to subsidize low-pay work, not leisure in the form of unemployment, whether voluntary or involuntary.

Since the majority of unemployed persons are low-skill workers, the in-work benefit approach is likely to be most successful if accompanied by a drastic reduction or abolition of an official wage floor, i.e. minimum wage, activating the demand for low-skill labor. The in-work benefits would safeguard against sub-standard incomes as opposed to earnings. From a more dynamic perspective, this approach makes it much easier for low-skilled workers to enter employment at the low-income level and to accumulate work skill, which allow him to raise his productivity and consequently, his income over time.[28]

Additional measures to reduce the negative incentive effects of unemployment insurance exist and are applied in some countries. The self-insurance element may be strengthened by introducing a "stand-down" period, i.e. start benefit eligibility only several days/weeks after a person has become unemployed. Moral hazard may be reduced on the employee's side by restricting benefit payments to firings such as no benefits in case of leaving a job voluntarily, and on the employers' side by introducing experience rating, i.e. make the level of insurance contributions dependent on the frequency of firing workers.

Public welfare programs Unlike public health care and unemployment benefits which conceptually are based on collective insurance contracts to which individuals contribute in return for financial aid in case the insured event materializes, welfare payments are straightforward transfers, which the government provides to eligible individuals.[29]

The major dilemma with social welfare is that the more effective it is in providing adequate income to the needy, the greater the moral hazard will be, i.e. the disincentive for beneficiaries to earn their own income thus losing their eligibility for welfare payments. The stronger the problem is, the more rapidly benefits are withdrawn in case the beneficiary receives income from an alternative source (typically employment), as is the case under stringent means testing of welfare benefits. In these situations the effective marginal tax rates on earned income can reach 100% or in some cases even more, creating so called "poverty traps". In extreme cases, specific welfare programs may even raise the incidence of the particular emergency they are designed to address.[30]

The poverty trap syndrome may be mitigated by introducing a negative income tax or similar arrangements already discussed in the previous section. This may reduce the effective marginal tax rate, but has the disadvantage of paying transfers to households above the poverty threshold, however defined. It is therefore considered fiscally expensive. Whether it indeed increases the fiscal cost of welfare, depends on how recipients respond to the improved incentives.

A negative income tax may at best, only partly resolve the incentive problems generated by welfare payments. It cannot reduce the negative incentives, e.g. on income earning activities, linked to the income effect of the welfare payment, rather than to the high effective marginal tax rate resulting from strict means testing. The income effect on incentive may only be influenced by varying the generosity of the welfare benefits, a direct trade-off between equity and efficiency, or by introducing direct control and obligations in return for welfare benefits. An example is participation in training or community work schemes, generally known as work-fare in the United States.

Securing Sustainability: Flexibility and Adaptation

The preceding discussion has been largely based on the concepts of static efficiency and equity. While static efficiency is a necessary condition for overall efficiency, policy makers must take into account the economy's development over time to achieve optimal outcomes. Evaluating equity from a life cycle perspective may lead to different policy conclusions and interventions, than looking at it at each point of time in isolation. In addition, a dynamic perspective is essential in order to make a social security system sustainable. Since future developments are inherently uncertain, it is important to develop institutions which can survive changing situations and external shocks, either by being not very vulnerable to such changes, or by allowing swift adjustment in case of unforeseen changes in the environment.

For example, failure to foresee demographic changes such as fall in fertility rates and increases in life expectancy, when public health insurance and pension schemes were designed or upgraded in many OECD countries after World War II, has led to serious budgetary problems. This is because it turned out to be extremely difficult politically to make the necessary adjustments in the schemes. Unless the political opposition to either lower benefits or increase contributions to the public PAYG pension schemes in many OECD countries can be overcome, the schemes as currently designed, imply implausibly large increases in public debt in the future. Such problems will not arise with funded contribution-defined pension schemes.

Lack of foresight is not the only reason which may render social security programs unsustainable. Smetimes it is outright political opportunism to obtain short-term political advantages which leads to unsustainable programs. The introduction of universal old-age income in New Zealand financed from general tax revenue in the early 1970s, is a case in point. Once programs have been introduced, it is difficult to scale them down or abolish them, as current reform efforts concerning excessively generous public sector pensions in many countries such as Brazil, Italy, etc., testify.

There is no absolute safeguard against either unforeseen developments or even political opportunism. However, a statutory obligation to secure long-term financing, including pre-specified procedures of how to adjust to widening gaps between revenues and expenditures in case of changing trends or adverse shocks, may facilitate timely adjustment by avoiding time-consuming political haggling. The Canadian unemployment scheme which mandates automatic premium increases in response to a trend rise in the insurance fund's deficit, is a case in point.[31]

When designing programs aimed at improving equity, it is important to take into account that incomes can vary considerably over a person's lifetime. It is more important and more sensible to aim at the equality of lifetime incomes than of individuals' incomes in a given arbitrary sub-period.[32] Thus, the decision to provide free health care to all persons above a certain age in the United States will imply perverse income re-distribution whenever tax payments of low income working people contribute to the financing of free medical services of persons whose lifetime income has been large in comparison. Similarly, subsidies to higher education financed from taxes on working class people will often subsidize persons whose lifetime income will be much higher than that of the persons whose taxes help to finance their education.[33]

The most effective distribution policy from a dynamic perspective may be to invest in basic education, thus enabling persons to earn higher future incomes by increasing their human capital and earning power. This is particularly true if the society's primary concern is to bring people above the poverty threshold. Some countries, e.g. Mexico, combine static programs to fight acute poverty with a dynamic approach to improve equity by tying income subsidies in kind such as food and health care for poor families to the school attendance of the children of such families.

Summary and Conclusions

Various market imperfections and failures provide opportunities for government intervention to increase economic efficiency through the introduction of various types of social insurance. In addition, the failure of market processes in combination with given initial resource endowments to generate an income distribution considered socially optimal, requires government intervention to achieve collective equity objectives.

However, government intervention is subject to government failure. Market failure or income inequality alone, is not a sufficient condition for justifying government intervention. It must also be shown that the government is indeed capable of remedying the identified shortcomings, and that the intervention results in a net increase in social welfare. With regard to the preceding condition, it is important to note that government intervention in many cases, introduces distortions in the incentive structures of economic agents. This in turn, may induce dead weight losses.

The risk of government failure may be reduced by strengthening the transparency of and accountability for government intervention. Transparency may be improved by separating the income transfer from the redistribution function of given social security programs. This in turn, is facilitated by administrating different programs as independent insurance funds with their own balance sheets and annual budgets, subject to periodic independent auditing procedures.

Separating and thus, making explicit the income transfer component of social security programs, also helps to reduce the incentive distortions resulting from these programs. It allows the individual to link the cost of these programs to benefits, and thus to interpret his/her contributions as insurance premia rather than part of the general income tax. To take account of differences in individual preferences, an optimal social insurance scheme should consist of a compulsory minimum level of insurance with options for voluntary supplementary insurance whenever the problem of adverse selection can be overcome. Whenever possible, the provision of services offered by social insurance should be contestable by private providers to subject public sector performance to competitive market pressure.

To reduce the risk of moral hazard resulting from welfare programs or service provision under public insurance schemes, it may be necessary for the government to use its prerogative for compulsion, i.e. to oblige individuals who receive transfers or make claims on the social insurance scheme, to undergo controls or conform to certain rules aimed at avoiding abuse of these schemes. This is important to maintain the public legitimacy and consequently, the sustainability of the schemes.

In securing equity objectives, the government should pay due attention to equity from a life cycle perspective. In designing policies in pursuit of equity, the emphasis should be on equity of process rather than of outcome. In this context, supporting basic education may, from a dynamic point of view, constitute an important tool for improving the future distribution of income and reducing large inequities in economic opportunity.

Notes

1 The term covers different activities in different countries. In the United States, it refers to the provision of pensions to retired persons and their surviving dependents. In Europe, it also comprises health insurance, unemployment compensation and various welfare programs. In this paper, the broader European definition is used.

2 Not all early socialist movements advocated state intervention. Some of them considered private associations capable of meeting the pertinent objectives, while the most militant saw government-sponsored social security as an unwelcome attempt to preserve the capitalist system.

3 Some countries distinguish between Social Security Programs which supposedly aim at overcoming market failures to provide an optimal mix and amount of services (usually insurance against various adverse developments), but do not try to redistribute income, and Welfare Programs, the explicit objective of which is to shift resources from the well-off to the poor and to provide a subsistence minimum for the latter.

4 Pareto-optimality is a concept that refers to situations in which no individual can be made better off without making at least one other individual worse off; this corresponds to the concept of "efficiency" in common economists' parlance.

5   For a systematic enumeration and explanation of market failures, see Stiglitz (1988) where this issue is discussed in general terms, not only as applied to social security.

6 High income people often supplement the public insurance scheme by private insurance in order to secure better service. In some countries, high-income person can opt out of the public scheme altogether, making it compulsory only for people with incomes below a certain threshold.

7 This is a specific example of "second best theory", which states that one government intervention (welfare payments) may require another government intervention (forced pension saving) to reduce the distortions resulting from the first intervention.

8 In economic terms, tax increases are similar to compulsory ex post premium increases, a solution not normally available to private insurers.

9 Not all countries finance public pensions, health and unemployment insurance through earmarked payroll taxes. In Australia and New Zealand, all social security expenditures are financed from general revenue, as are of course, welfare payments.

10 An alternative mode of government intervention to respond to these externalities is to subsidize private poverty relief, often in the form of tax deductibility of private charity contributions. This is indeed a policy instrument used in many countries in addition to public welfare payments. It introduces some degree of digression and tax payers' influence on how welfare spending is to be allocated.

11 Note that not all points on the utility frontier are superior to point I inside the frontier; only points to the right or above the social welfare function W1 will be preferred to I, and only points to the north-east of point I will make all individuals better off.

12 If the latter condition is not met, the redistribution of initial endowments will result in a modification of the transformation curve.

13 In principle, a further distinction could be made in this group between nations defining poverty by absolute standards and those defining it in relative terms (in relation to the nation's average income). In practice, only the latter approach has been used in the past, but more radical reform proposals in OECD countries are proposing the absolute poverty standard as the relevant concept guiding social security activity. Indexing benefits to consumer prices rather than average incomes is a partial switch from a relative to an absolute definition of poverty.

14 In the institutional literature, this is known as the "principal–agent problem", i.e. the difficulty in assuring that a hired agent always acts in the best interest of the person employing him. Principal-agent conflicts are not limited to the public sector but are widespread in the private sector as well, whenever ownership is separated from control (e.g. in share holder companies).

15 Hirschman (1982) attempts to explain such periodic changes in public opinion concerning the appraisal of the government's appropriate degree of involvement in the economy. Both public preferences and technological developments seem to influence such changes.

16 The complicated interaction of various welfare state interventions and their overall effect on social welfare has led to major efforts at modeling social welfare reform. An interesting example of these efforts, using a general equilibrium approach, is presented in Gelauff and Graafland (1994).

17 To some extent, this problem may be reduced by government-sponsored health care information and consumer education.

18 Clearly, there are other reasons which have also contributed to the rising share of health care expenditures in government budgets and national income. Changes in the age structure of the population, new expensive medical technologies, and last but not the least, the tendency to spend relatively more on health care as people get richer.

19 The term "gate keeper" refers to control of access to medical services by independent experts.

20 Oxley and MacFarlan (1995) give a comprehensive overview of ongoing efforts to control spending and increasing efficiency in the provision, both public and private, of health care.

21 This is the principle underlying the operation of so-called health maintenance organizations (HMO). One of the perceived shortcomings faced under this or similar systems is the need to limit patients' freedom in selecting their own physician.

22 In practice, the operation of such a system is complicated by large differences in medical needs among different individuals. Health insurance operators try to get around this problem by computing "risk adjustments" to the capitation fees offered, depending on the composition of the population covered by the provider. Obviously, the larger the groups covered by different HMOs, the less they tend to differ from the population average.

23 A variant of this approach is to establish a ceiling as percentage of disposable income, up to which each individual is expected to cover his personal health care expenditure. If expenditure exceeds this ceiling, public health insurance kicks in with remedial payments.

24 One of the most vociferous advocates of this thesis is Martin Feldstein of Harvard University.

25 A radical minimalist approach would modify the above scheme by introducing an opting out clause, allowing individuals to cease contributing to the second pillar once their cumulative savings are equivalent to the discounted present value of the minimum pension so that they will not claim welfare in retirement.

26 The work condition for benefit receipt may be replaced by a requirement to participate in job training programs aiming to upgrade skills and/or to re-train workers. This solution has been popular in Scandinavian countries, but critical observers have questioned its effectiveness.

27 To maintain the correct incentives, employment conditions and pay in such "residual employment schemes" needs to be less attractive than under alternative "competitive" employment.

28 This approach constitutes a variant of the negative income tax. It is currently being implemented in the United States as the "earned income tax credit" and in the United Kingdom as the "family benefit" and similar schemes in several other countries (OECD, 1998)

29 To the extent that welfare transfers are financed from general government revenue (including income taxes), one could consider that part of the income tax constitutes "poverty insurance", matched by the government's commitment to help people in need.

30 Murray (1985) claims that the aid to dependent children program in the United States has contributed to the rapid increase in the number of single teenage mothers.

31 These increases are lagged and phased in gradually so as to avoid pro-cyclical behavior.

32 The reason is that individuals facing a very volatile income stream may use precautionary savings as a buffer to smooth their consumption stream.

33 The net effect on equity of such an arrangement will of course depend on other things as well, in particular on the progressivity of the income tax.

References

Estelle, J. (1998), 'New Models for Old-Age Security: Experiments, Evidence, and Unanswered Questions', *The World Bank Research Observer*, Vol 13, No. 2.

Gelauff, G.M.M. and Graafland, J.J. (1994), *Modelling Welfare State Reform*, North-Holland, London and Tokyo.

Gramlich, E. M. (1998), *Is it time to Reform Social Security?*, University of Michigan Press, Ann Arbor, MI.

Grolier Inc. (1992), *The Academic American Encyclopedia*, (Electronic Version), Danbury, CT.

Haveman, R. (1996), *Reducing Poverty while Increasing Employment: A Primer on Alternative Strategies, and a Blueprint*, OECD Economic Studies No 26, Paris, France.

Hirschman, A.O. (1982), *Shifting Involvements: Private Interest and Public Action*, Princeton, New Jersey.

Leibfritz, W., Rosevaere, D., Fore, D. and Wurzel, E. (1995), *Ageing Populations, Pension Systems and Government Budgets - How do They Affect Saving?* OECD Economics Department Working Paper 156, Paris, France.

MacFarlan, M. and Oxley, H. (1996), *Social Transfers: Spending Patterns, Institutional Arrangements and Policy Responses*, OECD Economic Studies No 27, Paris, France.

Maddison, A. (1984), 'Origins and Impact of the Welfare State, 1883–1983', *Banca Nazionale del Lavoro Quarterly Review*, No 148.

Murray, C. (1984), *Losing Ground: American Social Policy, 1950–1980*, Basic Books, New York.

_____. (1998), *Benefit Systems and Work Incentives*, Paris, France.

Nye, J.S. Jr., Philip, D. Zelikow, D. and King, C. (1998*)*, *Why People Don't Trust Government*, Harvard University Press, Cambridge, MA.

OECD. (1988), *Ageing Populations - The Social Policy Implications*, Paris, France.

_____. (1988), *Reforming Public Pensions*, Paris, France.

_____. (1988), *The Future of Social Protection*, Paris, France.

_____. (1991), *Private Pensions and Public Policy - The Issues*, Notes by the Secretariat (SME/MAS/PP(91)1), Paris, France.

_____. (1997), *Making Work Pay – Taxation, Benefits, Employment and Unemployment*, Paris, France.

Oxley, H. and MacFarlan, M. (1995), *Health Care Reform: Controlling Spending and Increasing Efficiency*, OECD Economic Studies No 24, Paris, France.

Petrie, M. and Sturm, P. (1991), *Old Age Income Maintenance - Basic Problems and Alternative Responses*, OECD Economics Department Working Paper No. 100, Paris, France.

Prebble, M. and Rebstock, P. (eds.) (1992), *Incentives and Labor Supply: Modeling Taxes and Benefits*, Institute of Policy Studies, Wellington.

Stiglitz, J.E., (1988), *Economics of the Public Sector*, 2nd ed., Norton, New York.

US Social Security Administration. (1997), *Social Security Programs Throughout the World* Washington, D.C.

Van den Noord, P. and Herd, R. (1993), *Pension Liabilities in the Seven Major Economies*, OECD Economics Department Working Paper 142, Paris, France.

9 Institutional and Regulatory Issues in Pension System Reforms: Country Experiences and Policy Options

Iyabode Fahm

Introduction

The focus of this paper is on building and sustaining the institutional capacity for successful pension reform, particularly in African countries. In this regard, it is a contribution to the burgeoning debate on how Africa takes care of its old. The problem of old-age poverty is rarely the focus of policy in African countries, mainly because of the low life expectancy. However, changes in demographic trends occasioned by better health facilities, suggest that a grayer population is in the making. In addition, recent macroeconomic reforms and public sector downsizing has pushed pension reforms to the forefront of social policy agenda. Therefore, it becomes necessary to address research issues affecting the maturing population, both in order to understand the dynamics of poverty in the society as well as be able to make relevant policy prescriptions.

Some of society's most vulnerable groups may be found in the ranks of the old. In most African countries, only a small percentage of the old is taken care of through pension income accumulated while working in the formal sector. The larger majority relies on traditional safety nets, having spent their working life outside the formal sector. Pension reforms have important implications on poverty alleviation because pension income is a major link to the two main approaches to poverty alleviation, namely, economic growth and income redistribution. Experiences of emerging economies suggest that sizeable reduction in poverty is often achieved through the use of policies that stimulate growth and employment. With employment, income is provided for the poor, and with redistribution of income, those who are unable to benefit directly from the growth in employment, are taken care of.

This paper examines the pension system of Nigeria, Tunisia and Zambia against the experiences of some OECD and Latin American countries. Theoretical and institutional issues in pension policy are analyzed. A discussion of the experiences of Nigeria, Tunisia and Zambia follows after which international experiences of France, Japan, UK, USA, and two Latin American countries, i.e. Argentina and Chile, are featured. The paper concludes with recommendations on building the institutional capacity necessary for pension reforms. The main questions answered are:

- What should be the proper framework for the operation of pension schemes in African countries?
- In the absence of pension coverage, what poverty alleviation policies can be pursued for the benefit of the informal sector?
- What should be the proper role of government?
- How should African countries build the capacity that will sustain whatever reforms are put in place?

Theoretical and Institutional Issues in Pension System Reforms

Pension reform debates often revolve around the mode of financing, benefit administration and regulatory framework. The debate has been largely informed by the changes in demographic trend in advanced countries which affect the fiscal equilibrium in pension funds. In general, major issues of consideration in the design of pension schemes are income replacement and redistribution, fiscal and actuarial viability and efficiency.

Financing of pension plans is often based on a choice between defined contributions and general revenue financing. Sometimes, the expected benefit becomes an issue in the choice of the financing method. It has been argued for example that flat rate benefits should be financed from general revenue, since benefits are not dependent on income levels. Earnings-related benefits, on the other hand, depend on the level of contribution. Under the first option, the twin objectives of pension income, i.e. income replacement and redistribution, are satisfied. In reality, most public pension systems are a mixture of the two forms of financing, even if they may differ in the manner of funding.

Table 1 Demographic indicators, circa early 1990s

	Percentage of Population			Dependency Ratio	
	Over 60 years	Over 65 years	Over 75 years	Over 65	Over 60
Africa					
Nigeria	3.8	2.3	0.5	4.4	9.8
Tunisia	6.5	4.1	1.2	7.0	14.3
Zambia	3.6	2.3	0.6	4.7	10.0
OECD					
France	18.9	13.8	6.5	20.8	35.3
Japan	17.3	11.9	4.7	17.1	30.9
UK	20.8	15.7	6.8	24.0	38.8
US	16.6	12.3	5.0	18.7	30.3
Latin America					
Argentina	13.1	9.0	3.2	14.8	26.9
Chile	8.7	5.9	2.1	9.3	17.0

Source: World Bank (1994).

In fully funded schemes which all defined contribution plans are, contributions are invested and benefits linked to asset performance. The Pay As You Go (PAYG) scheme on the other hand, finances current pension obligations from current contributions and/or budget transfers. The advantage of a PAYG system is that benefits are available for distribution in a start-up pension program, and it improves solidarity among generations. Funded systems lack the element of redistribution. In addition, in an economy that lacks macroeconomic stability, capital markets may not be sufficiently developed to handle long-term investments efficiently. This applies very much to African countries, where the markets are limited in scope and the economies are in a state of flux, with wild swings in interest and inflation rates. Such volatility may not be conducive for long-term investments.

Benefit administration is often determined through a statutory retirement age and a minimum contribution period. In countries with older population like the OECD countries (Table 1) retirement age is usually in the early to mid-60s. However, in African countries with younger population and lower life expectancy, retirement age may be as low as 45 in some cases. Some countries have different age requirements for males and females, based on the assumption that women have higher life expectancy, and are expected to draw pension income for longer periods than males. The demographic make-up of a country has important implications on fiscal equilibrium in a pension system because a high percentage of older population means larger pension expenditure. In addition, the ratio of older people to working-age people, i.e. old-age dependency ratio, is important for the determination of financial equilibrium in unfunded schemes. Public pension schemes in advanced countries have been under considerable pressure in recent times because of the demographic transition pattern, which results in an increasing ratio of older to younger persons as fertility and mortality rates decline. Demographic projections for African countries suggest that this will be the trend as health facilities and general quality of life improve (Table 2).

Table 2 Projected percentage of population over 60 years: 1990 - 2050

	1990	2000	2010	2020	2030	2050
Nigeria	3.8	4.0	4.4	5.1	6.5	11.7
Tunisia	6.5	7.3	7.4	10.5	14.9	23.1
Zambia	3.6	3.2	3.0	3.4	4.4	8.9

Source: World Bank (1994).

Most pensions are indexed to the minimum wage or the inflation rate. The importance of indexation lies in the fact that if pensions are fixed in nominal terms, their real value declines at inflation times. In the absence of indexation and with high inflation rate, most pensioners slip to below the poverty line. This is more so in Africa where *ab initio*, benefits are low and the macroeconomic environment is unstable.

The role of government *vis-à-vis* the private sector is a major issue in pension reform. Most countries have a multi-pillar pension system made up of a general publicly administered mandatory plan with universal coverage of the working population, a second pillar of occupational schemes and a third pillar made up of personal savings and investments, some of which are linked to income tax benefits. In most countries of Africa, coverage in the occupational scheme is very limited, mainly because the majority of the labor force is either employed in the informal sector or is in the non-wage economy. Except for countries like Tunisia, very few countries have extensive publicly managed systems. Most have a provident fund system, and some, like Nigeria, are converting from provident fund to the social insurance system. Some occupational plans and private pension investment exist, albeit limited in scope.

Support system in the absence of formal pension, is extensive in Africa. The key basis of income support in old age is the extended family. Children often bear the responsibility of providing for their aged parents and siblings on a regular basis. A study of the old in Nigeria shows that 97% of the urban old and 93% of the rural old reported receiving financial and material assistance from family or kin (Ekpeyong *et al*, 1986).

In addition to the extended family system, community organizations often develop in the urban areas, and these contribute money to provide some infrastructure in their communities especially during their annual homecoming festivals. There are also organizations based on religious ties which provide for the poor through voluntary contributions and services. Moslems often take care of the poor through *zakat, a* religious tax earmarked for the needy, and *sadak'a,* a substantial donation decided by and for the purpose determined by the donor.

While traditional systems work well in the absence of market-based alternatives, as in the case of those outside the formal economy, there is nothing systematic about them. Thus, income redistribution from the rich to the poor cannot be efficiently handled within the framework. In addition, the income transferred may not be enough, and in any case, there is no certainty. Moreover, as society becomes more differentiated and complex, such unorganized systems cannot be expected to survive. However, to the extent that they contribute significantly to the reduction of old age poverty, and given the impossibility of integrating certain segments into the formal economy, they continue to be relied upon. They could be integrated into reforms in the short term, with a view to formalizing as the labor market condition changes.

The regulation of pension schemes has become a major issue as the movement towards privately provided pension plans starts gaining momentum. Supervision of most public plans falls under a department of the government. With the increasingly dominant role played by pension funds in the mobilization of savings and investment, extensive regulations have become the norm in most countries. Chile's privately managed pension system is one of the most regulated in the world. Some regulations are designed to provide participants with the best information about pension funds, while others are to prevent pension funds from engaging in speculative investments. Considering the constraints under which existing plans operate, if the use of private pension providers becomes extensive in

African countries, only few will have the technical and administrative capacity to supervise and regulate efficiently.

The foregoing review of institutional issues in pension reform has important implication on the reform of pension systems in African countries. Countries will have to choose the type of funding, benefit administration and regulatory framework that best suits their current level of development, demographic make-up and labor market conditions. These are by no means easy choices, but with the benefit of the experience of advanced countries, informed decisions may be taken.

The Experiences of Nigeria, Tunisia and Zambia

In this section the experiences of Nigeria, Tunisia and Zambia are examined. While all three countries have schemes offering survivorship and disability benefits in addition to pension, the focus of this study is on pension only. The state of the pension system in these countries reflects their colonial heritage and peculiar socio-economic circumstances. For example, Tunisia like most North African countries with a long history of association with European markets, has a well developed social security system with comprehensive coverage. On the other hand, Nigeria and Zambia have relatively underdeveloped systems, mainly because their systems arose out of the need to provide for the small crop of expatriates working in the former colonies.

Nigeria

Structure   The pension system in Nigeria is very fragmented, with no single coordinating body for all the pension plans. In the government sector, the Federal Civil Service had a pension scheme that was non-contributory until 1996 as it was financed from the general revenue. Each of the quasi-government organizations, autonomous units such as the Central Bank, the Railway Corporation, utility companies, universities, research institutes and the Ports Authority, has its own separate pension plan. The 36 state governments and local government authorities administer their own pension plans, mostly treated as expenditure items in the annual budget. In the private sector, the only general pension plan available is the National Social Insurance Trust Fund (NSITF), formerly known as the Nigeria Provident Fund (NPF). In addition, there are company-sponsored schemes in a fairly large section of the formal private sector. Most of these schemes are negotiated between management and unions, with some of them non-contributory. Finally, some insurance companies recently commenced the operation of private pension investment. Overall, the NSITF estimates that there are more than 500 different pension schemes in Nigeria.

Coverage   Public sector-based plans cover all employees in the Federal Civil Service, quasi-government corporations, government parastatals, state and local governments pension plans. In addition, government autonomous units have been directed to cease membership to the Federal Civil Service Pension plan. The NSITF estimates that the combined public sector pension scheme, including those of autonomous agencies, has a current working membership of about 3,000,000 and existing pensioners number over 1,000,000.   Private sector-based plans include the Nigeria Social Insurance Trust Fund, membership of which is mandatory for companies with 5 or more workers. Self-employed persons join voluntarily, while public servants, diplomats, and expatriates covered under equivalent foreign program, are exempted from participation. From 1961 when the NPF was established until the beginning of 1994 when the assets were inherited by the NSITF, there were 5,680,475 cumulative members. In addition to the NSITF, there are self-administered company-based schemes in most parts of the formal private sector. Employer-sponsored retirement schemes are estimated to have about 2.5 million members. The combined membership of private and public plans is estimated to be about 7 million, less than 7% of a labor force of 47 million.

Funding   In January 1996, contributions for those who joined the service after January 1993 became mandatory. However, the payment of pensions and gratuity to federal and state civil servants continues to be charged out of the consolidated revenue. Some autonomous organizations, research institutes and educational institutions have funded schemes with private insurance companies. For the NSITF, contribution is 2.5% from the employee and 5% from the employer on the first 48,000.00 Naira (about $600.00) of annual basic salary. There is no standard or uniform contribution in company-based plans, as contributions of employers and employees are usually negotiated internally. They are usually comparable with what obtains in the public service, but because wages are considerably higher, they are deemed more generous.

Eligibility requirement   To be eligible for benefits in the public service, an employee must have served for at least 5 years in the case of lump sum benefit and at least 10 years for pensionable income. Voluntary retirement age is 45 years, while compulsory retirement age is 60 years or 35 years of service, whichever comes first, except in the judicial services where retirement age ranges from 62-65 years. The eligibility requirements are similar in most of the quasi-government organizations. Participants in the NSITF who have reached the retirement age of 60 years, have 120 months of contribution and are retired from regular employment, qualify for a retirement grant and a monthly pension income. A member who has reached retirement age and has no less than 12 months of contribution qualifies for a lump sum retirement grant.

Benefits   The public service retirement benefits are a lump sum gratuity and pension for qualifiers. Employees with more than 5 years but less than 10 years of service obtain a lump sum payment of between 100% to 140% of terminal salary. Employees with 10 – 35 years of service obtain a lump sum payment of between 100 – 300% of final terminal salary, and an annual pension of between 30 – 80%. Benefits in the NSITF is 30% of final average monthly insurable earnings plus 1.5% of those earnings for each 12 months of contributions paid or credited over the first 120 months. In addition, a contributor obtains a lump sum amount equal to final monthly contributions multiplied by the number of months of contributions. Minimum pension payable is 80% of national minimum wage, while the maximum pension is 65% of final average monthly contributions.

Overview   The main problems of the Nigerian pension system are fragmentation, lack of systematic policy on benefits and contributions, and absence of regulation. Another problem is the lack of portability, as years of service accumulated outside of the unified public service are not countable elsewhere, while in the private sector, pensions are firm-specific. In addition, the ceiling on contribution and benefit, results in very low income for pensioners, which is compounded at high inflation times when the value of pension income is eroded.

   The lack of a systematic pension policy sometimes results in pension benefits being increased by administrative fiat, without serious actuarial analysis of the financial implications. Such actions usually create fiscal disequilibrium for agencies, especially in the public sector, with the result that many are not able to meet their pension obligations. Finally, there is little linkage between benefits and contributions. For example, period spent in acquiring education is counted towards pension, and with a pension qualification age of 45, periods on pension income often exceed periods on wage income in the public service.

In general, the private sector and autonomous agency schemes seem to be well managed, to the extent that much of the negative publicity of pensioners is that of public sector pensioners. In addition, the NSITF seems to have overcome some of the shortcomings of the NPF era, and is performing better, within the limits of its enabling decree. By the time the assets of the NPF were transferred to the NSITF in 1994, it inherited an organization with low benefits and contributions, low compliance rate, poor record keeping and poor investment policy. The NSITF seems to have rectified some of these problems in the short period of its existence. The exposure to government securities has been greatly reduced, and investment income went up by 17% in the first year (see Table 3). In addition, contribution jumped to 79% in the first year. With adequate legal backing, the NSITF was able to enforce compliance and contribution from litigation and warning amounted to 2% of total contributions in 1996.

The major problem observed with the NSTIF is the low contribution rate which, inevitably, results in low benefits. The implication of this is that contribution and benefits are not impressive, and the income provided barely exceeds the poverty level. In addition, it suffers from administrative and management problems. The Ministry of Labour and Productivity, its supervisory agency, is barely able to supervise effectively. The investment portfolio is too skewed towards real estate (see Table 3) and some equity investments are made in non-publicly quoted companies. Finally, no audited accounts have been available since 1995.

However, the least efficient of the pension schemes in Nigeria is the public sector scheme. As a result of this, government agencies are always at loggerheads with their pensioners. In addition, because of low public service remuneration, and the fact that the benefits are not indexed, inflation has eroded the real value of retirement income for a majority of pensioners. Tor most of them, the pension benefits are not worth the trip to the pension agency.

In the light of the above, the pension schemes with the larger coverage in Nigeria are not in a position to protect the old and redistribute income among the different economic groups. Indeed, redistribution seems to favor the rich, as some schemes have contributions based on wage salary alone while benefits are based on terminal wage salary, plus non-wage cash benefits. The difference between the two sometimes runs as high as 400% of wage salary. Apart from the fact that such a contribution/benefit ratio is actuarially infeasible in a fiscally sound system, it encourages the joining of certain services late so as to take advantage of such generous pensions.

Clearly, the pension system stands to gain a lot by instituting a comprehensive multi-pillar system. The issues of retirement age, contribution and benefits have to be addressed in a more systematic manner, rather than the current *ad hoc* methods used. An increase in retirement age from 45 to 55 in the public sector is long overdue, and so is an actuarial study of government's pension obligations.

The NSITF may be strengthened to form the mandatory basic pillar, which will cover all wage earners in the formal sector, public and private, based on a fully funded defined contribution system. A special scheme may be established for informal and agricultural sector workers who do not have steady earnings profile, with proportional pension benefit based on the total number of contributions. In addition, the 48,000.00 Naira ceiling on contributions should be removed, while benefits should be in multiples of the minimum wage. Existing firm-specific pension schemes may form the basis of a second occupational pillar, to be organized along trade union lines. In this case, one or two central organizations, like those in France, may be formed to serve as umbrella organizations for the existing firm-based schemes. This should take care of the problem of portability and ease labor mobility. Finally, private providers of pension who currently operate as regular insurance companies, may be subjected to a stricter regulatory environment in line with the practice in countries with private pension providers.

Tunisia

Structure   The Tunisian social security system which ranks as one of the most advanced in Africa, recently has undertaken major reforms aimed at improving on the previous level of coverage, income distribution and job creation. The pension system is a partially-funded, defined-benefit system administered by two main organizations: the *Caisse Nationale de Retraite et de Prevoyance Sociale* (*CNRPS*) which covers all employees in the public sector, and the *Caisse Nationale de Securite Sociale (CNSS)* which covers employees in the private sector. Some of the sub-schemes under *CNSS* are the *Caisse d'Assurance Vieillesse, Invalidite et Survie (CAVIS)*, which operates seven schemes for private sector employees, while the *Caisse de Retraite et de Prevoyance de Services Publics de L'Electricite, Gaz et du Transport (CREGT)* is for employees of public utilities.

Table 3 Membership, investment income and portfolio of the NSITF

	1994	1995	1996	1997
	(In Percent of total investment)			
Federal Govt Stock	8.89	6.21	1.01	0.69
Loan Stocks and Debentures	25.20	14.75	7.37	4.13
Equities	21.27	21.90	33.09	36.19
Bank Deposits	4.63	11.41	6.86	0.79
Treasury Instruments	7.84	7.50	7.38	0.71
Real Estate	32.17	38.24	44.29	57.16
	(Units)			
Registered Contributors	653,257*	83,140**	128,312**	99,794**
Contributions Collected***	151,329,503	680,290,000	953,970,000	1,115,760,000
Benefits Paid***	n.a.	6,839,950,000	8,814,000,000	15,537,000
Investment Portfolio***	1,403,753,586	1,775,310,000	2,186,410,000	3,110,200,000
Total Investment/ Investment Income	10.3	9.1	15.2	12.5
Total Investment	100	100	100	100

*Includes former NPF members.
** New regustration only.
*** In Nigerian Naira.
Source:NSITF Annual Report, various years.

Coverage   The *CAVIS* operates a general scheme that covers employees in the private sector. In addition, there are six other schemes for self employed people in the non-agricultural sector, namely, the basic scheme for agricultural workers, the improved scheme for agricultural workers, the scheme for independent farmers, and the scheme for Tunisians overseas. Finally, there is a scheme for non-agricultural employees earning in excess of the minimum wage. The *CNRPS* operates a main scheme for public sector employees and three schemes for members of government, parliament and governors. The *CREGT* covers employees in the electric, gas and public utilities. Eighty seven percent of participants in all the pension schemes belong to the *CAVIS* general scheme and the *CNRPS*. The public sector scheme has a current coverage of about 700,000 workers. All the private sector schemes under the *CNSS* have a membership of 1,100,000.

Funding   Contributions are based on pensionable salary, years of service, a vesting period and retirement age. As a result, they vary considerably from one scheme to the other. For the *CNSS* for example, non-agricultural private sector employees pay 3.25% of their earning, while agricultural workers pay 1.75% of the agriculture minimum wage or 2.5% of earnings. Farmers contribute 7% of profits, and non-agricultural self-employed pay 7% of earnings. Migrant workers not insured abroad contribute 5.25%. The employer portion of these contributions are 2.5% of payroll for non-agricultural self-employed, 3.5% of earnings for agricultural workers, plus 4.25% deduction in advance to the social security program to cover short-term benefits. One of the recent reforms undertaken by the government was to put responsibility on the employer's part to cover contributions for newly employed fresh graduates in the private sector for the first five years. The effect of this was to ease the financial burden of firms as well as stimulate employment. In 1996, the contribution rates in the *CNRPS* were increased from 6% to 8.2% of salary for the insured and from 12% to 13% for employers.

Eligibility requirement   Employees covered by the plan draw pension after the age of 60 or at age 50 with proportional pension, if unemployed for six months for economic reasons or prematurely aged, provided they have put in fifteen years of service. Public sector employees can retire at 55 years of age provided they have accumulated 35 years of service. Employees in the public service are expected to have worked for a minimum of 15 years, 10 years for manual workers in the public service and private sector employees and 25 years for utility employees. The length of service required for proportional pensions is considerably lower. Full pension is payable at 50 years with 180 months of contribution to working mother of 3 children.

Benefits   The range of benefits varies from scheme to scheme. Private sector employees get a basic 40% of average earnings in the last 3 or 5 years (whichever is higher) plus 0.5% for every 3 months of contribution beyond 120 months. The maximum pension is 80% of earnings, or 6 times the minimum wage, whichever is higher, while the minimum pension is 2/3 of the minimum wage. Workers with more than 5 but less than 10 years of contribution obtain proportional pension, subject to a minimum of 50% of the minimum wage. Public sector employees on the other hand have a maximum pension of 90% of gross pensionable income.

Overview   The Tunisian pension system is one of the few in the developing world that meets the challenges of old age poverty and income distribution. In the last decade, efforts have been made to reform the system to take care of the problems endemic in the old system. Prior to the reforms, the fragmentation of the Tunisian system created a lot of distortions in the labor market in particular and social policy in general. Contributions were low relative to benefit, and evasion was rampant. In addition, there was little coordination between the public and private sector schemes and poor investment plagued the system, resulting in problems of financial disequilibrium. Like similar organizations in less developed countries, the funds are expected to hold a sizeable amount of government instrument in their portfolio, most of which yield negative rates of return.

Indexation is another problem in Tunisia. In the public sector, pensions are indexed to wage inflation, thereby protecting against the adverse effect of inflation on the real value of retirement income. The private sector pension is only indexed to the minimum wage, i.e. minimum pension is at least 2/3 of minimum wage. However, the maximum pension does not have such a protection, thereby being susceptible to erosion by inflation.

However, most of these issues have been addressed in the reforms that took place in the 1990s. For example, the calculation of pension benefit is now based on total salary and benefits. In addition, pensions benefits are now linked to movements in the prevailing wage. To take care of the problem of non-portability, contributions in the *CNRPS* and *CNSS* can now be merged. Reforms are undertaken on regular basis to create balance between contributions, benefits, retirement ages, etc., between the two funds. The effect of the reforms is that coverage increased from 52% in 1986 to about 77% of the working population in the mid-1990s. In addition, the financial health of the funds has improved considerably, with social security services provided increasing from US$295m to US$710m from 1987 to 1996.

While the two main schemes in Tunisia enjoy financial stability arising from the reforms, forecasts indicate that things may worsen in the next ten years for several reasons. In the first place, the change in the calculation of benefits from basic salary to both basic salary and benefits is bound to exert some financial pressure on the funds, as the system matures. Secondly, a wave of movement from the public to the private sector has been on the increase, with the recruitment of a large number of public sector workers into the private sector, most of which are pension-eligible. Future reform efforts in Tunisia should address the issue of regulation and institutional capacity, as well as the impending system maturation, which if not properly handled, may lead to fiscal disequilibrium.

Zambia

Structure   In Zambia, as in most developing countries yet to reform their pension system, the system is fragmented. The three statutory schemes in operation are the National Provident Fund (ZNPF), the Civil Service Pension Fund (CSPF), a funded defined benefits scheme, and the Local Authority Superannuation Fund (LASF), a defined-benefits scheme. In addition to these, there are occupational schemes, separate for each organization but supervised by the Zambia State Insurance Corporation (ZSIC).

Coverage   More than 500,000 workers, representing about 90% of the formal sector labor force are covered by the three main pension schemes. The ZNPF covers all private sector employees, agricultural workers, domestic servants in rural areas, and apprentices. Casual workers, the self-employed and workers in cooperatives are excluded. Voluntary affiliation is allowed for some categories of rural workers and others exempted from mandatory coverage. The CSPF provides retirement pensions to non-contractual civil servants, armed forces and teachers. The LASF covers employees of all local authorities, the Zambia Electric Supply Corporation, the National Housing Authority and LASF personnel. In addition to the statutory schemes, there are other non-statutory schemes, such as the ZNIC, which covers mainly the private sector, and some parastatals and the Mukuba Pension Fund.

Funding   The ZNPF operates as a compulsory retirement savings plan. Employees pay 5% of their earnings per month, while lower rates are applicable to domestic workers in the urban areas and others earning less than 67.5 per day. Employers contribute 5% of the payroll, or higher in the case of low-wage earners. The maximum monthly contribution on an account can not exceed K15,000.00 a month. For the CSPF, contributions of 7.5% each are payable monthly by the employers and employees, based on the pensionable monthly salary. The LASF is a defined-benefit plan based on a contribution rate of 10% for the employees and 23% for the employers. The private pension funds managed by the ZSIC have contribution rates that vary usually between 12.5% from the employer and 6.25% from the employee.

Eligibility requirements   Contributors to the ZNPF qualify for old-age benefit at age 50 and upon retirement from regular employment, or emigration from Zambia. For those who joined the ZNPF before April 1,

1973, the respective age is 50 and 45 years. The civil service pension is based on a retirement age of 55 years, with a minimum of 10 years service. Early retirement at any time within 5 years of retirement age is also permitted, although payment of pension for retirement prior to age 55 is borne by the government. In the LASF, retirement age was recently reduced from 60 to 55 years, subject to a minimum of 10 years service. Pension benefit is computed based on the last annual salary. For most of the private pension scheme, pension age is usually 55 years, and if earlier, there is an actuarial benefit reduction.

Overview   As with most less developed countries, the pension system in Zambia has a low coverage rate. The estimated labor force is 4 million, but combined coverage of all the schemes is about 12%. Apart from the private pension plans run by the insurance companies, Zambia has yet to have a system that successfully delivers on the goal of providing for retirement. Management problems and institutional incapacity beset the ZNPF. Required contributions were stagnant from 1966 to 1995, in the face of inflation and serious macroeconomic dislocations. As a result, the benefit level has also been very low. This is partly due to low returns on investment, inflation and poor administration. The problem is complicated by the institutional framework which mandates an investment of at least 50% in government instruments, and another 35% in parastatals, most of which are non-performing financially. According to the 1994 World Bank report, the average annual investment return for the ZNPF was -23.8% for the period 1980 – 1988.

The CSPF also suffers from similar fate. Between 1991 and 1997, there were no employers' contributions made by the government. On the contrary, about $186 million of its reserves were borrowed by the government (Queisser *et al.*, 1997). With little scope for investments, investments in government instruments and real estate dominate their portfolio.

All the funds suffer from low compliance, low investment income, increasing expenditure and poor administration. Sometimes, benefits are delayed for up to 1 year, and there are up to 5 years of backlog in updating contributors information.

Pension reform in Zambia is long overdue. The provident fund should become an optional savings plan, which may be converted to an annuity at retirement. A fundamental reform addressing issues related to coverage, investment, membership and benefit administration, needs to be undertaken.

Comparison of the Three Countries' Pension Systems

The problem with the three pension systems reviewed so far is fairly representative of those of many less developed countries in Africa and Asia. Coverage is restricted to formal sector employees. The demographic pattern is similar with young, but growing population (see Table 2). For most countries, the system commenced in the early 1960s, so they are just going through system maturation. Fragmentation also is high and evasion rampant. Contributions and benefits are mismatched. The management organizations are beset with administrative problems. Benefits are low, and in addition, retirement age, vesting provisions and portability regulations do not seem to take cognizance of the real purpose of providing pension income. Consequently, distortions in the labor market and perverse income distribution are created..

Most of these problems may be addressed by changing the rules and regulations governing pension operations. The real challenge, however, is in building and sustaining the capacity that will make such reforms succeed.

Pension System in OECD and Latin American Countries

France

As in most industrialized countries, France has a multi-pillar pension system based on public and private coverage, both of which are unfunded. The public pension plan covers approximately 70% of the working population. In addition, there are special schemes for agricultural, mining, railroad, public utility, public employees and self-employed individuals. Membership is voluntary for non-working housewives and unemployed persons caring for invalid family members. The scheme operates as a PAYG system, with the insured paying 1.4% of pensionable earnings, subject to a maximum. Survivor benefits carry an additional 0.1% contribution. Employers contribute 8.2% of payroll. To qualify for benefits, individuals must be 60 years of age and must have contributed for at least 150 quarters, with reduced pension payable to those with less than 150 quarters of contribution. Benefits are usually 50% of average earnings in the ten highest years after 1947.

The second pillar of pension in France is a complimentary scheme structured along occupational lines. It is unique in the sense that unlike occupational schemes in other countries, it is unfunded. The plans are the

AGIRC (*Association Generale des Institutions de Retraites des Cadres*), which covers managerial and technical staff in the private sector of industry and commerce, and the *ARRCO*, (*Association des Regimes de Retraites Complimentaires*), a federation of twenty-six schemes which covers non-managerial employees in the same sector. These plans insure three categories of workers: the self employed (13%), state-employed (17%) and private sector employed (70%). All private sector employers must insure their workers in the statutory scheme and contribution is 6.55% per employee and 8.20% per employer. The schemes provide personal retirement pension, survivor's pension and reversion rights in the case of death. As with the public pillar, full rate pension is 50% of the average earnings over the best 10 years for those having at least 150 quarters of contributory service. Deductions depend on whether the contributor is a managerial or non-managerial employee. Pensions are revalued twice a year by the government taking into consideration the cost of living. Because participation in the occupational schemes is mandatory and arranged by collective bargaining, coverage is one of the highest for any occupational schemes in the world. A third tier of pension is an optional complimentary scheme, in which contributors may opt to contribute more than the compulsory minimum rate.

France's system is indexed to the real wage, as it operates through the "points" system which is independent of the monetary unit. Pensions are revalued regularly in accordance with the value of points. This could be once or twice a year, but is usually tied to the evolution of income of contributors, thereby protecting against inflation, and making the increase in pension comparable to that of wages.

The administrative cost of the pension schemes is shared between employer and employee through collective bargaining. The French system has no minimum number of years of affiliation or residency. Therefore, mobility between different segments of the labor market is not impaired.

Japan

Like most industrial countries, Japan has a public pension scheme administered by the national government providing old age, disability and survivor benefits. The National Pension, which is the public pension scheme, provides basic mandatory pension coverage to all Japanese citizens. It was originally designed for those not covered by other existing pension schemes, especially farmers and the self-insured. Joining is mandatory for all Japanese citizens aged between 20 and 60. Spouses of employee pension subscribers are required to enroll in the National Pension program. In the mid-1990s,

68.4 million citizens were enrolled, and more that 40% depended on it as their sole pension coverage. Insured and employers bear 2/3 of the cost of benefits, while the National Treasury picks up the remainder. Supplemental coverage is provided by the Employees Pension Insurance program, which currently covers about 32.0 million private sector employees. The other supplemental scheme is the Mutual Aid Association pension, which enrolls an additional 4.9 million public employees and teachers.

The cost of the supplemental plans is usually covered by equal contributions between employer and employee proportionate to the employee's wage rate, and benefits are indexed to net wages. Retirement age in Japan is 60 for men and 55 for women, and a 40-year contribution period is required for full pension.

UK

The public pension in the UK is a PAYG system, incorporating two schemes, a flat rate pension and an earnings-related pension. Retirement age is 65 for men and 60 for women, and 40 years of contribution is required for full pension. The scheme is financed from contributions made by the employer, employee and the self-employed, while the government bears the full cost of income-tested pensions. Earnings-related pension attracts additional contribution over the basic flat rate pension from the employee. In addition, employers may contract out of the earnings-related scheme and opt for private pensions instead, provided that the employer scheme is as good as the government additional pension. As of the end of 1996, occupational schemes had about 9.2 million members, and in 1994-95, 5.4 million people contracted out of the state earnings-related scheme and took out private pensions. In addition, personal pensions are available from banks, building societies, insurance companies and other financial institutions. After the 1977 reforms, over 11 million people belong to occupational schemes and 5 million to personal pension plans.

The UK system has a pensions' ombudsman office, which deals with maladministration and disputes of facts or law. A pension registry also helps to trace lost benefit. In addition, in 1991, the European Union proposed a new directive on the freedom of management and investment of funds held by institutions for retirement. However, this had yet to come into effect as at the end of 1997. The Directive sought to establish common prudential rules for pension fund investing, bearing in mind the diversity of pension systems in the European Union and security, quality, liquidity and profitability of the pension institutions portfolio.

USA

The public scheme in the US is a partially funded system based on a universal coverage social security system designed to provide income and services to individuals in the event of retirement. The scheme covers gainfully employed persons, including the self-employed, and it is funded through equal contribution from employers and employees, while the government bears the whole cost of income-tested allowances. The retirement age is 65 for male and female, and 10 years of contribution is required to qualify for full pension.

In addition to the public pension scheme, occupational schemes abound in the US, with more than 55% of the labor force covered by occupational schemes. The federal, state and local governments as well as several employers of labor have separate pension plans for their employees. In addition, several provisions in the tax law permit the self-employed and employees not covered by private plans, to establish pension plans for themselves with tax advantages similar to those given to corporate pension plans.

Pension funds are highly regulated in the USA. The Employee Retirement Income Security Act of 1974 (ERISA) provides basic protection for the individual for money invested in private pension schemes, while public pension plans are subject to the laws of the states or local governments where they operate. Operators of pension funds have important fiduciary duties regarding the choice of pension investment, and there are limitations to the extent to which plans can hold speculative investment. Participants are to be provided with disclosure statements describing the plans' benefits and investment objectives, and pension funds are required to submit to the Department of Labor an annual report, which includes detailed balance sheet and investment schedule. Finally, the Pension Benefit Guarantee Corporation, created by the ERISA guarantees a portion of the retirement benefit of a vested employee in a defined benefit plan.

Argentina

By the end of the 1970s, the Argentine pension system was the oldest and most mature scheme in South America, with high coverage, evasion and increasing dependency ratio. By the turn of the decade, defaults on pensioner obligations were rampant. Most of the initial attempts made at reforming the system were more concerned with managing the problem rather than changing the system. These included increasing the retirement age so as to reduce financial obligations, and tightening eligibility requirements. However, following the successful implementation of the Chilean pension reform, a reform that allowed the co-existence of private and public schemes was introduced.

The first pillar of the Argentine pension system is the public pension scheme, which is operated as a PAYG system. It provides a basic pension and contribution is mandatory. The reformed pension scheme offers employees the option to move from the public PAYG, which is a defined benefits scheme to a private, fully funded contributory scheme with individual accounts. Enrolment is mandatory in either of the two, and members who do not choose are automatically placed in the private scheme. In both schemes, the retirement age is 60 for male and 65 for female, and a thirty-year work life is required before the minimum pension can be received.

The private pension pillar is very similar to that of Chile, which seems to have set the pace for the continent. Three and one half percent of the contribution goes to the managing firm, while the government guarantees a minimum pension, which translates to about 40% of average wages over a working life of 30 years. The performance of the scheme after reforms seems encouraging as about 50% of private sector employees enrolled within the first year. It is particularly attractive to the younger generation.

Chile

The reform of the Chilean pension system was informed by the fact that the previous publicly managed, benefit-determined scheme was unable to achieve the planned benefits level and national coverage. In addition, it was beset with a crisis of credibility, which eventually led to its abandonment, and replacement by a government-mandated and regulated but privately administered, individually capitalized, contribution-determined system.

Under the new system, all private and public civilian wage earners must join except those who opt for the old arrangement. Past contributions in the old public system were carried into the new system as a premium in the form of treasury bonds. Contribution is 10% of insured wages for pension and an additional 2.5 – 3.7% for disability and survivors' benefits. There are no state or employer contributions allowed. Managing companies called *Administradors de Fondos de Pensiones (AFP)*, deduct commission and invest the proceeds in a separate account for each worker. All benefits, annuities and pensions are denominated in "UF", a reference unit, the value of which is adjusted daily according to the Consumer Price Index (CPI). At retirement, some of the savings may be withdrawn in lump sum provided contribution has been for at least 10 years, and there is enough in the savings account to provide for a pension equal to at least 12% of average wages of 10 years prior. The state guarantees a minimum pension for those who have at least 20 years of contribution, have reached retirement age, but whose account can only support less than 22 – 25% of the average wage.

One of the more remarkable things about the Chilean system is the tight regulatory environment that the *AFPs* operate. Regulation is the responsibility of the *Superintendente de Administradoras de Fondos de Pensiones (SAFP)*. There are detailed regulations governing operations, audit and financial reporting of the private pension companies. Assets and liabilities of the company and those of contributors are to be completely separated.

In addition to general supervision of operations and provision of guidelines, the investment of the *AFPs* is strictly monitored. The credit rating of financial instruments is used to determine the eligibility of a security for investment by a private pension fund. Since 1988 when the Chilean government made it compulsory that all publicly offered securities be rated by at least two private rating agencies, only high quality issues are eligible for investment. The government also ensures the adequacy of the rating service. In the event of bankruptcy of an AFP, members' contributions are guaranteed by the state.

The reforms may be considered to be successful in all the relevant areas. In the first place, coverage is much better than in the past, with 93% of the formal sector workforce being covered by private pension. With respect to benefits, these were higher than the pre-reform days with 40% difference.

Comparison of Pension Systems

The twin objectives of pension income have been brought out clearly in the above analysis of the pension system in OECD and Latin American countries. Public pension system, co-existing with private earnings-related plans, are able to satisfy both the objectives of income replacement and redistribution through both means-tested and defined-contribution pension. Jointly, they constitute vital instruments for poverty alleviation. In addition, pension funds are significant participants in the capital market, contributing to the deepening of the financial system. In Chile, after the reforms of the 1980s, private pension plans grew rapidly, with their value totaling US$22.3

billion or 43% of the GDP by mid-1994 and the savings rate increasing from 16.7% of the GDP pre-reform to 26.6% of GDP post-reform.

In the US, pension fund is the largest institutional investor group. Between 1950 and 1994, funds operated by private plans grew from US$17 billion to about US$4.7 trillion. Currently, they own more than 25% of the total corporate stocks outstanding. Similarly, in the UK, pension funds account for close to 30% of securities in the London Stock Exchange in 1996, while the total British pension fund assets was 566 billion pounds.

The implication is that properly managed pension schemes can serve as financial intermediaries for the mobilization of capital on behalf of small savers. To the extent that they contribute to growth and development of the capital market, pension reforms have positive effects on financial market deepening. According to James (1997) after the reforms in Switzerland, the national savings rate rose from 6 to 8.5% of GDP in the decade after the funded second pillar became mandatory and the entire increase occurred in pension funds and related institutions.

These facts are instructive for the design of an efficient pension system in a developing country. Most advanced countries have higher percentage of aging population (see Table1), a fact that creates fiscal disequilibrium in most PAYG systems. While the expectation of adverse demographic trends have often shaped pension debates in these countries, for developing countries, the issues are likely to be different, since demographic trends are relatively favorable. The focus of attention has to be directed to building the capacity to make reforms successful.

Building the Capacity for Successful Pension Reforms

In comparing the experiences of OECD and Latin American countries with those of African countries, three main issues stand out.

In the first place, the dynamics of the African labor market, with the coexistence of formal and informal sectors imply that formal methods of poverty alleviation such as pensions can only apply to a limited percentage of the population. Secondly, existing pension schemes are beset with institutional problems, and they lack the administrative and technical capacity for efficient pension administration. Finally, the macroeconomic environment is relatively unstable, with important reforms in tax administration and financial market yet to be undertaken. In the light of these, the focus of the following recommendations will be on the formal sector, informal sector, the role of the government, and building the capacity for reforms.

Formal sector pensions should be built around a multi-pillar system with contributions very closely linked to benefits, which should be indexed to the minimum wage. The first pillar should be a publicly mandated but privately managed scheme with mandatory coverage of formal sector employees, financed with contributions from employers and employees. The short to medium-term reality in most African countries, rules out any system that has to be financed from taxation. This is mainly because of the lack of efficient tax administration and transparency. In addition, the national budget may be overburdened by such a task. Rather, a fully contributory system in the short term, with the scope for the inclusion of means-tested program in the long term is suggested. This can be easily achieved by turning the existing general scheme into the first pillar, and many countries can build on existing social insurance scheme or the provident fund. The advantage of a scheme that is not financed partly by government revenue is that since such a scheme can only be limited to the formal sector, government transfer payment means that those not covered by the scheme are subsidizing the covered; a situation of perverse income distribution.

The second pillar should be structured along occupational lines. Many countries have occupational schemes, what is lacking in centralized organization to which all occupational schemes can belong. A few organizations, possibly organized along trade union lines, as in France, may be used for this purpose. The advantage of such a scheme is that it makes pension benefits portable as employees move from one job to another. In addition, individual firms are relieved of the full and direct responsibilities for their workers' retirement pension as the established funds pool resources and risks among firms. Regulation is also relatively easier than dealing with several private sector firms.

The third pillar should be that of personal savings and pension investment. While the scope for investment is limited in some countries, they are already in wide usage in other countries, and there is no reason why they cannot be more useful. In this regard, provident funds can still serve some use. Although they operate on the principle of lump sum payment which may not be available to provide for long-term retirement income, but, as is the practice in Chile, provident fund contributors may be given the option to purchase annuity with their lump sum benefit.

With the multi-pillar system specified, most employees in the formal sector will have adequate coverage and benefits in old age.

For informal sector employees, the possibilities are limited. There is little or no capacity for schemes based on personal contributions, as incomes are either very low or are non-wage, and cannot therefore be the basis of generating long-term savings. Even if there is the ability to contribute, evasion is high in the informal sector. The lack of efficient tax administration rules out means-tested program financed from general revenue. Poverty targeting among the old in this group therefore has to follow a gradual approach. In the short to medium term, governments could initiate policies that improve their working conditions and therefore, income. Complimentary policies that target the root causes of poverty such as lack of useful education, health care and employment should always be at the top of the social policy agenda. In the meantime, traditional institutions that take care of the old such as the extended family systems and religious obligations, may be strengthened through appropriate policies. In the long term however, the goal should be the pursuance of policies that generate employment and economic growth, which will draw the labor force away from the informal sector.

The role of government is very critical to the realization of these objectives. Governments have to pursue macroeconomic policies that will guarantee stability in the financial and labor markets. These include fiscal, monetary, exchange rate and labor market policies. For example, the fiscal implication of pension reforms is very important. Even if there is no tax-financed scheme, some of the changes that will come with pension reform, will require fiscal discipline from the government. Public pension agencies will no longer be required to finance the government's deficit through the purchase of treasury instruments at negative interest rates. In addition, government will no longer be able to treat its (employer) contributions as mere expenses in the budget, which may or may not be met, but as any other insurable risk, underwritten by an insurance company. All these require a lot of discipline and transparency, which may not currently be the norm.

The most important task is that of regulating the schemes. The first task in this regard will be the replacement of *ad hoc* changes of the past with fundamental reforms. During the transition period, extensive regulations will be required for coverage, retirement age, years of contribution, vesting, benefit administration and provision for workers in the previous system. In addition, new institutions will have to be set up, with clear requirements about capitalization, investment responsibilities and financial reporting. All regulatory policies will be undertaken based on existing realities and future possibilities.

Whereas it is easier to identify the issues and set out rules and regulations, the most difficult aspect of social policy reform is often the extent of local capacity to manage those reforms. An efficient pension system must be able to handle problems of compliance, communication with regions, record keeping and delivering the benefits. Extensive information and statistics will be required about labor and financial market conditions. These cannot be efficiently handled without some degree of technical know-how, administrative and management capacity which may currently be lacking. In addition, regulatory agencies may lack the technical manpower to supervise effectively. Progress in these areas will therefore be incremental. In the long term, governments will have to make substantial investments in human capital, while in the short term, training of current employees locally and through technical aid program might be beneficial.

The effect of pension reform on poverty alleviation is instructive. Apart from the direct effect of providing income at old age, there are other advantages that, in the long run, contribute to increase in income for various groups. One of these is through the effect on labor markets. In an economy with less than full employment, an efficient and transparent pension system leads to increases in employment in the formal sector, where suppliers of labor will prefer to work so as to qualify for pension income. Secondly, through its effect on financial deepening, pension funds increase the stock of financial savings, which are available for investment, and impacts positively on growth.

References

Ahmad, Ehtisham. (1991), 'Social Security and The Poor: Choices for Developing Countries', *The World Bank Research Observer*, 6 (1), pp. 105-127.

Ahmad, Ehtisham. (ed) (1991), *Social Security in Developing Countries*, Oxford University Press, Oxford.

Chand, Sheetal K., and Albert Jaeger. (1996), *Aging Population and Public Pension Schemes*. IMF Occasional Paper 147, International Monetary Fund, Washington, D.C.

Chu, Ke-Young and Hemming, R. (eds.) (1991): *Public Expenditure Handbook*, International Monetary Fund, Washington, D.C.

_____ and Sanjeev Gupta. (eds.) 1998, *Social Safety Nets*, International Monetary Fund, Washington.

Ekpeyong S., Oyeneye, O.Y. and Piel, M. (1986), *Reports on the Study of Elderly Nigerians.*, University of Birmingham, Birmingham.

Gillion, Collin and Bonilla, Alejandro. (1992), 'Analysis of a National Private Pension Scheme: The Case of Chile', *International Labour Review*, 131 (2) pp.171-195.

Gruat, J. V. (1990), 'Social Security in Africa: Current Trends and Problems', *International Labour Review*, 129 (4) pp. 405-421.

Iver S. N. (1993), 'Pension Reforms in Developing Countries', *International Labour Review*, 132 (2).

James, E. (1997), *Pension Reform: Is There a Tradeoff between Efficiency and Equity?*, Policy Research Working Paper 1767, World Bank, Washington, D.C.

Kopits, George and Gotur, P. (1980), *The Influence of Social Security on Household Savings: A Cross-Country Investigation*, IMF Staff Papers 27 (March) pp. 161-190.

National Social Insurance Trust Fund, Nigeria (various years), *Annual Report*.

Nigeria Economic Society. (1997), *Poverty Alleviation in Nigeria: 1997* Conference Proceedings, Ibadan: The Nigeria Economic Society.

Queisser, M., Bailey, C. and Woodall, J. (1997), *Reforming Pensions in Zambia*, Policy Research Working Paper 1716, World Bank, Washington, D.C.

U.S. Department of Health and Human Services. (1997): *Social Security Programmes Throughout the World -1997*. Research Report No. 59, US Department of Health and Human Services, Washington.

Vittas, Dimitri. (1993), *Options for Pension Reform in Tunisia*, Policy Research Working Paper 1154, The World Bank, Washington, D.C.

_____. (1994), *Averting the Old Age Crisis*, World Bank, Washington, D.C.

von Braun, Joachim. (1991), 'Social Security in Sub-Saharan Africa: Reflections on Policy Changes', in Ehtisham Ahmad (ed), *Social Security in Developing Countries*, Oxford University Press, Oxford.

World Bank. (1994), *Zambia Poverty Assessment*, World Bank, Washington, D.C.

Zambia National Provident Fund. (Various years), *Annual Report*.

PART IV:
BASIC HEALTH SERVICES

10 A Framework for Primary Health Care Reforms

George L. Dorros, Marianne Jensen and Gary D. Robinson

The Experience and Global Context

One of the main strategies of Health for All (HFA) is Primary Health Care (PHC). PHC is essential health care made universally acceptable to individuals and families in the community by means acceptable to them, through their full participation and at a cost that the community and country can afford. It forms an integral part both of the country's health system of which it is a nucleus, and of the overall social and economic development of the community.

Operationally, PHC is based on the following principles:

- Food, water and shelter are essential to maintain and improve health;
- Health is indivisible and has to be seen as the responsibility of self-reliant individuals, families and communities, not just the health services;
- There is a need to make optimum use of available resources in the community; and,
- All community members have the right to access essential health care that is affordable, socially acceptable, relevant and jointly planned and monitored by the health services.

Many of these principles call for the full involvement of the community and imply intersectoral support to meet the basic needs required for health. The implementation of the policy in many countries focuses on the extension of PHC services and the delivery of specific public health programs such as immunization, TB control, nutrition, maternal and child health, and water and sanitation. Major efforts have been made to build the capacity of the health services by training health workers to deliver discrete health interventions and by training health teams to plan and manage health programs at the local levels. Unfortunately, for the most part, these efforts in capacity building have been short term and usually tied to donor-funded programs. The result therefore has been unsustainable fragmented approaches to health services development and policy implementation.

More recently, the frustrated efforts to implement sustainable PHC gave way to the health sector reform movement. The emphasis is still on health services development but with a focus to improve outcomes of health interventions and the integration of service components in cost effective packages. The shift is towards building capacity for efficiency, cost effectiveness and most importantly, sustainability.

A meeting in Helsinki in 1997 issued a report entitled *Health for All Renewal: Building Sustainable Health Systems from Policy to Action* (WHO, 1998). It acknowledges the relevance and need to adhere to the principles of PHC. In the current socio-economic context, it also highlights the need to develop sustainable health systems with a focus on health outcomes. Emphasis is on redefining the roles and building the capacities of government ministries of health and public and private sector providers for delivering efficient and effective health care.

The context for building and sustaining capacity for PHC has also undergone dramatic changes in recent years as a result of globalization. A universally accepted definition of globalization is that it is the process of increasing economic, political and social interdependence and global integration which takes place as capital, traded goods, persons, concepts, images, ideas and values diffuse across state boundaries. Globalization increasingly affects, not only the sustainability and performance of health systems, but also the daily lives of individuals, families and communities living even in remote areas.

Still the challenge remains on how to build and sustain the capacity for PHC reform. The Helsinki meeting established a common understanding of sustainable health systems in the global environment. The report states that: "Sustainability refers to areas of human resources, institutional structures, and political will. But it also depends on good governance, the involvement of partners and civil society, and moral leadership based on a clear vision and explicit values, and responding to the needs of the people". It also asserts that: "Many health systems are not sustainable and their performance often inadequate".

The full participation of a self-reliant community as stated in the principles of PHC, is a neglected, yet pivotal component for building and sustaining the capacities of systems for health. A new framework is needed where building and sustaining capacities begin in the community.

A Framework for PHC Reforms

A reform of PHC is called for based on the experience of countries to date. This experience indicates that fundamental changes in both the structures and processes of systems for health are needed to deploy a reformed policy. People are central to the framework. They are both the object and the actors of their development in the dynamics of PHC reforms. This framework is outlined below.

The framework focuses on three subsystems which represent interdependent stakeholders. Each has different roles, interests and values, priorities and contributions to health. The degree to which the health system is sustainable, depends on the degree to which each subsystem has the capacity to play its role, adapt to its environment and establish and maintain a unique interrelationship with each of the other subsystems.

The three subsystems include:
- The government and its line ministries as central coordinator of health policies, including intersectoral strategies;
- The health care providers, both public and private, who engage in intersectoral cooperation; and,
- The community which responds to its health needs in a holistic manner and through collective actions, seeks to maintain and improve its health.

A Vision of the Functioning of the Framework for PHC Reforms

By inference from experiences at community level, a vision of the functioning of this framework may be outlined. These subsystems interact at different levels in qualitatively different ways. The community plans, organizes and manages its own health and addresses its priority health issues and concerns. The interaction between the community and service providers is focused on support to the program and on the accessibility, quality and efficiency of the health services provided. A process of joint planning and monitoring provides the information needed to prioritize action and identify complementary intersectoral support required to attain and sustain health improvements.

Local government authorities disseminate national health and development policies, build capacities to implement them and allocate resources based on local needs. Priorities are negotiated with elected representatives and service providers. With the facilitating role of the local authorities, different modalities of cooperation are developed at this level, both within sectors and across sectors, in order to:

- Address major socio-economic determinants impacting on the health of the population;
- Take advantage of complementary actions which would increase efficiency in the use of resources; and
- Create opportunities for synergy in health development activities.

Traditionally, the central or national level coordinates health work in a country through policy, legislation, allocation of resources and development of legal frameworks. Within this framework however, the central level plays other critical roles, including buffering the negative effects of the external environment on both the health system and the community. In this context, identifying and understanding the socio-economic determinants of health is an important role at the national level in order to act proactively in an inter-sectoral context.

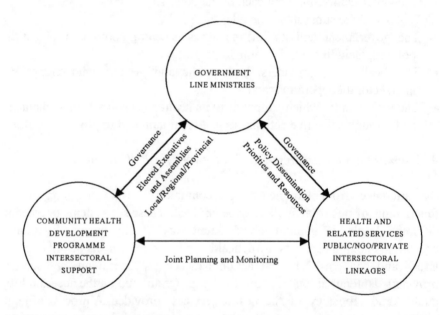

A Framework for PHC Reforms

This framework proposes a top-down and bottom-up approach to policy implementation, coupled with a side-by-side approach in cooperating to develop shared vision and sustaining capacity to attain it.

In practical terms, health and social policy may be developed jointly between national authorities, sector institutions such as health, and selected communities side by side. Once formulated and agreed upon, deployment of those policies for sustainability is an iterative both top-down and bottom-up process of adjustment, complemented by a side-by-side mutually supportive process of capacity building at all levels and among all subsystems to ensure effective implementation.

Characteristics of Successful Community Health Development

As a result of these iterative processes, country experiences point to an emerging consensus on the approach to implementing PHC reforms in communities. It may be described in generic terms as a process of community health development and defined as an action program implemented by the community. It is facilitated and supported by the district or local health system in cooperation with other development agents or service providers in other sectors. It adopts strategies which empower people to pursue their highest potential and the well-being of all and seeks to sustain development while optimizing the use of available resources. It is a community-led program, which means that the community is collectively empowered to:

- Analyze its own situation;
- Express its own vision and plan its own path of development;
- Set its own goals and priorities;
- Design its own programs to achieve these goals and priorities;
- Contribute financially and implement its programs;
- Monitor its programs and adjust them continuously in order to optimize their effectiveness.

Further analysis of two country experiences, namely Syria and Zimbabwe, reveals four key characteristics of successful implementation of this approach (see Table 5).

High Participation

Community Health Development (CHD) is a highly participative process which operates in top-down, bottom-up and a side-by-side approach. National management takes the initiative in the process, but confers throughout the process with the sectoral and community participants to take their views and priorities genuinely into account. Communities and sectoral representatives confer in the development and implementation of the community plan.

Joint Responsibility

While the national level is ultimately responsible for goal achievement, the CHD process does not draw a formidable boundary between the national government's responsibility for goal formation and sectoral and community responsibility for goal achievement.   All three levels are responsible for planning and development of goals and methods. This joint responsibility is developed through the use of participative methods and consensus building that produces understanding and commitment among the three levels. An added benefit of this joint responsibility is shown when things get off track. Both the sectoral and community engage in joint problem solving to fix things rather than ascribing blame on the other.

High Accountability

Another characteristic of the CHD process is that it makes individual and group accountabilities very visible. Goals are quantified. Methods of achieving the goals are made explicit and roles and expectations are agreed on.   Regular reviews are conducted to measure, with facts and data, both progresses toward goals and the effectiveness of the methods employed. Results are made accessible and openly communicated among relevant parties.

Equal Attention to End Results and to the Process for Achieving Results

End results are monitored and measured for all the obvious reasons. In addition, measures of the end results are also used as indicators of the extent to which the methods designed to produce the end results are effective. Direct measures of the methods employed are also recorded to assess: (a) what methods are being employed; (b) whether they are being employed correctly; and (c) whether these are the methods which should continue to be used.

Intended Systemic Outcomes of PHC Reforms

When the national level properly deploys a policy, many common constraints to implementation are reduced. In addition to the primary purpose of goal achievement, the process also strengthens the three subsystems at all levels by achieving the following outcomes. Once again, examples from Syria and Zimbabwe illustrate these results (Table 5).

Key Features of the Model

- Focuses on the vital improvement areas of opportunity and places trivial activities into their proper perspective;
- Aligns efforts by providing a common long-term vision with mid-range and annual goals and methods agreed upon for achieving the goals and the vision;
- Strengthens the country's achievement through the development of reliable methods, systematic improvement processes, quantified goals, high visibility and accountability, and rigorous review and measurement;
- Increases commitment through participation, joint responsibility, shared influence and consensus building;
- Promotes the development of planning at all levels of the health system; and;
- Provides the national government with an efficient method to be in touch with the realities of the communities' actual performance and the people.

Grounding the Framework: The Cases of Syria and Zimbabwe

The two examples used to illustrate how the new concept is useful in practice are Syria and Zimbabwe. The two countries are distinctly different in culture, health indicators, and geographic area and in the way they deal with the challenge of health development at the community level. A comparison of country profiles is provided in Table 1. Their purpose for undertaking the challenge also differs. The Ministry of Health (MOH) of Syria began a program of Healthy Villages in 1995 as a way of implementing a policy framework to meet the basic development needs of its communities. The MOH of Zimbabwe initiated a similar community health development activity in 1992 as a demonstration project intended to guide the ministry in the further development of a policy for improving community health.

Country Profiles

A comparison of demographic and socio-economic characteristics of the two countries shows a number of differences. Table 1 shows that while

Zimbabwe is twice the size of Syria, its arable land is only 25% that of Syria. Syria is less than half the size of Zimbabwe but has 30% more population and a population density three times higher. The GNP per capita in Syria is twice that of Zimbabwe.

There are major health disparities between the two countries. Life expectancy (LE) is much lower in Zimbabwe with 49 years than in Syria with 69 years and will decrease even further over the next decade, due to the HIV/AIDS pandemic. The infant mortality rate in Zimbabwe is also twice the rate of Syria (69 versus 33 per thousand). However, Zimbabwe has a higher literacy rate.

This general overview of the two countries shows distinct differences with regard to health status and economic situation. However, both countries have followed similar paths in trying to improve the health of their populations.   Neither is satisfied with the country's level of health and has initiated community approaches to improve health. The program parameters for these two initiatives and specific features of the two approaches are compared and contrasted in the following section.

The Program Parameters

Syria began its program with a pilot in three villages in three provinces in early 1996.   The second phase was begun in July 1997 in 36 villages in all provinces and has now been expanded to 55 villages and is expanding rapidly. The program is supported by the MOH, as well as WHO and UNICEF.

The initiative in Zimbabwe began in 1992 in the Chinyamukwakwa Ward in the Chipinge District. Its aim was to improve the health care delivery and ultimately the quality of life of the vulnerable rural communities. Survival itself has been a struggle in Chinyamukwakwa against periodic droughts and the subsequent harsh economic times. The community itself has requested development projects numerous times. Chinyamukwakwa Ward is made up of 6 villages over a 110 sq km area with a population of nearly 10,000 people living in 1,240 households. In addition to the MOH, WHO and various other international donor agencies contribute to the project on an *ad hoc* basis.

Table 1 Country profiles

	Syria	Zimbabwe
Population	16, 137,899	11,423,175
Population density per sq mile	225	75
Pop. In urban areas (%)	53	34
Geographic Area (sq miles)	71,498	150,872
Government	Republic	Republic
GNP per capita (US$, 1995)	1.120	540
National budget (US$, 1995)	3.4 billion	2.2 billion
Arable land	28%	7%
Life expectancy (both sexes)	69	49
Births per 1000	39	32
Deaths per 1000	6	19
Average annual growth rate, 1975-95 (both sexes)	3.3	3.0
Hospital beds	1 per 911	1 per 514
Physicians	1 per 966	1 per 6,909
Maternal mortality rate (per 1000, 1990)	180	570
Infant mortality rate (per 1000, 1997)	33	69
Education	Compulsory, 6-12 yrs	Compulsory, 7-13 yrs
Literacy (both sexes)	71%	85%

Source: World Health Organization, 1998; *The World Almanac and Book of Facts*, 1998; UNDP, 1997.

Policy, Principles and Philosophy

Syria's broad comprehensive approach to improve community health follows the Basic Development Needs approach of the WHO Eastern Mediterranean region. Zimbabwe on the other hand, is more concerned with specific projects focused on problem areas such as water and sanitation. They both seek to improve health status through these interventions as revealed in the principles underlying their policies. Notable is the concurrence of both on the importance of equity as a policy and the focus on the community as the master of its own destiny. Nevertheless, the underlying assumptions differ. With Zimbabwe, community development is a means of improving the health of the population and teaching people how to become self-reliant. Syria, on the other hand, views health as an entry point to initiate and sustain community development and improve health status. They both seek to learn, but use different approaches.

Objectives and Components

Objectives of the two efforts highlight the broad approaches taken by both, yet in this instance, the Zimbabwe approach focuses on specific problem areas. Components reveal the broader criteria approach by Syria and the specific problem-solving approach of Zimbabwe. Each reflects the felt needs of the community, which is, in both cases, a challenge of considerable ambition. Noteworthy is that Zimbabwe considers mobilization of assistance from foreign donors as one of the components of its initiative.

Organization and Operational Management

In Syria, the MOH supports the Healthy Village Program at the national level, which provides its counterparts in the local health services with technical support in training village workers and organizing the communities. Health workers at this local level also seek the cooperation of other sector representatives to support the community program. In Zimbabwe, the MOH initially sponsored the project through its District Health Office. In time however, the coordination of the project was transferred to the district administrator who assigned a community development worker from the Ministry of National Affairs to work directly with the community. This worker also acts as the liaison with other sector representatives at this level to organize support for the community's projects.

Table 2 **Comparison of Syria's and Zimbabwe's community health initiatives: policy, principles, philosophy, objectives and components**

Country Indicator	Syria	Zimbabwe
Policy	Development ideology; Health making; Equity and universality; Community based, managed and partially financed; Bottom-up planning; Community partnership, leadership and ownership Role change; Comprehensive package approach.	Adult literacy; Pre-school education; Equity in health care delivery; Free health services in rural areas; Free health promotion and prevention; Aggressive PHC delivery; Decentralization; Poverty alleviation; Food for work; Establish cooperatives; Welfare assistance.
Principles	Comprehensive approach; Helping people help themselves; Continuous learning process; Decentralization and integration; Community methodology.	Community becomes the center of development and plays a major role in determining its own development needs and priorities; Community participates as partner.
Philosophy	Create a developmental oriented mentality among community members; Help people help themselves; Address all health and health-related areas in a holistic integrated way.	Health is a prerequisite component to development; The achievement of health objectives is an important measure of development strategies; Health status is a reflection of successes and failures - health status can therefore be seen as a measure of development.
Objectives	To accelerate and strengthen attainment of health for all by the year 2000; To improve the quality of life in high risk areas through Basic Development Needs; To perform comprehensive social development based on peoples' partnership and intersectoral collaboration approach; To ensure protection and promotion of health of the people at highest risk, especially women and children.	To improve health care delivery; To improve the quality of life; To strengthen sectoral linkages for development activities through joint planning, support and monitoring of interventions for development as selected by their communities.

Table 2   Cont

Country Indicator	Syria	Zimbabwe
Components	Basic Development Needs; Self Care; Community school; Village information centre; Health lifestyle; Baby-friendly home; Baby-friendly community; Women's development; Protection and promotion of the environment; Community entertainment/sport center; Scouting for intellect and innovation.	Malaria control; Income-generation activities; Decentralized health care, training and service; Improved agricultural services; Literacy training for women; Assistance to orphans; Water supply improvements and toilet construction; Mobilization of assistance from foreign donor.

Identified Community Needs

In both Zimbabwe and Syria, the community identifies priority projects. In Syria however, a broader framework is used for data collection, analysis and priority setting.

Table 3   Comparison of Syria's and Zimbabwe's community health initiatives: organization, operational management, identified community needs and training

Country Indicator	Syria	Zimbabwe
Organization	Village District Province National	Ward/village District Province
Operational Management	Organize villages by dividing them into sectors consisting of 10-15 houses, with one male and female representative from each; Village Development Council; Specialized sub-committees.	Supervisory committee; Loans Committee; Education Committee; Advisory Committee.
Identified Community Needs	As determined by community but generally relating to: Primary health care; Basic education; Health housing; Income generation activities; Food supply and safety; Clean water, sanitation and hygiene.	Low family income; Poor grain storage and distribution; Poor transport; High illiteracy; Unclean sources of domestic water; Poor sanitary facilities; Poor hygiene at homesteads.

Table 3   Cont

Country Indicator	Syria	Zimbabwe
Training	Training methodology according to levels: National Providence District Village.	Two-day orientation at District level.

Training

In both countries, training is provided at the community level. Little, if any, is organized at higher levels of the system. Training in Zimbabwe appears to be focused on specific content related to the identified community needs. The Syrian approach is to train village volunteers on basic health issues, problem-solving and organizing, and managing health development activities.

Comparison of Results of CHD Efforts

To understand more fully the experiences of the two countries, it is useful to compare their characteristics.

A comparison of the characteristics of development processes used indicates that in practice, the two countries have taken distinct approaches. For example, Syria has pursued community participation within its own framework for "Healthy Villages", while in Zimbabwe, each village simply develops its own health or health related projects such as water systems, communal gardens, etc., without the benefit of guiding principles to help focus its collective efforts. With respect to the process of joint planning and monitoring between the community and local health service providers, Syria seems to have established stronger linkages whereas in Zimbabwe, these joint efforts appear to be weak due to high turn over of staff in health facilities. In Syria, systems of accountability are established both at the village level as well as at the level of health care provider. In Zimbabwe, accountability remains only within the village. In Syria, the process and its outcomes are seen as a focused effort to establish a systematic approach to improve the health of villages in the country as part of the development of the national health system. In Zimbabwe, the process remains at the level of experimental and discreet projects and is not part of a focused national development effort.

Table 4　Comparison of country characteristics

Country Characteristic	Syria	Zimbabwe
High Participation	The number of villages participating has increased to 55 in the two years of the program. There is a Village Development Council (VDC) and sub-committees in which everyone is eligible to participate. Everyone is encouraged to attend Council meetings and, through them, decide upon priorities for action.	Each development project has its own management committee. At local level, a management committee is established with participation of the community. There are sub-committees (super, loan, education and advisory).
Joint Responsibility	Villagers accept their responsibility for health through the VDC. Through the VDC, the village decides on the action it wishes to take. One village decided the cost of smoking was too great and agreed to stop smoking and invest the money previously spent on tobacco on other things, including health.	Management committees plan, manage and monitor the development activities. The extension worker in the Ministry of National Affairs at the village level is responsible for joint planning with other sectors. Joint planning does not go beyond this level.
High Accountability	The village measures its accomplishments through achieve- ment of plans made through the VDC. In this way, it tracks progress and is accountable.	Accountability is limited to loans for the projects.
Equal attention to end results and methods for achiev-ing results	As important as the goals achieved is the training and experience gained by villagers in taking responsibility for their own health and well-being. Achievement of the goals themselves may not be as important as the increased capacity of the village to manage itself.	Increased capacity to take responsibility for their own health and development is an important component of the project, giving extensive attention to the process.

These two experiences demonstrate that successful and sustainable community health development processes have to be part of a national policy framework for health improvement. They also must be an integral part of the continuous process of reorienting health systems and component services through similar policy mechanisms. In both cases, the role of a facilitator to assist the community in organizing itself and initiating and managing health development projects, is a critical factor in guiding productive community participation.

It is one thing to review the results in terms of the characteristics of the model. More important is whether it brought about the intended outcomes postulated earlier in the paper. Table 5 presents these data.

Table 5 Comparison of intended outcomes

Country Outcome	Syria	Zimbabwe
Focus on vital areas	Focuses the need for working with the community on issues they feel important.	Brings focus on community-centered development at local level.
Aligning of efforts	Three levels of the system (national, provincial and local) are aligned, but great attention is required to maintain this.	Strong links district/ward/village but highly dependent on individuals.
Strengthening the country's achievement	Has built 17 new health centers, and improved health indicators.	Has improved health indicators in the project area.
Increasing commitment	Commitment is verifiable at all three levels but is fragile, particularly at the provincial level.	Commitment verifiable at district/ ward/village level.
Promotion of planning at all levels	Started with a pilot of 3 villages and expanded to 55 at present.	No replication to date.
Efficient method to be in touch.	Performance is readily visible and people feel a direct connection to the government. Requires great maintenance effort.	No connection between local and national level.

This Table shows that Syria's efforts have greater potential for sustainability. The lack of connection with the national authorities and limited connection with the district level in Zimbabwe is one indicator of the lack of potential for sustainability.

Conclusion

In the light of the framework proposed for building and sustaining capacity for reforming PHC, a number of important conclusions may be drawn from the review of Syria's and Zimbabwe's experiences.

Effective implementation of the policy must start with the community but must be based on a jointly tested approach with selected communities, sector stakeholders and national government ministry representatives. Bottom-up project approaches disconnected from a clear national policy or a commitment to implementing such a policy are not sustainable. Their value is primarily as a means to clarify or further develop approaches for implementing policies.

The health development activities in Syria and in Zimbabwe seem to share many of the characteristics of the "community health development approach" outlined in the framework. They reconfirm a growing consensus on how to build the capacity to improve the health of underserved communities. Health is an effective entry point for community development in these contexts.

Each country's experience, in its own way, demonstrates the importance of the partnership between the communities and the sector representatives in effectively planning and implementing solutions to priority issues.

Both countries are still in the early stages of evolution of these efforts, particularly in Syria. Little may therefore be said about developing the capacity of sector institutions and government structures to provide sustained support for reformed PHC implementation. It may be inferred however, that there would be a need for a significant and fundamental redesign of organizational structure and processes.

Finally, the experiences in Syria point to three important factors in building and sustaining capacity for PHC reform:

- The empowerment of the community through its continued active participation in decision-making processes and actions related to health.
- The gradual expansion of a pool of human resources in the health sector with the capacities and skills to implement community health development approaches.
- Exchange visits and intracountry meetings of individuals engaged in similar approaches greatly increase the potential for transfer of knowledge and capacity.

References

Loubser J., and Dorros G.L. *Draft Framework for Community-led, People-Centred Development*. Unpublished document.

Ministry of Health, Syria. *Healthy Villages Programme (1997-2000)*, in collaboration with the World Health Organization and United Nations Children's Fund, Unpublished project document and field reports.

Ministry of Health, Zimbabwe. (1998), *Chinyamukwakwa Ward, Chipinge District*, Draft Report in collaboration with the World Health Organization.

Nugroho G, Dorros G.L, and Macagba R.L., *Building CommuHealth. A Practical Guide*, Unpublished document.

Robinson, G.D. (1977), *Interorganizational Cooperatiion in Human Services Administration – A Third-Party Intervention Process Model*, Unpublished Dissertation, Case Western Reserve University, Cleveland.

UNDP. (1997), *Human Development Report, 1997*, Oxford University Press, Oxford.

World Almanac Books. (1998), *The World Almanac and Book of Facts*, World Almanac Books, K-111 Reference Corporation, Mahwah, N.J. USA.

World Health Organization/UNICEF. (1978), *Primary Health Care, Report of the International Conference on Primary Health Care*, Alma-Ata, USSR, 6-12 September 1978, Geneva, World Health Organization

_____. (1998). *Health for All in the Twenty-First Century*. WHO document A51/5. Geneva, World Health Organization.

_____. (1998). *Health for All Renewal. Building Sustainable Health Systems: From Policy to Action*, Meeting Report, 17-19 November 1997, Helsinki, Finland. WHO document WHO/ARA/PAC/98.1, World Health Organization, Geneva.

_____. (1998). *World Health Report, 1998, Life in the 21st Century. A Vision for All*, Geneva, World Health Organization.

11 Evaluating Health Care Policy Reforms in Africa: A Lesson from the Use of Precision Service Delivery Techniques in Animal Health Care Management

Isaac A.O. Odeyemi, N.B. Lilwall and R.L. Wilson

Introduction

Mr Mudzawa Kuimba is a communal farmer in Chivhu District of Zimbabwe. His household of six now resides in a resettlement area. They own four indigenous breeds of cattle, six chicken and four goats. He uses his cattle mainly for draught power, but the family also depends on the cows for milk, and the occasional bull will be reserved for his son's dowry. Health care services for his family as well as others in his village, are provided at the district health center several miles away. Similarly, veterinary services for Mr Kuimba and nearly half a million communal farmers like him all over Zimbabwe, are provided by animal health assistants either at the cattle dip, a trek of five kilometers away or at the animal health centers, thirteen kilometers away. They seldom see a veterinarian as they will need to travel at least thirty five kilometers to the nearest veterinary clinic. Human, as well as veterinary services for Kuimba and other rural farmers, have in the past, been subsidized by the government. Recently however, news is filtering through that they will now have to pay for most of these services. Even worse, a number of facilities in the communal areas will have to be shut down, as part of the government restructuring and privatization exercise. Says Mr Kuimba: "We will now have to travel even farther. I think the government is just not interested in our welfare."

All over Africa and in other developing economies, persistent budgetary constraint is forcing governments like Zimbabwe to undertake both social and health care reforms. Such policy reforms involve the privatization of health care delivery services hitherto provided free by the government. Consequently, drug and input supplies will be liberalized and the participation of the private sector in the provision of clinical services. This will result in down-sizing or closure of some government veterinary facilities and the retrenchment of surplus government personnel. However, the dilemma for the authorities and planners is the difficulty of quantifying and qualifying availability and demand for services. Resources such as personnel and clinical facilities are therefore not optimally allocated or managed with consequences for millions of rural and poor households dependent on agriculture such as Mr Kuimba's. It is estimated that by the turn of the century, less than one quarter of the rural livestock population in Africa will be receiving adequate clinical services, with grave economic and health consequences for the rural population (Odeyemi *et al.*, 1998a).

The on-going social and health care reforms in developing countries, especially within sub-Saharan Africa, have brought to the fore the problem of monitoring the efficiency of service delivery and the equity of access by all the population (Lavy *et al.*, 1996, Bolduc *et al.*, 1996). Although the need for developing a framework for the systematic evaluation of the delivery of health care services is apparent to a lot of scholars, a universally acceptable and workable framework does not yet exist. A major difficulty encountered by planners, especially in Africa, is the inherent diversities within their delivery systems. These differences make the development of a universally applicable methodology or even framework, difficult. In particular, epidemiological and socio-economic differences have been recognized as influencing the type and efficiency of health care delivery systems (Odeyemi, 1997; Majok, 1995). The recognition of such a phenomenon within populations is indicative of the need for area-specific methodologies and interventions which will identify and address the specific health care needs of the different segments of the population (Odeyemi *et al.*, 1998b). This way, in addition to achieving efficiency objectives, equity of access may be ensured. The complexity of the task has led Doyle (1992) to suggest the combination of predictive models and other decision support tools as the only means of analyzing the delivery system.

Structural Dynamics of Delivery Systems

Health care delivery systems may be described as the interaction of the constituent tri-partite institutions composed of the providers of services, recipients of services, and the prevailing socio-economic environment within which services are to be provided. Most modern health care delivery systems work on a provider-purchaser arrangement. The purchasers may either be the direct beneficiaries themselves or some prevailing financial institution such as medical insurance.

Irrespective of the structure, two important characteristics of the delivery system influence the efficiency of service delivery. Firstly, it is recognized that these interactions do exhibit spatial variations. Thus, any framework for evaluating the delivery system would entail the analysis of the various constituent components and their interaction over space. The introduction of a spatial dimension to the framework would ensure that health care needs and resultant interventions are area-specific and therefore more appropriate. The complexity of developing such a framework is greatly reduced when one considers that whatever spatial variations are exhibited within the whole system, they are simply a combination of individual situations at one particular place and time, and each of these may be individually analyzed. Secondly, the efficiency of delivery of animal health services would depend on the levels and appropriateness of the services *vis-à-vis* the specific health care needs of the population. Since no population is homogenous, it then implies that health care needs are likely to be varied among the various socio-economic groupings or prevailing stratification within the population. It then follows that the efficiency of delivery of health care services would also depend on how services are targeted to meet the needs of the different strata of the population.

A framework for evaluating the efficiency of health care delivery would therefore involve the identification and qualification of the various constituent population, their spatial distribution, specific health care needs and the socio-economic environment within which they exist. The accuracy with which the above elements of the population are defined and integrated within a working framework, will inform the level of efficiency and appropriateness of health care interventions within the delivery system (Lavy et al., 1996). The above therefore makes the case for the concept of Precision Service Delivery in a health care delivery system.[1]

Framework for Precision Service Delivery (PSD)

Recent advances in science culminating in the development of better analytical tools, accurate positioning systems and information processing and management technologies, have improved the prospects of greater efficiency in the planning, evaluation and implementation of health care policies and interventions. The concept of Precision Service Delivery (PSD), which is not dissimilar to its equivalent in agriculture, is based on the premise that population is not homogenous, and thus health care needs for the various segments of the population would be variable. Furthermore, because population is often distributed unevenly over space, a spatial dimension needs to be considered in health care delivery.

PSD is therefore aimed at adjusting and fine-tuning the delivery of services so as to meet the specific health care needs of the different segments of the population in the context of their geographical distribution. The concept is inherently demand-led, thus different services would be adapted to different population groups residing in different locations, resulting in specific and targeted service delivery. A major limitation of the procedure however, is the likelihood of sampling inadequacies since population characterization which is an important component of the analysis, will be based on samples to be drawn from within the whole population.

Five Steps in the Development of a PSD Framework

Step 1   Qualifying the various elements of the delivery system. This involves the identification of any existing strata or categories within the population, and the statistical validation of the categories as distinct units relevant to the health care issues being considered. Statistical techniques such as factor analysis would be useful in achieving the required categorization. This process permits the profiling of the population with regards to specific health care indices.

Step 2   Quantifying the health care demand indices. This involves determining the levels of specific health care needs for the different segments of the population as identified in Step 1. This will usually involve quantifying the level of disease or health care demand variable in the various segments of the population and/or the economic value of the same, through some epidemiological and/or socio-economic survey techniques. These are then extrapolated to the whole population.

Step 3   Spatial desegregation of demand and supply. Through the use of Geographical Positioning System (GPS) and geo-spatial modelling techniques such as Location-Allocation models, the specific health care demands of the various population segments, as well as infrastructure for service delivery, may be geo-referenced.

Step 4 Rationalize service delivery options. When the various health care needs of the population and their distribution over space is known *vis-à-vis* available supply resources, it is possible using decision support tools such as mathematical models to simulate and predict various service delivery policy options. This will permit a more rational decision-making process depending on the policy objectives being pursued.

Step 5 Dissemination and implementation of policy decision. When various service delivery options have been identified and rationalized, it is often necessary to disseminate the information before, during and after implementation. Geographical Information System (GIS) tools are now available to assist with the management and display of such information.

PSD has several advantages over orthodox planning techniques and these include:

- Enhanced efficiency of allocation of resources thereby reducing waste.
- Specific targeting of services which will bring about equity in resource allocation.
- Because services are demand-led, uptake of interventions will be enhanced with the resultant economic and health benefits.
- Decision-making process will be greatly enhanced due to better information.

Characterization of the Delivery System

Qualifying the delivery system essentially involves the characterization of the various elements within the system such as the recipient population, the provider groups, as well as the environment within which services are provided. This is done on the premise that there are differences in the type and level of health care needs by different categories of the population, and these needs may require different provider institutions. In human health care delivery, categorization often includes the identification and classification of the population on the basis of their socio-economic and cultural attributes such as household income levels, education, nationality or race, as well as economic activities engaged in (Lavy *et al.*, 1996). It is shown for instance that humans in the lower income brackets often have poor health or that community based primary health care providers are more appropriate for rural populations (Ettner, 1996).

The provider classification is either related to the level of professionalism, in which case they are either qualified doctors/veterinarians working in clinics or various cadres of para-professionals providing community-based primary health care in rural areas. Another area of analysis is the provider's sector of employment such as private practitioners and fund holding GPs or government employees working for national health service boards or similar institutions. As discussed earlier, the validity of the classification of these groups is tested using appropriate discriminating statistical techniques. Where classes are confirmed to be valid and distinct in relation to a particular health attribute, populations within the various different categories are determined for the whole population, either through taking a census of the whole population or sampling and extrapolation.

Indices of Health Care Delivery Systems

Various attributes of the delivery system have been indexed, thereby providing a means of comparing different population groups within the system. The objective of the evaluation exercise will inform the type of indexing used. Depending on the objectives of the study therefore, socio-economic as well as health care indices for the various categories of the population, are determined. This can thus permit accurate profiling of the various segments of the population with regards to specific social or health care indices. A careful examination of existing indices in use in health care delivery systems suggests that these may be categorized into three groups: (a) Health indices; (b) Health-economic indices; and (c) Socio-economic indices. The following represent some of the indices with potentials for evaluating the health care delivery system.

Health Indices

These are indices that are used in evaluating the state of health of a population. Different indices are currently in use to evaluate different aspects of health.

The disease index   The disease index is more of an epidemiological entity, and is used to quantify and compare prevailing diseases in different areas or countries. In animal health, a table of disease indices for every country is produced annually in the FAO-OIE Animal Health Year Book which also classifies all the reported diseases according to the FAO-OIE classification (AHYB, 1992). The indexing system simply allocates units (+), to countries according to the level of each prevailing disease in that country. Disease indices can become a useful tool for providing economic information for various reported diseases. It is important to note that the economic value of a disease for a practice or a country may not correspond to the relative importance of the disease based on the FAO-OIE classification, but rather the client's perception of the disease. McInerney (1996) suggests a possible re-classification of livestock diseases based on their economic rather than veterinary characteristics.

Quality Adjusted Life Years (QALY) index This is an index which measures health in terms of quality adjusted life-years especially in humans. This involves computing a quality-of-life score which is a form of utility score, utility deriving from the fact that the level of well-being influences the ability to provide for oneself (Culyer, 1989). The QALY score is calculated by weighting each remaining year of life by the expected quality of life in each year.[2] The efficiency of service delivery would then be measured by the sum of the QALY for the whole population. Under such circumstances, health care policy objectives would be to maximize the QALY for the whole population. It is suggested that health maximization using QALY may result in inequity of resource allocation (Wagstaff, 1994; Bleichrodt, 1997). Harris and Nease (1997) criticized QALYs calculations for not discriminating between values due to co-morbidities and that due to the index condition (principal disease). QALY is particularly criticized for discriminating against older people (Johanesson and Johansson, 1997). The difficulty of developing similar index in animal health emanates from the fact that livestock are seldom kept until old-age, and contrary to the situation in human health, older animals would be valued higher than younger animals, but the objective is seldom to prolong life expectancy.

Health Economic Indices

These are indices derived from economic analysis employed in evaluating health care interventions. Such economic analysis includes: Cost-Effectiveness Analysis (CEA), Cost-Benefit Analysis (CBA), Cost-Utility Analysis (CUA) and Cost-of-Illness Analysis.

Cost-of-illness analysis This index, rather than just measuring the level of disease in a population as in the disease index, provides an index of the economic value or monetary cost for a disease in an individual or population. It often includes the direct cost of treating the disease as well as indirect costs attributable to production losses from the illness. This index which is widely used in human health, provides a means of undertaking a cost-benefit analysis of disease control programs even in animal health. There is quite clearly the difficulty of including indirect costs in the evaluation of the Cost-of-illness analysis especially in human health (Ratcliffe, 1995).

Cost-utility analysis   Economic analyses of available health care such as the CUA have been developed using related quality of life measurements (Dolan *et al.*, 1996). CUA compares the costs of a health care program with its benefits and measures the impact of the disease control program on the length and quality of life years.

Cost-effectiveness analysis   The monetary value of an intervention is compared to the physical effect of disease averted by the intervention (Weinstein, 1990; Johannesson, 1996; Gold *et al.*, 1996). Thus, it is possible to compare the money to disease (death) values of two or more alternative interventions.

Cost-benefit analysis   Unlike the CEA, the CBA compares the monetary cost of interventions with the monetary value of the benefits derived from implementation of the intervention (Johannesson, 1996). In either case, the efficiency of interventions is measured, and a comparison made possible by the analysis.

Socio-Economic Indices

Most socio-economic non-disease related characteristics especially of the human population within a health care delivery system, often result in nominal categories for which metric indexing is inappropriate. These often involve special indices generated to provide a picture of particular areas of policy interest. For instance, a useful index commonly generated is that of the level of resources available to the health care consumer. In particular, poverty indices have proved useful, where equity of access is being evaluated. In similar vein, level-of-well-being index is often required in certain epidemiological studies where predisposition to diseases is related to well-being.

Poverty indices in human health are related to the amount of income or household consumption associated with acceptable minimum levels of nutrition (Carvalho and White, 1997). More often however, income levels are simply ranked and grouped in quintiles from the highest quintile (top

20% or the richest), to the lowest quintile (lowest 20% or the poorest). Other composite socio-economic indices have been developed and used for categorizing populations (Jolley *et al.*, 1992). Such indices include the Underprivileged Area (UPA) score which relates to the level of GP (doctors) work-load each area has per unit of the population. The Townsends Index, on the other hand, aggregates the absence of a car, unemployment, housing tenure and overcrowding into an indexing system. Whether in human or animal health, it is quite often difficult to agree on empirical values for indexing poverty, despite the usefulness of the index.

Modelling Health Care Services

Determining health care indices for a population is only of importance when used in the decision-making process and particularly when accurately desegregated within the population. For instance, a decision analysis model may be used to provide a means of assessing and comparing the viability and sustainability of facilities in different locations. A better picture of how the particular health care variable is distributed within the various segments of the population for the whole country will then emerge. The concept of PSD even goes further, and involves the development of hybrid models, which combine geo-spatial models with econometric models resulting in decision support tools which permit more efficient targeting of health care interventions (Birkin *et al.*, 1996).

Geo-Spatial Models in Health Care Delivery

The spatial characteristics of populations *vis-à-vis* location of health care facilities have been identified as influencing access to health care. The development of geo-spatial models has simplified the otherwise complex problem of analyzing the spatial characteristics of populations. Hitherto, most geo-spatial activities have been limited to cataloguing, projection and display of socio-economic and health care variables so as to permit comparison across regions (Delehanty, 1992). Geographical Positioning System (GPS) machines permit accurate geo-referencing of populations and facilities under study, while the Geographical Information System (GIS) computer software programs allow data management and display especially of model output. The development of search and optimization models, such as Location-Allocation (L-A) models on the other hand, has provided planners with a means of determining the best position for the location of facilities with regards to the distribution of population being served.

It has long been recognized that the problem of equity and access to facilities for any population, is a function of the location of the population in relation to the facility they use (Hodgart, 1985; Rushton, 1988). L-A models address the problem of locating facilities such that they are as accessible as possible to the population, by allocating population centers (demand points) to their nearest facility (supply points). The models use the coordinates of the population centers and those of the existing or planned facilities as input data, the population figures, any existing road network as well as the production or socio-economic coefficients of each population unit. Depending on whether the objective is to minimize the aggregate travel distance or maximize attendance (usage) of the facilities, the models may compute the aggregate travel distance (cost) by the whole population, the mean travel distance (cost) and the proportion of total population allocated to each facility within any specified distance ring. The output data from the L-A models may be manipulated in a decision analysis, using coefficients derived from population sample surveys to produce appropriate indices for evaluating different aspects of health care service delivery (Revelle *et al.*, 1977). L-A models have been used to help determine the optimum location for veterinary facilities making them more accessible especially to poor and rural farmers (Odeyemi *et al.*, 1998a).

The model has also been used in determining the viability of the facilities, so that decisions to support non-viable facilities for poorer communities could be taken in a more informed way (Odeyemi *et al.*, 1998b). With such information available, resource needs, including manning levels could be better ascertained by health care management authorities, while health professionals that would want to set up private practices have a means of establishing the best location for viable practices. On-going work has equally shown the ability of these models to permit the economic evaluation of disease control programs by providing insight into their potential uptake and hence, the viability and sustainability of the disease control initiatives. Preliminary evidence suggests that the model may also be used in the assessment of the environmental impact of some animal production and health policies.

Mathematical Models

Mathematical models provide decision makers with decision-support tools on the optimal allocation of often scarce and fixed resources among competing health care demands. Such models have been used to compute various economic health care indices such as the CBA and CEA. Linear programming models for instance, have been used to formulate CEA values for health care services. This involves maximizing objective functions of effectiveness of the service subject to budgetary constraints (Stinnett and Paltiel, 1996).

e.g.

maximize: $\sum x_i e_i$

subject to: $0 \leq x_i \leq 1$ (for all i)

$$\sum x_i c_i \leq C$$

$$\sum x_i \leq 1 \text{ (for i} \in M \text{)}$$

where e_i and c_i are the effectiveness and cost of program i if fully implemented, C is the total budget available, M is a set of mutually exclusive programs and x_i is the percent implementation of program i. LP models have also been formulated to evaluate the choices that are open to practitioners following privatization of clinical facilities the constraints being their Practice Viability Indices (PVIs) and the travel costs to the clinics (Odeyemi *et al,*, 1998b). Integer models as well as mixed models constitute variations to the linear programming models. Figure 1 is a framework involving decision analysis and this has been used to achieve similar objectives as those for LP models in computing the PVI. Other decision-support tools could be developed using dynamic programming and systems simulation models (Dijkhuizen, 1986).

The techniques described above are just a few of the techniques that have potential applications in improving the delivery of health care services especially to poor and rural communities that are likely to be further marginalized by policies promoting market economies and privatization. Such policies tend to neglect issues of equity of access, which quite often are not so obvious to planners especially in the absence of tools and techniques which can assist in quantitatively determining the inherent inequities likely to be created by the policies.

Figure 1   Veterinary practice viability decision analysis

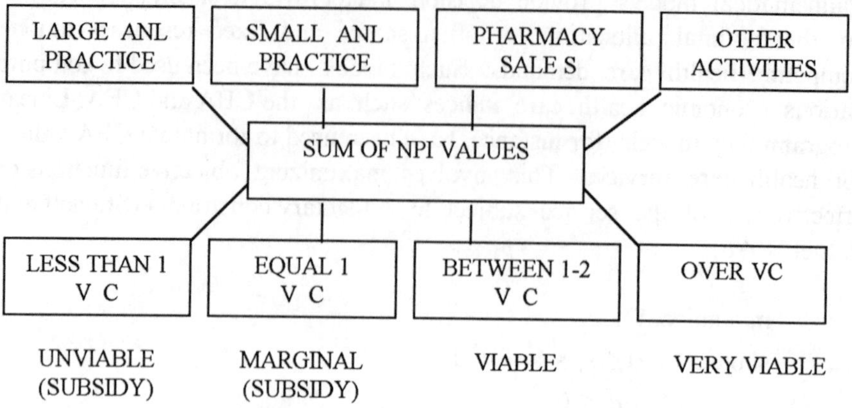

Viability and Equity Issues in Health Care Delivery in Zimbabwe: A Case Study

Zimbabwe has a cattle population of about 5 million, comprising of about 1.6 million managed under intensive commercial production systems in farms or ranches, and 3.4 million managed under extensive production systems in communal and small-scale resettlement farms scattered all over the country. The Directorate of Veterinary Services, in addition to its other roles, provides clinical services to the cattle farmers through a network of some 63 locations with veterinary clinics. They are potentially manned by veterinarians, and supported by animal health inspectors and veterinary extension assistants serving predominantly the communal and small scale resettlement farmers. In the face of declining government budgetary allocations to the veterinary department, the government of Zimbabwe is currently engaged in a privatization and restructuring exercise of its veterinary facilities. Hence, this study should be of relevance. Aspects of the PSD technique were used to evaluate *ex ante*, the impact of privatization on prevailing inequities inherent in the delivery of animal health services in Zimbabwe.

The case study involved:
- A questionnaire survey of livestock producers in Zimbabwe was conducted with a view of identifying any prevailing socio-economic stratification within their animal health delivery system. In all, four different livestock producer groups were interviewed.

- Indices of health care uptake such as veterinary expenditure and veterinary coverage were then quantified for the different livestock production systems.
- Existing animal health care facilities were then evaluated in terms of their efficiency of location and allocation using the L-A (geo-spatial) model.
- Equity issues relating to the economic impact of a privatization program were investigated using results of the L-A modelling exercise.

Results

PSD Step 1   Although four categories of livestock producers were interviewed based on *a priori* government categories. Discriminant Analysis results suggest that they are more accurately classified into just two economic groups, commercial and non-commercial (Odeyemi, 1998b). These results thus helped to achieve the first step of the PSD technique which is that of characterizing the stakeholders within the delivery system.

PSD Step 2   Further statistical analysis of the results of the questionnaire survey helped develop indices of health care delivery. As an example, Table 1 below provides a summary of some of the responses by the farmers in the two different production systems in the country. The established indices of health care uptake may then be extrapolated to the whole population when applied to population census figures. Using such information, it is possible to determine the total animal health care expenditures, or veterinary uptake in a country or region.

Table 1   Comparative analysis of veterinary uptake and veterinary expenditure in different production systems in Zimbabwe

Producer Type	Cattle Ownership.	Vet.Expend. per Head	Vet. Visit Per Year
Commercial farms	410	£3.2	6.6
Communal/small scale	20	£0.9	6.9

PSD Step 3   Geospatial analysis, involving the L-A model (GRAFLOC) was then used to model the optimality or locational efficiency of the current location of clinical facilities in relation to the distribution of Zimbabwe's livestock population. The model suggests that each livestock has had to make an extra 9 km when visiting the nearest clinic due to the inefficiency or non-optimality of the current clinic locations. Thus, travel costs savings equivalent to 9 km per visit would be made if the facilities were relocated. Table 1 shows the average cattle population of communal (rural) and commercial farms, and the number of visits made annually to or from the veterinary clinic.

PSD Step 4   When these figures are used in conjunction with the travel cost savings as predicted by the L-A model (GRAFLOC), substantial financial savings potentially may be made in Zimbabwe as illustrated in Table 2.

Table 2   **Annual efficiency savings to Zimbabwean rural livestock farmers following relocation exercise as predicted by GRAFLOC**

	Predicted unit mean travel distance savings (km)	National travel cost equivalent (km)	National travel cost equivalent (Zimb. $)
GRAFLOC	8.76 km	10.6 million	42.4 (0.4)* million

Cost of travel in Zimbabwe is Z$4 per km.
Amount in ( )* represents contribution in Z$ millions of commercial farmers.

Discussion and Conclusion

In addition to dwindling financial resources, the most important problem encountered by planners involved in the delivery of health care services has been the difficulty of quantifying and qualifying the demand for such services. Consequently, resources are inadequately allocated to meet these demands resulting in poor uptake of otherwise well intended and potentially beneficial policy initiatives. The concept of PSD involves a five-step process of qualifying, quantifying, dis-aggregating, rationalizing and disseminating data and information relating to a delivery system.

This procedure, through a combination of tools, has provided a means of resolving such resource management problems relating to the animal health care system in Zimbabwe. The different measures of demand from the allocated population were derived from surveys and other statistical analysis conducted on the sample population, and when applied to the output of the L-A model, allowed more informed decisions to be made with regards to the population under study.

Immediately apparent with the analysis carried out on the cattle population of Zimbabwe, is a significant efficiency savings in travel costs, over Z$40 million annually, following the relocation of existing veterinary infrastructure using the various techniques described above. The importance of this analysis becomes even more apparent when travel costs are taken into consideration, hitherto been borne by the government either entirely, or mostly subsidized. With market-led reforms such as privatization and cost recovery, these costs are passed on to the farmers, the bulk of which are borne by rural farmers as indicated in Table 2.

Since travel costs between clinics and farms are recurrent and incurred annually by the farmers for as long as the facilities and the farms remain in their current locations, it becomes obvious that over time, say ten years, savings to farmers from a relocation exercise are likely to defray the cost of the relocation exercise itself. This is especially because the latter is likely to be a one off-cost. The above analysis makes the case for relocating veterinary facilities nearer to the farmers, especially rural ones, in the event of any cost recovery or privatization exercise.

In this paper, use has been made of L-A models and Decision Analysis to highlight the economic impact of the current market-led reforms on poor and rural livestock dependent communities through the extra travel costs they are likely to incur. Similar aspects of human health care delivery could quite easily be evaluated using the same tools. Potential applications of the model include the planning, budgeting and monitoring of uptake and socio-economic benefits of policies, determining viability and sustainability of projects, relocation alternatives for facilities as in restructuring, evaluating issues of equity of access as well as the determination of manning levels and manpower projections for the health care in a country (Odeyemi, 1997, Odeyemi *et al.*, 1998a).

Notes

1 Locational efficiency is inferred here, and relates to optimum location and allocation of health care facilities such that the whole population enjoys the best possible access.
2 Life expectancy has been used as an index in health care in some studies, suggesting the targeting of different age-groups of the population (Johansson, 1996).

References

Animal Health Year Book. (1992). FAO-OIE Publications.

Birkin, M., Clarke, G., Clarke, M. and Wilson, A. (1996), *Intelligent GIS: Location Decisions and Strategic Planning*. GeoInformation International, Cambridge, U.K.

Bleichrodt, H. (1997), 'Health Utility Indices and Equity Considerations', *Journal of Health Economics*, 16, pp 65-91.

Bolduc, D., Lacroix, G. and Muller, C. (1996), 'The Choice of Medical Providers in Rural Benin: A Comparison of Discrete Choice Models', *Journal of Health Economics*, 15, pp 477-498.

Carvalho, S. and White, J. (1997), *Combining the Quantitative and Qualitative Approaches to Poverty Measurement and Analysis*. World Bank Technical Paper. No. 366, World Bank, Washington, D.C.

Culyer, A.J. (1989), 'The Normative Economics of Health Care Finance and Provision', *Oxford Review of Economic Policy*, 5, pp 34-58.

Delehanty, J. (1992), 'Spatial Projection of Socio-Economic Data Using GIS: Results from a Kenya Study in Strategic Implementation of a Livestock Disease Control Intervention', in K. Dovak (ed), *Social Science Research for Agricultural Technology Development. Spatial and Temporal Dimensions*, pp 37-50.

Dolan, P., Gudex, C. Kind, P. and Williams, A. (1996), 'Valuing Health States: A Comparison of Methods', *Journal of Health Economics*, 15, pp 209-231.

Doyle, J.J. (1992), 'What Kind of Animal Strategies for Different Agricultural Production Systems?', Seventh International Conference of Institutions of Tropical Veterinary Medicine, Volume II, Conference Proceedings, pp 391-399.

Ettner, S.L. (1996), 'New Evidence on the Relationship Between Income and Health', *Journal of Health Economics*, 15, pp 67-85.

Gold, M.R., Siegel, J.E., Russell, L.B. and Weinstein, M.C. (1996), *Cost-Effectiveness in Health and Medicine*, Oxford Press, New York.

Harris, R.A. and Nease, R.F. (1997), 'The Importance of Patient Preferences for Co-Morbidities in Cost-Effectiveness Analysis', *Journal of Health Economics*, 166, pp 113-119.

Hodgart, R.L. (1985), 'Developments in Location/Allocation Modelling', *Geographia Polonica*, 51.

Johannesson, M. (1996), *Theory and Measurements of Economic Evaluation of Health Care,*: Kluwer Academic Publishers, Dordrecht, The Netherlands.

_____ and Johansson, P.O. (1997), 'Is the Valuation of a QALY Gained Independent of Age? Some Empirical Evidence', *Journal of Health Economics*, 16, pp 589-599.

Johansson, P.O. (1996), 'On the Value of Changes in Life Expectancy', *Journal of Health Economics*, 15, pp 105-113.

Jolley, D.J., Jarman, B. and Elliot, P. (1992), 'Socio-economic Confounding', in P. Elliott, J. Cuzick, D. English, and R. Stern (eds), *Geographical And Environmental Epidemiology: Methods For Small-Area Studies*, Published on behalf of the World Health Organisation Regional Office for Europe by Oxford University Press.

Lavy, V., Strauss, J., Thomas, D. and de Vreyer, P. (1996), 'Quality of Health Care, Survival And Health Outcomes in Ghana', *Journal of Health Economics*, 15, pp 333-357.

Majok, A.A. (1996), 'The Role of Epidemiology among Socio-Economically Different Livestock Production Systems', in K.H. Zessins (ed), *Livestock Production and*

Diseases in the Tropic: Livestock Production and Human Welfare. Proceedings of the VII International Conference of Institutions of Tropical Veterinary Medicine, Berlin, Germany, Vol 1, pp 257-267.

McInerney, J. (1996), 'Old Economies For New Problems-Livestock Diseases: Presidential Address', *Journal of Agricultural Economics,* 47(3), pp 295-314.

Odeyemi, I.A.O. (1996), 'Economics of Private Veterinary Practice In Africa. Concepts On Viability', Proceedings of the Tanzania Veterinary Association Conference, Arusha, December 1996.

_____ (1997), 'Location-Allocation Modelling of Veterinary Services in Africa: A Case Study of Zimbabwe and Kenya', A research conducted for Livestock In Development for Submission to DFID Policy Research Programme.

_____, Finnigan, D.C., Hodart, R.L., Lilwall, N.B., and Wilson, R.N. (1998a), 'Managing Agricultural Services Delivery in Less Favoured Areas: A Role for Geospatial Models', Proceedings of the First International Conference on Geospatial Information in Agriculture and Forestry, Buena Vista, Florida, USA, June 1-3 1998. Vol. 2, p 245.

_____, Lilwall, N.B. and Wilson, R.N. (1998b), 'Socio-Economic Characterisation ff the Livestock Production Systems in Africa: An Animal Health Delivery Perspective', Paper presented at the IXth International Conference of the Association of Institutions of Tropical Veterinary Medicine, Harare, Zimbabwe, 14-18 September, 1998.

Ratcliffe, J. (1995), 'The Measurement of Indirect Costs and Benefits in Health Care Evaluation: A Critical Review', *Project Appraisal,* Vol. 10 (1), pp 13-18.

Revelle, C., Bigman, D., Schilling, D., Cohon, J. and Church, R. (1977), 'Facility location: A Review of Context-Free and EMS Models', *Health Services Research,* No.5, pp 129-146.

Rushton, G. (1988), 'Location Theory, Location /Allocation Models and Service Development Planning in the Third World', *Economic Geography,* Vol. 64, No. 2.

Stinnett, A.A. and Paltiel, A.D. (1996), 'Mathematical Programming for the Efficient Allocation of Health Care Resources', *Journal of Health Economics,* 15, pp 641-653.

Wagstaff, A. (1994), 'Health Care: Qalys and the Equity-Efficiency Trade-Off', in R. Layard and S. Glaister (eds), *Cost-Benefit Analysis,* Cambridge University Press, pp 428-447.

Weinstein, M. (1990), 'Principles of Cost-Effective Resource Allocation in Health Care Organisations', *International Journal of Technology Assessment in Health Care,* 6, pp 93-103.